APPROACHES TO MEDIA LITERACY

APPROACHES TO MEDIA LITERACY

A HANDBOOK

SECOND EDITION

ART SILVERBLATT • JANE FERRY • BARBARA FINAN

M.E.Sharpe
Armonk, New York
London, England

Library of Congress Cataloging-in-Publication Data

Silverblatt, Art.
Approaches to media literacy : a handbook / Art Silverblatt, Jane Ferry,
Barbara Finan.—2nd ed.
    p. cm.
Includes bibliographical references and index.
ISBN 978-0-7656-2264-8 (cloth : alk. paper)—ISBN 978-0-7656-2265-5 (pbk. : alk. paper)
1. Media literacy—Handbooks, manuals, etc. I. Ferry, Jane, 1941- II.
Finan, Barbara, 1937- III. Title.

P96.M4S59 2009
302.23—dc22   2008047124

Printed in the United States of America

The paper used in this publication meets the minimum requirements of
American National Standard for Information Sciences
Permanence of Paper for Printed Library Materials,
ANSI Z 39.48-1984.

∞

CW (c)	10	9	8	7	6	5	4	3	2	1
CW (p)	10	9	8	7	6	5	4	3	2	1

To Monkey, with love
2nd edition
To my "third generation" of friends:
Paul, Looie, Mark "The Claw," Johnny C., and Richard K.
—Art

In memory of Dick
For Megan, Maureen, and Sean
2nd edition
To Camilo, who loves movies with "trouble"
—Jane

To the Coach and our sons, Tony, Mike, and Tom
2nd edition
To my grandchildren
—Barb

Contents

Preface

When one of the co-authors was a doctoral student, his final course was a required Shakespeare class. On the first day, the elderly professor addressed the class: "There is one Truth to Shakespeare," he intoned. "And I know what that Truth is." Having set the ground rules, the game became clear. We, as graduate students, were to climb into the professor's dusty brain and extract that Truth.

Our intrepid co-author then raised his hand and mentioned that the university library was filled with books that offered different perspectives ("truths") about the Great Bard. This apparently was unwelcome news to the professor. It was not a pleasant semester.

This is not that kind of book. *Approaches to Media Literacy* offers a range of approaches to the study of media literacy. In that regard, the book is expansive rather than reductive. Becoming familiar with these various approaches is intended to provide students with strategies to make media content accessible and understandable. Ideally, these approaches will enable you to see media content from different perspectives. And, depending on the specific area of study, one approach may be more useful than others. The old professor not withstanding, there is no one truth to media content. The key is not that there is one truth to any content area, but that you select critical approaches that provide fresh insight into media content. However, in that regard, it is critical that you become familiar with various critical approaches (as tools), so that you can systematically analyze media content (with support from the media "text").

It should be emphasized that these are not the only critical approaches to media literacy analysis. Others include narratology, dramatological approaches, and *Keys to Interpreting Media Literacy*

(Silverblatt). The more critical tools you have at your command, the better.

This edition contains updated examples, text corrections, and new concepts and insights into media literacy. Many thanks to research assistants Margaret Finan and Lee Ann Tapscott for their diligence and hard work.

APPROACHES TO
MEDIA LITERACY

1

Ideological Analysis

Overview

An ideological approach to the study of media is designed to help people become more sensitive to the ways in which the media *reflect, reinforce,* and *shape* ideological systems.

Ideology refers to the system of beliefs or ideas that help determine the thinking and behavior of a culture. Although ideology typically refers to a political orientation, cultural historian Raymond Williams observes that ideology may involve a "more general way of seeing the world, human nature, and relationships."[1] However, even this expanded notion of ideology has political implications, containing assumptions about how the world should operate, who should oversee this world, and the proper and appropriate relationships among its inhabitants.

Ideological analysis has its roots in the discipline of *cultural studies.* The focus of cultural studies is not on aesthetic aspects of text, but rather what these texts reveal about social systems. The fundamental principles of cultural studies are as follows: (1) there is inequitable distribution of power in our cultures; hence, it is possible to detect race, gender and class power profiles; (2) forces of domination and subordination are central in our social system; (3) the same ideology is repeated in a variety of texts; and (4) audiences bring this cumulative information to new material, which reinforces this dominant ideology. Professor Linda Holtzman describes the dominant class as follows: "Dominant groups have greater access to privileges, resources and power because of their membership in a particular group.... For example, in the United States, men traditionally have had greater access to positions of power (e.g., Senators, CEOs of corporations).... Conversely, women have had less access to positions of power."[2]

3

Certainly, there are instances in which the dominant culture imposes its will on the subordinate class through force. However, the members of the dominant culture also maintain their superior position by cultivating a worldview that presents the dominant culture's own interests as being aligned with the welfare of society as a whole. In adopting this worldview, the subordinate class willingly consents to the continued preeminence of the dominant class.

The media have emerged as a principal means by which ideology is introduced and reinforced. One of the central tenets of cultural studies is that the worldview presented through the media do not merely *reflect* or *reinforce* culture but in fact *shape* thinking by promoting the dominant ideology of a culture through *cultural hegemony;* that is, the ability of the dominant classes to exercise social and cultural leadership in order to maintain economic and political control over the subordinate classes.

As a product (and beneficiary) of the prevailing system, the media generally reflect the predominant ideology within a culture. Historian Nikolai Zlobin observes that even seemingly innocuous media programming promotes the dominant ideology of the culture: "Take a textbook on history—U.S., Russian, French, and German—and read a chapter about World War II. It will be like reading about four different wars. Why? Because we construct different ideas about world history and our own histories, and the media supports this."[3]

The dominant ideology frequently assumes a disarming "naturalness" within a text, which makes it particularly effective in promoting and reinforcing the prevailing ideology. (*Text* refers to different types of media presentations, such as articles, videos, billboards, and Web pages.) These media presentations begin with unquestioned assumptions about the correctness of this order. For example, in police dramas, basic assumptions about the origin and nature of crime and criminals are adopted by actors with whom we identify. While a media program may be open to several interpretations, the text generally dictates a *preferred reading,* which reflects the social position or orientation of the media communicator. The preferred reading asks the audience to assume the role, perspective, and orientation of the primary figure, so that the sympathies of the audience are aligned with the values and beliefs of the dominant culture. Within this construct, the audience assumes a passive role in the communications process.

Ideological Approach to Media Literacy

Ideology is integral to all aspects of media production, distribution, exchange, and consumption. A primary objective of the ideological approach, then, is to move beyond the description of a media production into a discussion of the values implicit within the presentation, as well as whose interests are served by such ideas. The objectives of ideological analysis include the following:

- Examining media text as a way to identify its prevailing ideology;
- Becoming more sensitive to the impact of ideology on content;
- Understanding the impact of media content as a vehicle that shapes, reflects, and reinforces ideology within a culture;
- Broadening the public's exposure to the unique experience and contributions of subcultures in society;
- Identifying ideological shifts within the culture; and
- Encouraging an ideological detoxification, that is, a healthy skepticism toward ideologically-based explanations of the world conveyed through media presentations, by challenging the media's representations of culture.

A Cautionary Note

Identifying the ideology of a media presentation is a far more complex matter than the discussion thus far would suggest, for several reasons:

- Although a media communicator may establish a *preferred reading* for the text, the audience may assume a far more active role in interpreting media content, based on their own personal experience. (For further discussion, see "Audience Interpretation of Media Content" in Chapter 2, "Autobiographical Analysis.")
- Every community has its own local media outlets, such as alternative community newspapers.
- International media presentations, such as newspapers, videos, and blogs, are now readily accessible through the Internet.
- Media technology now enables individuals to produce and distribute their own perspectives without corporate middlemen.
- The emergence of media produced by members of subcultures offers alternatives to the single voice of dominant culture. Filmmaker

Spike Lee has enjoyed commercial success by appealing directly to the interests and concerns of the African American community, while building a white, mainstream audience as well.

• In some cases, the interests of the dominant culture and subgroups coincide. Len Masterman observes, "The idea that ruling groups impose a dominant ideology upon subordinate groups does less than justice to the fact that dominant ideas are often not simply imposed but often appear to be acceptable, and even to speak to the interests of subordinate classes."[4]

While the ideological approach may not account for all media messages, this perspective can provide considerable insight into media content, as well as the behaviors, attitudes, values, and preoccupations of media audiences and the culture.

Analysis of Ownership Patterns

The ownership patterns of the media industry influence both what information appears in the media and how it is presented. There are three basic global media ownership systems, each of which exercises a distinct influence on the construction of media messages:

• State ownership
• Public ownership
• Private media

State Ownership

State-owned media systems make up a sizable proportion of the worldwide media operations. According to the United Nations' 2002 Human Development Report, 29 percent of the world's largest newspapers are state owned.[5]

In authoritarian countries such as China, Cuba, and North Korea, the function of the media is to promote the government's agenda. Under this system, the media is regarded as an instrument of the state. The government regards the media as tools to guide the people toward their social, political, and economic destiny. Consequently, all information, including criticism of the government, is tightly controlled.

Under this system of ownership, television programs, radio shows, films, and newspapers, as well as books and magazines, are produced and distributed under the close supervision of the government. The news information agencies belong to the state. For instance, in China, all news is filtered through the state news agency, Xinhua. Even foreign news is channeled through these state-run news agencies, but because independent sources of information are not readily available, stories often are difficult to substantiate, which undermines public confidence in the media.

News and editorial functions are performed by professionals who are committed to the goals of the government. As government employees, these editors, reporters, anchors, and TV producers are subject to state labor laws and practices.

State-owned media systems prevent access to sensitive topics, including pornography, religious materials, and political dissent. Significantly, the Chinese government entered into an agreement with search engine Google in 2006; in exchange for access to 100 million Chinese consumers, Google agreed to censor material that the government found objectionable. Thus, a standard Google search of "Tiananmen Square," the site of a 1989 student protest that turned into a massacre, generates links to images of protesters and tanks, as well as tourists, whereas a search of Google through the Chinese filter produces links only to benign images of happy tourists posing in the square.

State-owned media systems are under no particular pressure to attract high audience ratings or generate advertising revenue. As a result, presentations produced under this system provide insight into official government positions. At the same time, digital technology now furnishes perspective into alternative points of view within a country.

For example, in Bahrain, the royal family dominates; members of the family hold half the cabinet positions and the major posts in the security services and the University of Bahrain. The United States considers Bahrain crucial for its many regional military ventures (the U.S. Navy's Fifth Fleet is based there). With its monopoly over television and radio and the ability to shut down newspapers, the Khalifa dynasty was able to control those interested in democratic reform. However, bloggers now appearing on the Internet are promoting social change. Neil Mac-Farquhar explains, "One reason the Internet is so popular—scores of villages have their own Web sites and chat rooms—is that far more can be said about the ruling family online than through any other means."[6] Further, princes, Parliament members, opposition leaders, and others with an interest in politics say they consult Bahrain Online daily to find out what the opposition is thinking. One blogger wrote, "In Bahrain, glorifying the king means glorifying the nation, and opposing the king means betraying the homeland and working for foreign countries. Should we be loyal to the king or to Bahrain?"[7]

Public Media

In countries such as Sweden, the Netherlands, and Kazakhstan, the media are owned by the public but operated by the government. Under this system of ownership, revenue covering the operating costs of newspapers, television stations, and radio stations is generated through public taxes. Because of this system of public financing, regulations and policies in many of these countries are designed to guarantee a diversity of sources of information. For example, Swedish law stipulates that at least two newspapers must be published in every town. As Aleksander Grigoryev explains, "One newspaper is generally liberal, the second is conservative. In cases in which one of the papers (generally the liberal newspaper) is unprofitable, Swedish law stipulates that the town taxes and donations from the city go to support the struggling paper."[8]

Writers, editors, and media technicians are civil servants who maintain a degree of autonomy from whatever political administration happens to be in office. Because the money to produce programs and pay salaries is generated by public financing, media producers are insulated from market pressures, so that they are free to produce thoughtful and quality programming. At the same time, this system can promote an environment in which programming reflects only the narrow concerns and interests of the media communicators, ignoring the audience altogether.

Although these media operations are set up to serve as independent watchdogs, there are times when the administration in power attempts to influence programming. For example, the Public Broadcasting Service (including National Public Radio and Television), though partially funded through the U.S. government, are established as autonomous corporations. However, in 2003, the administration of George W. Bush hired a new chairperson, Kenneth Tomlinson, who, according to internal investigations, attempted to turn PBS into an instrument of the Bush-Rove propaganda machine by interfering with PBS programming, using political tests in recruiting the corporation's new president, and sending the information to the White House. Once these practices became public, the Corporation for Public Broadcasting inspector general Kenneth A. Konz instituted an inquiry into whether Tomlinson violated any rules that require that the corporation act as a buffer between politics and programming. Tomlinson resigned from his position in 2005.

Private Ownership

In countries such as the United States, newspapers, magazines, radio stations, film studios, and television stations are privately owned—either by individuals or, increasingly, by large, multinational corporations. Under this market-driven system, the primary purpose, or function, is to generate the maximum possible profit for the owners (or stakeholders).

Over time, the number of media companies shrinks as large corporations buy out the small, family-owned media companies. In 1981, forty-six corporations owned or controlled the majority of media outlets in the United States. However, as of 2007, that number had shrunk to eight corporations: Time Warner, Disney, Vivendi Universal, Viacom, Sony, the News Corporation, General Electric, and Bertelsmann. This ownership model fits F.M. Sherer and D. Ross' definition of an *oligopoly:* "Oligopoly refers to an industry characterized by a few mutually interdependent firms, with relatively similar shares, producing either a homogeneous product (a perfect oligopoly) or heterogeneous products (an imperfect oligopoly) Under such a market structure, the industry leader often sets the price."[9]

According to Ben Bagdikian, the corporate worldview has become prevalent in media programming:

> No sacred cow has been so protected and has left more generous residues in the news than the American corporation. . . . (At the same time), large classes of people are ignored in the news, are reported as exotic fads, or appear only at their worst—minorities, blue-collar workers, the lower middle class, the poor. They become publicized mainly when they are in spectacular accidents, go on strike, or are arrested. . . . But since World War I hardly a mainstream American news medium has failed to grant its most favored treatment to corporate life.[10]

The emergence of the media oligarchy affects the content of media programming in the following respects:

Ideology of Guests

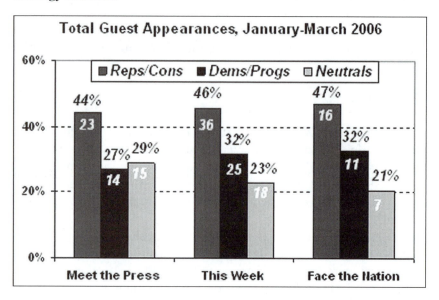

Support of Status Quo

These wealthy and influential media companies are beneficiaries of existing policies and regulations. Consequently, the changes that the media advocate are generally refinements of the current system, rather than a radical overhaul of structure or policy. The reason: The media ownership is never going to advocate their own overthrow.

Further, these major conglomerates sometimes exercise an enormous influence over regulations and policies. For example, in 2007 the Postal Regulatory Commission announced that postal rates for smaller periodicals would increase by as much as 30 percent; at the same time, the magazines with the largest circulation will face hikes of less than 10 percent. According to a document outlining the board's decision, this rate structure was first proposed by Time Warner, one of the elite eight media conglomerates. Katrina vanden Heuvel, publisher of the *Nation,* declared,

> What's at stake is the stifling, the future, the survival of an independent media that the founding fathers of this country thought was essential to a vibrant, flourishing democracy.
>
> We are publishers of magazines that don't make money, that believe in

information as a public good. We believe it is vital to the marketplace of ideas, which, you know, you would think this big behemoth Time Warner would be supportive of. But again, in an unprecedented move, again almost in the dark of night, we're seeing the Postal Board of Governors accepting a rate increase developed by the largest publisher in this country. . . .

If we are to remain a democracy, we have to have flourishing ideas and not one huge publisher conglomerate deciding what this quasi-government agency is going to do.[11]

Conflicts of Interest

These conglomerates sometimes have ties to the political establishment, creating conflicts of interest. For example, although the manifest function of Fox News, an ideological *broadcast news* outlet, is to inform the public, its latent function is to promote the agenda of the Bush administration. Filmmaker Robert Greenwald tracked Fox News in the lead-up to the 2008 presidential elections and found a concerted effort to paint Barack Obama as unfit to be president of the United States. Almost immediately after Obama announced his candidacy in December 2006, there were coordinated efforts to discredit him. In January 2007, the cast of *Fox & Friends* reported that *Insight* magazine, owned by the conservative newspaper the *Washington Times,* cited "unnamed sources" claiming that as a child, Obama had been enrolled in an Indonesian madrassa, a Muslim school that taught Wahhabism, a form of radical Islam.

This story was immediately debunked; as a child, Obama attended public school in Indonesia. However, Fox News continued its campaign to scare the electorate, pointing out that Obama's middle name is Hussein, a Muslim name. David Wallis explains the strategy of scaring people with Obama's name: "Obama's name tests the limits of American nomenclatural tolerance. Just say his full name to yourself. 'Barack' is unfamiliar but innocuous. 'Hussein' is the name of a loathed dictator and enemy. And Obama sounds eerily like the world's most wanted terrorist. (Right-wing Web site Freerepublic.com has featured a Photoshopped image of 'Senator Osama Obama,' and Rush Limbaugh has called him 'Obama Osama.')"[12]

Fox News even "revealed" another "dirty little secret" about Obama. Weatherman and commentator Steve Doocy asked, "What do we really know about Barack Obama? He is a cigarette smoker. . . . What else do we not know about Obama?"

Conflicts of interest may also arise from the close personal ties between owners of these conglomerates and politicians. For example, Clear Channel Inc., the largest radio conglomerate in the United States, with 1,200 stations scattered throughout the country, is a corporation whose vice chairman, Tom Hicks, has financial ties to President George W. Bush. Consequently, at the outset of the Iraq war, Clear Channel organized and paid for a series of prowar rallies in Cleveland, Atlanta, and Philadelphia, and banned artists from their stations who were critical of the war. Indeed, at the end of 2007, plans were under way for Clear Channel to be sold to Bain Capital and Thomas H. Lee Partners. The CEO of Bain Capital is Mitt Romney, the former Massachusetts governor who made an unsuccessful bid for the 2008 Republican primary for president of the United States.

Indeed, the CEOs of these large conglomerates occasionally interfere with decisions about the publication of stories. For instance, in 2007, it was revealed that Rupert Murdoch, the owner of the *New York Post,* had directed the editors of "Page Six," the paper's gossip page, to avoid items that could be seen as critical of China, where he was trying to do business:

> The harshest criticism of Mr. Murdoch . . . has been that he is willing to contort his coverage of the news to suit his business needs, in particular that he has blocked reporting unflattering to the government of China. He has invested heavily in satellite television there and wants to remain in Beijing's favor.
>
> Many of the charges have been reported before, but (former reporter for "Page Six" Ian Spiegelman) said that in 2001, he was ordered to kill an item on Page Six about a Chinese diplomat and a strip club because it would have "angered the Communist regime and endangered Murdoch's broadcast privileges."[13]

Homogeneity of Content

Although the number of media channels has increased over the years, the number of voices has actually *declined* over this same period. In a report, "The State of the News Media, 2006," the Project for Excellence in Journalism concluded, "The new paradox of journalism is [that] more outlets are covering fewer stories":

> As the number of places delivering news proliferates, the audience for each tends to shrink and the number of journalists in each organization is reduced. At the national level, those organizations still have to cover the big events.

Thus we tend to see more accounts of the same handful of stories each day. And when big stories break, they are often covered in a similar fashion by general-assignment reporters working with a limited list of sources and a tight time frame. Such concentration of personnel around a few stories, in turn, has aided the efforts of newsmakers to control what the public knows. One of the first things to happen is that the authorities quickly corral the growing throng of correspondents, crews and paparazzi into press areas away from the news. One of the reasons coverage of Katrina stood out to Americans in 2005 was officials were unable to do that, though some efforts, including one incident of holding journalists at gunpoint, were reported. For the most part, the public—and the government—were learning from journalists who were discovering things for themselves.[14]

The media outlets that are owned by a megacorporation are character- ized by a uniform style, content, and operating philosophy. For instance, Clear Channel radio affiliates use a standard list of songs that they play in each hour. The disc jockeys even tell the same jokes, sent to them from the "home office" via computer.

Further, many radio stations subcontract with national news ser- vices, reducing the number of local news operations. Metro Networks, a Houston-based company, reaches an audience of nearly 100 million listeners, providing news, sports, weather, and other information to more than 2,200 radio and television stations in more than eighty markets in the United States. Metro Networks even subcontracts with several sta- tions in one market; for example, Metro provides news and weather to 100 stations that serve the city of New York. Although the news staff at each station rewrites the copy to make it appear distinctive, this practice reduces the diversity of news sources.

For example, radio is a medium that was made up primarily of small, independent, locally owned stations. But with the relaxation of regula- tions governing ownership, small radio stations increasingly have been purchased by large conglomerates. For instance, Clear Channel has bought up many of these smaller stations and now owns 10 percent of all of the radio stations in the United States. Indeed, under these ownership provisions, one media conglomerate can dominate an entire region. Clear Channel owns all six commercial stations in Minot, North Dakota (the state's fourth-largest city, with a population nearing 37,000).

In 2007, the FCC passed a measure further easing the rules for com- panies owning both a newspaper and television or radio station in the same city. Thus, for example, News Corp. chair Rupert Murdoch would be able to own a television station along with the *New York Post* and the *Wall Street Journal.* Dissenting commissioner Michael Copps called the vote a "gift to corporations":

> In the final analysis, the real winners today are businesses that are in many cases quite healthy, and the real losers are going to be all of us who depend on the local news media to learn what's happening in our communities and to keep an eye on local government. Despite all the talk you may hear today about the threat to newspapers from the Internet and new technologies, today's order actually deals with something quite old-fashioned. Powerful companies are using political muscle to sneak through rule changes that let them profit at the expense of the public interest. They are seeking to improve their economic prospects by capturing a larger percentage of the news business in communities all across the United States.[15]

Programming as Product

In this corporate environment, decisions often are made for economic reasons rather than because of any commitment to media programming as a public service. In the early days of Hollywood, film studios were owned by "small businessmen" like Louis B. Mayer for a myriad of reasons—the glamour, the money, the starlets, and last (but certainly not least), a love of film. Instead, international conglomerates acquire media companies for cash-flow purposes. That is, films and music productions can generate box office revenues that, in turn, provide financing for other enterprises within the corporate empire. However, when programming is regarded simply as "product" rather than news, entertainment, or art, the quality of the productions can suffer. Jeremy Iggers explains, "Many observers worry about the impact that this state of affairs will have on our democratic future. Will corporate-owned media twist the news to promote their own narrow economic interests? But an even more vexing question is what happens to the story journalists tell when, under the thumb of corporate ownership, news is reconceived and repackaged as a product instead of being allowed to remain the complex process of informing citizens."[16]

Consequently, these conglomerates have adopted a corporate mentality, without thought of their responsibilities as mass communicators. The management of the Minneapolis-based *Star Tribune* sent a memo to its staff announcing that "the goal is to change Minnesotans' perception of the *Star Tribune* from that of a newspaper to 'the brand of choice for information products.'"[17]

This economic sensibility explains much of the content that appears in the media. For instance, some media presentations are used to promote other subsidiaries of the conglomerate.

Columnist Frank Rich explains this technique of *cross-promotion:*

> Nowhere has this problem been more acute than at . . . ABC News, where "Good Morning America" on-camera (personalities) were enlisted to promote a theme park of the network's parent company, Disney, and where Diane Sawyer all but turned the selling of "Ellen" into a full-time news magazine beat last season. But you can also find this incessant product-plugging in almost every local news show, as fake stories are dreamed up at 11 o'clock to promote network movies, series and specials. My enterprising local NBC affiliate in New York . . . has gone so far as to hyperventilate about previously little-known Nazi activity in World War II–era Long Island as a tie-in to its network's airing of *Schindler's List.*[18]

Many media organizations also carry *syndicated* programs to save expenses. A syndicated program is produced in one location and then sold to stations throughout the country. Thus, if a radio station carries Rush Limbaugh instead of producing its own local talk program, the station is spared the cost of hiring a host, producer, and engineer. But unfortunately, these radio listeners are denied the opportunity to hear and discuss issues from a local perspective.

Influence of Advertisers

Because of this corporate sensibility, U.S. media companies are inordinately sensitive to the objections and concerns of the primary sources of revenue—advertisers. In 2001, ABC announced a policy by which they would send unfinished scripts to advertisers for their approval. ABC Entertainment cochairman Lloyd Braun promised a group of advertising executives, "We're going to send all of you our scripts for this season. We think you'll enjoy reading them."[19] Because the advertisers indicated that they preferred shows that were "lighter in tone (and) broader in appeal," the network made "tonal adjustments" to the network's dramas, replacing *Once and Again,* a relatively dark saga of families and divorce with the wholesome family drama *Being Brewster.*[20]

Moreover, in their haste to attract the largest possible audience, the old news imperative of providing what the public *needs* to know has been replaced by what the audience *wants* to know. Consequently, entertainment is being presented as news, and news content must be entertaining. Michito Kakutani declares, "The sales imperative—be popular, be accessible, be liked—is . . . threatening to turn writing into another capitalist tool. In an effort to raise circulation, newspapers like *The Miami Herald* and *The Boca Raton News* have used reader preference surveys to determine their 'coverage priorities.'"[21]

This profit-driven imperative leads to a conservative environment, in which most of the media presentations are derivative, playing off of previous successes. For example, the fall 2007 television lineup consisted of the return of old stars such as Kelsey Grammer (*Frasier*) and Patricia Heaton (*Everybody Loves Raymond*) in *Back to You,* as well as the return of old hits such as *The Bionic Woman, The Wilderness Family,* and *Scarface.*

Organizational Analysis

The *internal structure* of a media organization also has an enormous impact on content. The available resources of the media operation, such as the size of the staff and available technological support, influence the quality of programming. For example, in 2004, the profit margins of some of these news organizations were very healthy:

- Tribune Company publishing division: 25.9 percent
- Gannett: 32 percent
- E.W. Scripps: 31.3 percent
- Lee: 27.4 percent
- Journal Register: 27.3 percent[22]

However, at the same time, these conglomerates are devoting *fewer* resources to the coverage of the news. Between 2000 and 2006, news organizations eliminated more than 3,500 staff positions, a drop of 7 percent.[23] In 2006–2007, the following newspapers reduced their staffs as a cost-cutting measure:

- The *Philadelphia Inquirer* announced that it planned lay off sixty-eight to seventy-one employees, or about 17 percent of the newsroom staff, just seven months after a group of local businessmen took over the newspaper.
- The *Washington Post* cut eighty newsroom jobs through voluntary buyouts, the second such offer in just over two years, and attrition.

- The *Dallas Morning News* announced that more than 100 of its 580 newsroom staff members accepted severance packages, reducing the size of the newsroom by roughly 20 percent.
- The *Cleveland Plain Dealer* announced plans to cut 17 percent of its staff.
- At the *San Jose Mercury News,* 101 jobs were eliminated.
- The *St. Paul Pioneer Press* cut forty full-time positions at the paper.
- The owners of the *Los Angeles Daily News* laid off the paper's publisher and twenty other employees.

Apart from the high-visibility anchors in large markets, the salaries of TV reporters are frightfully small, so that the news staff consists largely of young reporters who lack experience and contacts. Further, news editors are asking their staffs to do *more* with *fewer* resources. At the *Los Angeles Times,* the nation's fourth-largest newspaper, publisher Jeffrey Johnson and editor Dean Baquet were fired by executives of the Tribune Company after they defied orders to eliminate more newsroom positions.[24]

These economic cutbacks compromise the quality of a news organization's coverage of issues. For example, in 2007, the city of Chicago agreed to pay $20 million to four former death-row prisoners who had been tortured by Chicago police. The four men—all African American— sued former Chicago police commander Jon Burge and more than twenty officers who worked with him, alleging that they were coerced into falsely confessing to murder in the 1980s. This landmark decision was largely due to the articles of John Conroy, the investigative reporter of the *Chicago Reader* who followed this story for eighteen years. Conroy explains the significance of this story as follows:

> These four cases, they're four men who were pardoned by Governor Ryan in 2003, but they are just the tip of the iceberg, really. There were more than a hundred men who were tortured using electric shock with either a cattle prod, a hand-cranked device much like an Army field phone, or a third device which I believe was a now-extinct medical device called a violet ray machine, which was once a cure-all. Hundreds of thousands of them were manufactured here in Chicago. And in addition to that, some men were suffocated. Some were hung by handcuffs. Mock executions were conducted on others. Some were subjected to severe beatings.[25]

But in December 2007, Conroy was laid off by the *Chicago Reader.* Conroy explains, "I was laid off last week. Four writers from the *Reader* were given the boot. We don't fit into the future plans of the company which purchased the *Chicago Reader* last summer. The company is based in Florida."[26] It is highly unlikely that this story would have come to light without the efforts of this reporter or that, in a mercantile environment, stories like this one will be uncovered in the future.

Because of staff shortages, news organizations sometimes rely on video news releases (VNRs), which are mailed to broadcast stations by public relations companies. Although VNRs look like news reports, they actually promote the products represented by the public relations firm. Media consultant Tripp Frohlichstein explains, "Corporate America routinely provides free video to television stations for newscasts that are actually commercials for their products or services, but since television has so much time to fill, they are using the video as if it is their own. Given budget cutbacks, skeletal news staffs, etc., using these videos as news saves time and money."[27] For example, in one instance, General Mills sent out a video "news" release announcing a university study that cited the health benefits of whole grain oats. As the voice-over discussed the study, the visuals depicted a well-dressed woman pouring Cheerios into an elegant crystal goblet in slow motion. This subtle ad for Cheerios was included in local news programs throughout the country. Frohlichstein declares, "Viewers are subtly being influenced by these commercials without knowing it, because they think it's news."[28]

But in addition, the U.S. government has begun to employ VNRs to serve propaganda functions as well. In January 2004 it was revealed that the Bush administration had violated federal law by producing and distributing VNRs to local news outlets throughout the United States promoting its Medicare program, disguised as television news segments. The video stories contained all of the formulaic elements of broadcast news stories, including a voice-over by a person who signed off, "In Washington, I'm Karen Ryan reporting." Investigation revealed that Karen Ryan was not a journalist but, instead, an employee of the public relations firm that the government had hired to produce the VNRs. The Government Accountability Office, an investigative arm of Congress, has determined that these videos "constitute covert propaganda" because the government was not identified as the source of the materials.[29] Thus, although the audience was expecting to receive an informative report about the Medicare program, they were instead presented with the Bush administration's "spin" about the program. Moreover, the use of this material violated the prohibition on using taxpayer money for propaganda.

The *demographics* of a media organization also reflect the ideology of the dominant culture. Media ownership by women and minorities is declining. For instance, as of 2007, women owned just 6 percent of all full-power commercial radio stations nationwide, and racial or ethnic minorities own just less than 8 percent. Significantly, stations owned by women and minorities are more likely to broadcast local content and diverse programming than ones owned by white men.[30]

The staffs of media operations are also largely homogeneous. In local radio, the minority workforce fell to 6.4 percent in 2005, down from 7.9 percent in 2004. (The highest level ever recorded was in 2001, when minorities held 24.6 percent of TV news jobs.) At the same time, the percentage of women radio news directors dropped from 24.7 percent to 20.4 percent.[31]

The problem is not so much that newsrooms are made up of hostile, active sexists or racists, but rather that they may be guilty of a *benign* racism. Because people are limited by their own experience, white, male editors may not be sensitive to issues that might be clearly offensive to a member of a subculture. An anecdote might help to clarify this statement. One of our authors participated in a seminar on press coverage of people with disabilities. One of the panelists displayed a series of headlines appearing in newspapers and clarified the meaning behind these labels:

- "People with disabilities" refers to an individual who has a disability (the preferred term)
- "Disabled person" suggests less than a whole person as a result of his/her disability
- "Victim of cancer" presents the person in a vulnerable position

After the seminar, a photojournalist complained to me, "All this is a lot of bull. After all, the operative principle in journalism is *economy*. If we can say something in fewer words, this leaves more space for additional ideas."

I said, "Fair enough. Bob, what is your ethnic background? Where are your ancestors from?"

He replied, "Italy."

I responded, "Well, I know a shorter word than 'Italian'" (thinking of the derogatory term for Italians, "wop").

Bob immediately protested, "Heyyyy . . ."

I said, "See, Bob, it depends on whose ox is being gored, doesn't it?"

A culturally diverse news staff is more likely to pick up these types of unintended slights against minority groups and women.

Ownership and the Digital Domain

The Internet represents a significant battleground with regard to ownership. Supreme Court Justice Paul Stevens praises the "democratic forum" of the Internet, which he describes as "the most mass participatory medium yet invented, . . . as diverse as human thought."[32] Kim Gordon, an international interactive technology producer and consultant, explains, "The Internet offers a decentralized source of information and interchange. Traditional mass media requires a press or operating license or significant capital investment. However, with the Internet, anyone with a little hardware can be an electronic publisher, as it were."[33]

The Internet has emerged as a virtual community, in which people throughout the globe communicate with others who share common interests. It is an almost limitless resource, providing access to a wide range of information, from areas of academic interest to pornography. The Internet also provides a forum for individuals representing a range of views ranging from prodemocracy unionists in Hong Kong to members of separatist hate groups in Germany.

In the United States, *citizen journalism* has emerged as a response to what is perceived as the corrupt, bottom-line sensibility of the mainstream press. Citizen journalism refers to the use of blogs and video to develop an audience-driven source of news production and distribution that circumvents the traditional gatekeepers of news and information such as newspapers, radio, and television news programming.

Citizen journalism performs an essential service, providing a glimpse into locations and issues that go uncovered by traditional media. An editorial in the *New York Times* calls attention to the important function of Bloggers with regard to the war in Iraq: "Reading the bloggers has helped to fill one of the big gaps in Americans' view of the war in Iraq. Danger in the streets and security fears for anyone seen speaking with Western reporters has made it increasingly hard to get real glimpses of what it's like for the people who have to live there."[34]

For example, during the February 2007 trial of Lewis Libby Jr., former top aide to Vice President Dick Cheney, Firedoglake.com, a collective of six liberal bloggers, covered the trial in rotation. These bloggers included a former prosecutor, a current defense lawyer, a PhD business consultant, and a movie producer, all of whom shared a Washington apartment rented for the duration of the trial.[35]

With no audio or video feed permitted in the courthouse, the Firedoglake "live blog" offered the fullest, fastest public report available. Indeed, many mainstream journalists used it to check on the trial. The Libby trial marks a courthouse coming of age for citizen journalism. This was the first federal case for which independent bloggers were given official credentials along with reporters from the traditional news media. During the trial, the audience for the blog grew steadily, reaching 200,000 daily visitors (about equivalent to the weekday circulation of the *St. Louis Post-Dispatch*).

Conservative sites such as American Thinker also dispatched bloggers such as Clarice Feldman to cover the Libby trial. One of the basic tenets of citizen journalism is that the principle of "objectivity of the press" is illusory and does a disservice to the audience. Consequently, these sites make it clear that they cover the trial from a distinct point of view. Scott Shane explains, "Even as they exploit the newest technologies, the Libby trial bloggers are a throwback to a journalistic style of decades ago, when many reporters made no pretense of political neutrality. Compared with the sober, neutral drudges of the establishment press, the bloggers are class clowns and crusaders, satirists and scolds."[36]

At this inception stage of citizen journalism, quality standards and practices haven't yet been established. While some blogs are well researched and fair in their coverage of issues, others are merely personal reflections. Citations and references are frequently not cited. And finally, there is no way to verify information on authors, including their background, credentials, and possible motives for contributing. However, the process of establishing standards of accuracy, thoroughness, fairness, reliability, ethics, and transparency are currently under way.

A good case in point is the emergence of film reviews on the Web, written by movie fans. Joe Baltake reports that the proliferation of film critics poses a threat to the Hollywood establishment:

> Hollywood is probably without peer in terms of controlling its product at every stage and managing what information is made available to the public. However, while the studios have their ways of dealing with the press, the public is something else. If a newspaper reporter or TV personality gets feisty and out of hand, asking the wrong question or saying the wrong thing, a film company can retaliate by threatening to drop its advertising (although they rarely do), ostracizing the reporter from movie

functions, or harassing his or her boss. . . . Hollywood always counted on the testimonials of average movie fans, but the fans don't think they're so average anymore. . . . Everybody is a movie expert now. Everybody is a critic. . . . How do you keep the audience from going on the Web to gripe about what they saw? You can't.[37]

As a result, the Internet poses a threat to the established media conglomerates, providing a way for producers of media to distribute their own work. For example, the music industry has long been dominated by two powerful organizations, ASCAP and BMI. These organizations have a vested interested in the distribution of music in all forms: performance, physical (CDs, records, tapes, etc.), and broadcast (radio, television, public usage, etc.). Thanks to interactive technology, enterprising musicians now can bypass the established distribution channels entirely by posting, or "publishing," their CDs directly on the Internet. Consumers then can make purchases directly bypassing ASCAP and BMI.

According to Gordon, the Internet has the potential to alter the established system of compensation for artists as well:

> For example, in a broadcast model, a radio station plays a particular piece regardless of whether or not anyone is actually tuned in to the station at that particular two- or three-minute interval. Odds are you do have an audience, but there is no feedback mechanism to confirm this. In an interactive model . . . we can tell *exactly* how many people requested a particular piece of music. We can tell how many people are tuned to that piece of music at that time. With feedback radio systems, I can "watch" you jump stations from your car until you settle on a piece of music. In these cases, the distributor would not pay compensation unless you as an individual were actually tuned in. Take this logically to its next level: Why not actually charge you as an individual [micro-cents] when you listen in?[38]

In the face of this unwieldy, egalitarian media system, corporations and entrepreneurs are scrambling to identify strategies to seize control of the Internet for commercial purposes.

Media and Government

Every country maintains its own policies with regard to the kinds of information that can be conveyed through its channels of mass communication. In the United States, the First Amendment to the Constitution declares that "Congress shall make no laws abridging the freedom of speech, or of the press." The First Amendment was established on the premise that the United States is a marketplace of ideas. All forms of ideas should be expressed, and each individual must be able to make his or her own decision about what is right and appropriate. Over the years, the term has been expanded to include any governmental body, local or federal.

In authoritarian countries, information, including criticism of the government, is tightly controlled. For example, in 2007, Pakistan's President Pervez Musharraf shut down the nation's private broadcast stations and newspapers as part of its "emergency measures" to fight terrorism. Only the government-run Pakistan Television remained on the air. Musharraf also blocked the reception by cable of international channels such as the BBC and CNN. In addition, the government imposed a "Code of Conduct" on newspapers that prohibited, among other things, "ridicule" of the government or armed forces. Penalties include fines, seizure of equipment, and loss of license. In addition, journalists were beaten, harassed, and intimidated by security forces and supporters of Musharraf. In September, dozens of Pakistani reporters, photographers, and cameramen covering a demonstration outside the Election Commission were beaten by police, some severely. Indeed, in 2006, 167 journalists were killed while engaged in news gathering. The three deadliest countries for journalists in the last decade were Iraq, Russia, and Colombia.[39]

However, thanks to technological communications advances, governments now are limited in their ability to regulate information. For instance, after the state of emergency was imposed, Pakistanis were able to get information through Pakistan-themed blogs and in Internet chat rooms.

In addition, the Internet eliminates borders, challenging governments' ability to impose tax systems and commerce regulations on individual entrepreneurs. Gordon raises this revolutionary scenario:

- I live in the United States.
- I open a new business.
- I do not manufacture a product—but provide an information service.
- It is entirely online.
- I deal in milli-cents for use of my service—the monetary transactions are credited to my account in the Netherlands.
- I bypass the local tax structure.
- I bypass the national tax structure.
- I bypass the international tax structure.

- In fact, I don't pay taxes anywhere.
- Does this mean the government (and which one?) has the right to monitor what I do on my own machine in my own home/business?
- How can the United States government require me to pay taxes if the machine and information and accounting transaction systems are *physically* located in South Africa?
- What if I am paying taxes there because they are lower?[40]

At the same time, however, freedom of speech is not solely determined by governmental regulation. In the United States, the media industry maintains an independence from the government. But at the same time, the media industry struggles with *freedom from market forces* that shape the coverage of issues. Seth Faison comments,

> When will the news media stop reporting so much about celebrities, sex, and violence, all that silly stuff none of us should want to read? Consider China. . . . Although Chinese society is much more open each day, firm principles still guide what can and cannot be printed in newspapers. As a result, there is no real danger of the privacy of movie stars or other celebrities being invaded by the Chinese media, nor of anything offensive or distasteful being published. The state, not the market, still rules the media in China. . . .
>
> For those who tire of all the violence and tragedy in the American media, domestic coverage in China might seem better at first, too; newspapers are dominated by good news. Of course, that ultimately means it cannot be balanced: reports are carefully filtered to praise the achievements of the authorities and, on some occasions, to point out problems that officials have decided should be addressed.[41]

For example, on April 16, 2007, on the campus of Virginia Tech, a student, Seung-Hui Cho, went on a shooting spree, killing thirty-two people. In this case, the television networks didn't necessarily want to saturate the airwaves with meaningless updates and unsubstantiated innuendo; however, they couldn't afford *not* to delve into the story, for fear of losing their audience to a competing station that did carry the story. Further, before going on his rampage, Cho had mailed a package of materials to NBC. Given this "exclusive," NBC chose to present the video, including photos and videos of Cho holding pistols and looking tough.

Each country has its own policies regarding both *what* can be covered and *who* can be covered. In the United States, people can be subjected to media scrutiny as "public figures" if they have met the following criteria:

- Voluntarily stepped into the spotlight
- Assumed an important role in the resolution of important public issues
- Had an impact on a public issue
- Became a public figure through means other than simply media attention[42]

In recent years, the lives of public figures have assumed an extraordinary amount of attention in the American press, overshadowing other topics of importance. These editing decisions convey messages about the relative importance of issues. As an example, on August 17, 2006, the amount of television news coverage of a U.S. federal court ruling on the government's warrantless wiretapping received considerably less attention than new developments in the 1986 murder case of the child beauty queen JonBenet Ramsey. All three networks led their nightly broadcasts with the Ramsey case, rather than the story of Judge Anna Diggs Taylor ruling that the NSA's wiretapping surveillance program was unconstitutional. Further, ABC devoted twice as much airtime, CBS devoted seven times as much airtime, and NBC devoted fifteen times as much airtime to the Ramsey story.[43]

Media and Political Proselytizing

Governments have long employed the media as a propaganda tool to promote their particular ideologies, both internally and in the global arena. Harold D. Laswell identified the following functions of wartime propaganda: (1) to mobilize hatred against the enemy; (2) to preserve the friendship of allies; (3) to preserve the friendship and, if possible, to procure the cooperation of neutrals; (4) to demoralize the enemy. In peacetime, propaganda serves the purposes of expansion, trade, tourism, and investment.[44]

Some critics argue that the media have emerged as an instrument of elite control. Clearly, the overwhelming amount of information circulated throughout the globe is Western (primarily from the United States). Four of the five major news agencies are Western, and these agencies account for 90 percent of the global news flow.[45] In the twentieth century, the United States relied on such channels as Radio Free Europe as a propaganda device.

During the George W. Bush administration, the United States established a "public diplomacy" program, in which information was planted through payoffs to members of the legitimate, mainstream media:

- In 2003, newspapers throughout the United States received letters from local servicemen and women serving in Iraq, emphasizing how well the United States was doing in Iraq. However, it was disclosed that the letters were part of a propaganda campaign, written by the Bush administration.
- In 2005, the Lincoln Group, a public relations firm, planted more than 1,000 articles in the Iraqi and Arab press and placed editorials on an Iraqi Web site. Lincoln paid newspapers from $40 to $2,000 to run the articles as news articles or advertisements.[46] The Lincoln freelancers planted stories with the following headlines:

  - "The Sands Are Blowing Toward a Democratic Iraq"
  - "Iraqi Forces Capture Al Qaeda Fighters Crawling Like Dogs"
  - "Iraqi Soldiers Improve Leadership Skills"
  - "Renovated Facilities Help to Bolster Security in Mosul"
  - "Iraqis Electing the Future"
  - "Border Security Is in Full Swing on All Levels"[47]

- In 2005, it was revealed that the military operates thirty radio stations in Afghanistan but does not disclose their American ties. In addition, Muslim scholars were paid by the U.S. government to serve as "expert" sources in these propaganda articles.[48]
- In September 2006, the *New York Times* revealed that the Bush administration's Office of Cuba Broadcasting paid ten journalists to provide commentary on Radio and TV Martí, which transmit to Cuba government broadcasts critical of Fidel Castro. The group included three journalists at *El Nuevo Herald,* the Spanish-language sister newspaper of the *Miami Herald,* which fired them after learning of the relationship. Pablo Alfonso, who reports on Cuba for *El Nuevo Herald,* received the largest payment, almost $175,000 since 2001.[49]

In addition, entertainment media programming has been an *indirect,* but far more effective means of promoting the American way of life to a global audience. Josef Joffe declares, "One has to go back to the Roman Empire for a similar instance of cultural hegemony. Actually, there is no comparison. The cultural sway of Greece and Rome, or France in the age of Louis XIV and Napoleon, or Germany between 1971 and 1933 reached much beyond the economic and educational elites of the world. But America's writ encircles the globe, penetrating all lay-society. Modern mass culture, for better or for worse, is American."[50]

The American media saturate the globe with *cumulative messages* about American culture. Cumulative messages occur with such frequency over time that they form meanings that are independent of any individual production. These messages are reinforced through the countless hours of media that repeat the cultural script. While there are a multitude of messages (indeed, conflicting cumulative messages may exist at the same time), the ultimate test of a cumulative message is its *universality,* that is, the degree to which an audience is able to recognize a cumulative message that is conveyed through a variety of media channels and programs.

The cumulative messages found in these media presentations promote the following attributes of the American system:

- *Freedom of expression.* Films and music discuss personal angst and societal taboos, and even poke fun at politicians. This freedom of expression is very attractive to members of other cultures. Panrawee Pantumchinda, a Thai graduate of Webster University, observes that *Cosmopolitan* magazine enjoys phenomenal success in Thailand: "The content [of *Cosmopolitan*] emphasizes women's strengths, ways to be successful in relationships and their careers. . . . This content is attractive to Thai readers because the magazine is like their representative to speak about women's issues and sexuality, which are things [Thai women] want to do but cannot because of Thai customs. Moreover, they learn to express their feelings to others from the magazine."[51]
- *Personal empowerment.* American media programming sends messages about freedom of choice. Characters are faced with making a choice between several alternatives. Heroes and heroines are in control of their destinies, so that they make those decisions that are in their best interests. Many ads present their products within the context of personal freedom. Some ads have even equated consumerism with American democracy. A McDonald's TV ad featured a young man lauding the choices and convenience of breakfast at the fast-food restaurant: "Is this a great country, or what?" he asked. Freedom has been translated into the freedom to *buy.*
- *Individualism.* Films such as *The Cinderella Man* (2005) and *Seabiscuit* (2003) focus on the underdog (or horse) who triumphs despite

great odds. Although the hero is written off by other characters, he (and the audience) knows that he can meet whatever challenges present themselves.

- *Celebration of life.* American media programs are characterized by an infectious energy. Popular music is a celebration of youth and revives the youthful spirit in us, regardless of age. This high-intensity vigor and enthusiasm also reinforce the message that the United States is a young country—in terms of both its history and its veneration of youth culture.

However, since 2000 citizens of other countries have overwhelming objected to the politics of the Bush administration. Within this context, U.S. media programming and personalities have met with a negative response from global audiences. For instance, during the 2007 Miss Universe contest, held in Mexico City, Mexico, the television audience booed the U.S. contestant, Rachael Smith, each time she was announced. Reporter Marc Lacey points out that, although the manifest of the program was entertainment, the audience saw the contest in ideological terms: "The complaints included arrogance by the Bush administration and frustration over American immigration policy, the war in Iraq and the historical grievances Mexico harbors against its neighbor. . . . So, Mexicans say, the booing at this pageant was never about Miss U.S.A. herself. It was those letters on her sash."[52]

Other factors also have contributed to the decline of the U.S. media as a global influence. Countries including France, Israel, and Canada imposed quotas on the percentage of international media programs that could be played on their channels of mass communication. Indeed, it is common in Central America for domestically produced music to command up to 70 percent of market share.[53] In addition, the media industries in other new countries compete with the United States for global influence. For instance, the films of India—called "Bollywood" reach up to 3.6 billion people around the world—a billion more than the audience for Hollywood.[54] Tyler Cowen notes, "American popular culture will continue to make money, but the 21st century will bring a broad melange of influences, with no clear world cultural leader."[55]

Worldview

In producing a program, media communicators construct a complete world based on certain fundamental assumptions about how this world operates. Consequently, media presentations establish *who* and *what* are important within the worldview of the program. The following questions related to worldview are useful in identifying the ideology of a media presentation:

  I. What culture or cultures populate this world?
     A. What kinds of people populate this world?
 II. What do we know about the people who populate this world?
     A. Are characters presented in a stereotypical manner?
     B. What does this tell us about the cultural stereotype of this group?
III. Does this world present an optimistic or pessimistic view of life?
     A. Are the characters in the presentation happy?
     B. Do the characters have a chance to be happy?
 IV. Are people in control of their own destinies?
     A. Is there a supernatural presence in this world?
     B. Are the characters under the influence of other people?
  V. What does it mean to be a success in this world?
     A. How does a person succeed in this world?
     B. What kinds of behavior are rewarded in this world?[56]

Examining media programming can furnish perspective into the ideology of a given culture. Media programs can serve as a text that discloses the sources of power and authority in a culture, the class system, and the hierarchy of values. The following cumulative media messages provide insight into the belief system that defines American culture.

A World Preoccupied with the Self Rather Than the Collective Good

In the narcissistic world of media programming, the *greater good* has been reduced to *individual satisfaction*. Ads announcing that "we deserve a break today" urge the audience to indulge their own needs. A hierarchy of values is established in media programs, in which personal amusement is valued over societal well-being. Even programming set within a social-political context such as *Bury My Heart at Wounded Knee* (2007) incorporates a love story into the narrative, so that the program focuses on how these historical events affect the main characters on a personal level.

Because political issues are reduced to personal experience, the appearance of successful minority members in entertainment programs and advertising tends to negate the existence of social problems. Sut Jhally and Justin Lewis found that that the depiction of race in the American media conveys the message that there is no lingering impact from a history of racism, that there are no institutional barriers to success, and no class divisions—only individual failures. Thus, media programming contributes to the belief that racism is no longer a problem in this country, and that African Americans who do not succeed are simply individually inadequate.[57] Consequently, media programming does not encourage its audience to look beyond one's immediate needs to consider the public good.

A World of Immediate Gratification

In media programming, the solution to a problem is never far off. To revise an old adage, nothing worth having is worth waiting for. One explanation for the swift resolution to problems can be found in the competitive nature of the media industry. Entertainment programs, in competition for ratings, must attract audiences by holding nothing back. There is no value in patience or subtlety. The preponderance of violence in media programming gives viewers greater doses of instant stimulation to maintain their interest. One clear media message is that violence is indeed an effective solution to problems. Change is swift, immediate, and dramatic.

The instant-gratification syndrome in media programming also responds to the audience's longing for resolution. People enjoy clarity and certainty in their entertainment programming, possibly in reaction to the uncertainty in their own lives. A film such as *Sleepless in Seattle* (1993) plays on the audience's desire for resolution by postponing the inevitable meeting of the couple. The momentary delays add an edge to the anticipated meeting. However, this process had to be handled delicately by the filmmaker; keeping the audience waiting too long would cause the film to lose them altogether.

The time constraints of media programs further contribute to this sense of urgency. In TV situation comedies, as many as three subplots (all involving some conflict or predicament) must be resolved within a half hour. In film, one must wait for up to two hours for a resolution.

Advertising also accelerates this push toward immediate gratification.

Advertising measures its success by its ability to influence the consumer to buy an advertiser's products as soon as possible. Some ads actually command the consumer to act and act quickly by using directive words such as *hurry* and *now.*

Television commercials operate according to a formulaic plot that reinforces this notion of instant satisfaction. First, a person is introduced who has a particular problem, need, or desire. Within seconds, the product is presented as the solution to this problem. Finally, the viewer can see that the character is entirely transformed by the acquisition of the product. Print ads are even more streamlined, eliminating the establishment of the problem. We see the model, beaming with delight, showing the product. The audience is left to imagine the "problem" stage by seeing how fulfilled the consumer is with the problem solved.

A World That Expects Simple Solutions to Complex Problems

Media programming offers simple solutions to complex problems. Given America's market-driven media system, media communicators are compelled to present a world that is easy to identify and understand. Consequently, the world of entertainment programs and ads is populated by uncomplicated characters who personify a particular value or point of view in the story. Popular films and television programs generally deal in absolutes (e.g., good vs. evil, or right vs. wrong). Heroes are virtuous without fault, and villains are simply evil. There is no room for subjectivity or ambiguity. No one does the wrong thing for the right reason, or vice versa.

To be sure, some programs focus on complex problems that relate to the personal experiences of the audience: relationship issues, socialization pressures, and obstacles to success and happiness. However, the time constraints of media presentations require a swift, tidy resolution to these issues—so that the conclusion is frequently simplistic and illogical.

A Cynical World That Sees the Political System as Dysfunctional

In the world of media programming, the political system is corrupt. For example, Clint Eastwood's *Dirty Harry* series (made between 1971 and 2007) features Detective Harry Callahan, a lone-wolf police detective who is frustrated by the inadequacy of the legal system. At the beginning of each episode, the audience witnesses criminals in the act of committing a crime. Significantly, this point of view establishes the guilt of these characters, so that the principle of "innocent until proven guilty" does not apply. However, constitutional rights concerning the presumed innocence and search-and-seizure laws prevent the cops from bringing to justice those characters who Harry (and the audience) knows are guilty. Harry Callahan always faces *two* adversaries in each film: the perpetrator of the crime that Harry is trying to crack and the bureaucrats in the police department who impede Harry's attempts to get the job done. In this world, bureaucracy only gets in the way. In this environment, the audience has diminished expectations about the value and purpose of our system of justice.

A World Operating According to a Romantic Ideal: If You Wish upon a Star . . .

The romantic ideal presumes the existence of an ordered universe that is a microcosm of heaven. This world operates according to an absolute value system, consisting of *truth, beauty, justice, faith,* and *love.* These values are fixed and interchangeable. For example, the external beauty of heroes and heroines is a reflection of inner virtue. It is a just world, in which good always wins in the end. Faith is an integral part of the romantic ideal, as epitomized by Disney films. As Jiminy Cricket advised Pinocchio, "When you wish upon a star, your dreams will come true." In other words, if you believe hard enough and are deserving, good will be rewarded.

A World in Which Consumerism Is the Cardinal Ideology

The consumer ideology holds that success is defined in terms of material acquisition, replacing other avenues of fulfillment. Personal problems and metaphysical issues have been transformed into consumer needs. Are you lonely? Have money problems? Are you aging? These issues all find resolution through a wise consumer purchase.

Consumerism has emerged as a principal form of recreation and lifestyle in America. The average American shops six hours each week while spending only forty minutes playing with his or her children.[58] As the spokesperson for an ad for Potomac Mills Mall declares, "You can buy happiness. Just don't pay retail for it."[59] Significantly, however, success (as defined by consumer culture) does not bring happiness; according to polls, the pinnacle of happiness in America was reached in 1956.[60] In 1974, economist Richard A. Easterlin found that despite stellar economic growth in the United States since World War II, "higher income was not systematically accompanied by greater happiness."[61] Significantly, Easterlin later found that other countries adopting consumer culture were also no happier; people were no happier in Japan in 1987 than in 1958, despite a fivefold jump in income.[62]

Today, Americans are working more and saving less. People suffer from chronic stress, (the cumulative load of minor, day-to-day stresses), which results in short-term symptoms (headaches and depression), as well as long-term consequences such as heart attacks. And in 90 percent of divorce cases, arguments about finances play a prominent role.[63]

But despite their personal experiences, people are conditioned to participate in the consumer society without questioning its basic assumptions. The film *Blue Collar* (1978) addresses these issues. Jerry (Harvey Keitel), a Detroit autoworker, is in perpetual debt but continues to buy lots of "stuff" he doesn't really want—motorcycles, cars, elaborate home furnishings. His buddy Smokey (Yaphet Kotto) explains, "Why do you go on the [assembly] line on Friday? Because the finance man will be at your house on Saturday. And that's what the company wants . . . to keep you on the line." Thus, the system perpetuates itself by cultivating a longing for possessions.

The media play a pivotal role in shaping and reinforcing our involvement in consumer culture. Media programming depicts a world in which social problems are resolved through consumerism rather than political action. By purchasing the right products, we can move into another social class (or at least maintain the illusion of upward mobility). We celebrate our democratic (or rather, capitalistic) system by participating in the market economy. As Stuart Ewan has observed, the concept of the "citizen" has been replaced in the American vernacular by the label "consumer."[64]

Advertising also plays a critical role in reinforcing the values of consumer culture in the mass audience. By the age of twenty, the average American has seen 1 million commercial messages.[65] On average, each of us will spend one full year of our lives watching TV commercials.[66] But beyond any specific product endorsement, the cumulative message of the advertising industry exhorts the public to adopt a consumer mentality. In the world of advertising, personal problems are transformed into consumer needs. Advertising positions products as keys to emotional well-being and happiness. In the TV commercial for Potomac Mills Mall discussed earlier, the spokeswoman whispers seductively that "shopping is therapy"—a way to soothe yourself. A derivative strategy used in children's advertising equates the purchase of goods with parental love and approval. Heeding a child's plea for a product is part of being a good parent. This approach pits children against their parents, pressuring the adults to feed into this consumer sensibility.

Consumer ideology has an impact on the content of entertainment and news programming as well. Programs are structured so that the mood of television programs is upbeat or suspenseful at the commercial break in order to make people receptive to the commercial messages. (After all—who is in the mood to buy things if they are depressed?) Indeed, Robin Anderson observes, "[O]ften, topics which are antithetical to the product or its image are eliminated."[67]

The HBO television series *Entourage* (2004–) is an unapologetic celebration of the consumer ideology. The series tells the story of Vincent Chase, a handsome actor who is becoming a star in Hollywood. Vince is not particularly talented, and his success is attributed to shrewd handling by his agents. Vince's entourage—gofers and hangers-on, including his brother—profess to care for Vince while raking in the (considerable) crumbs of Vince's fame, including women and riches. Unlike other programs of this genre, in which the characters are unaware that they are being exploited, *Entourage* depicts a world in which its members are cognizant that they are part of a system in which they are used and, in turn, use others. Vince knows that his buddies are using him, but it doesn't matter. Rather than denying the system, he revels in it. If he is simply a commodity in Hollywood, for the moment, Vince is willing to parlay his good looks into fame and fortune.

But regardless of its manifest message, the latent message of media programming frequently supports the values of consumer culture. For example, the film *Jerry Maguire* (1996) stars Tom Cruise as a sports agent who goes through a personal reexamination about his goals and priorities and, consequently, is fired from his high-powered agency. He attempts to go off on his own, contacting his old clients and offering to provide services based on loyalty, concern, and personal attention. Unfortunately, none of his previous clients will return his phone calls, with the exception of one player: Rod Tidwell (Cuba Gooding Jr.), whose battle cry is "Show me the money."

As the film progresses, Jerry develops a close relationship with his one remaining client, Tidwell. The audience also gains insight into the special relationship that Tidwell enjoys with his wife, and how he struggles to maintain control and dignity in a sports world that seemingly only rewards clowns and showboats. In the final game of the season, Tidwell catches a key touchdown pass but is knocked unconscious. After a moment (presumably bolstered by the faith and support of his family—and Jerry), Tidwell gets to his feet and finally expresses his enthusiasm and passion for the game (i.e., clowning and showboating). At the conclusion of the film, Jerry's commitment to basic human values pays off—ironically, in the form of a $3 million, multiyear deal. This feel-good ending ultimately reinforces the ideology of consumer culture, as virtue is rewarded by a long-term contract with a no-trade clause.

A World in Which Style Has Become Substance

Before the media boom, the best one could hope for was to make appearance reflect reality. Now, image can be *better* than reality. As Andre Agassi put it so succinctly in his ads for Canon, "Image is everything." People devote their time and energies to reinventing themselves as more attractive (and marketable) human beings.

At the same time, the media industry undermines grassroots political movements. For example, an ad for Pizza Hut is a thinly disguised adaptation of Martin Luther King's apocalyptic sermon, "I See the Promised Land," delivered on the eve of his death on April 3, 1968. Knowing that he was the target of assassins, King concluded his remarks as follows:

> Well, I don't know what will happen now. We've got some difficult days ahead. But it doesn't matter with me now. Because I've been to the mountaintop. And I don't mind. Like anybody, I would like to live a long life. Longevity has its place. But I'm not concerned about that now. I just want to do God's will. And He's allowed me to go up on the mountain. And I've looked over. And I've seen the promised land. I may not get there with you. But I want you to know tonight, that we, as a people will get to the promised land. And I'm happy, tonight. I'm not worried about anything. I'm not fearing any man. Mine eyes have seen the glory of the coming of the Lord.[68]

In the Pizza Hut adaptation, the sermon takes place in a locker room during halftime of a football game. Using the same ministerial intonation as Dr. King, an African American coach gives a halftime motivational speech. Rather than going to the mountaintop, the coach has "been to the edge and back." What has he seen, the young men ask with their eyes? "What I've learned is . . . you don't need other crusts!" At Pizza Hut the toppings extend all the way to the edge of the dough. He begins to recite a litany of toppings: "Pepperoni . . . mushrooms." The ad cuts to close-ups of the players, who are stunned, amazed, and, finally, converted to Pizza Hut. This ad has reduced Dr. King's vision and, indeed, the civil rights movement, to a pitch for fast food. Once again, ideology has been diverted, and style has triumphed over substance.

The media industry also exploits the ideological significance behind a program, star, or genre for commercial purposes, leaving only the framework and style intact. When the image of a movement is co-opted, the original meaning is lost. For example, when Elvis Presley emerged on the American scene in the 1950s, he was regarded as dangerous by influential members of the dominant (white, middle-class) culture. He was firmly rooted in black culture; he was a white kid who sounded black. Elvis's hip gyrations and snarling lip emitted a sexuality that threatened the 1950s sexual mores. Following the grassroots success of Elvis, the record industry (with considerable help from Dick Clark) manufactured a series of clean-cut rock 'n' roll idols who maintained the image of Elvis, devoid of the ideological substance: Ricky Nelson, Fabian, Bobby Rydell. This pattern was repeated in the 1960s: The Beatles, who sang about revolution, led to the creation of the Monkees, who warbled harmlessly about that last train to Clarksville. This depletion of meaning culminated in a 1995 TV spot in which Ringo Starr teamed up with members of the Monkees . . . as spokespersons for Pizza Hut. Substance has been reduced to pure image.

Similarly, rap music originated in the streets as an expression of the concerns of inner-city African American youth. This genre of music began to be co-opted with the marketing of Vanilla Ice, a white kid who was nonthreatening to the white community. The commercialization of rap music is now complete, with clothes and jewelry associated with the genre sold at malls. Indeed, the familiar trappings of rap music (cadence, dance moves, etc.) are now being employed in commercials to sell potato chips, breakfast cereal—everything but insurance.

In like fashion, VH1's rock 'n' roll fashion awards show, *Fashion Rocks,* promotes a connection between rock music and the fashion industry, conveniently forgetting that the nonconformist ideology of popular music was intentionally *unfashionable.*

The consumer culture co-opts people as well. Before her death in 2007, Anna Nicole Smith was transformed into a commodity. Her appearance in a reality show, *The Anna Nicole Show,* was parlayed into a successful marketing gimmick to sell products—so that, in reality, she became a victim of the market-driven system. Athletes participating in the Super Bowl are now making tentative arrangements to promote products ("I'm going to Disney World"). Even as they walk off of the field, they cannot wait to capitalize on their success and fame.

A Hierarchal (Rather Than Democratic) World

The model society depicted in popular media programs is far from democratic. Only the major characters play significant decision-making roles, leaving the supporting cast with no choice but to follow their leaders. An example of this autocratic social structure occurs in the original *Star Trek.* Search parties typically consist of the main characters (Captain Kirk, Mr. Spock, Dr. McCoy) accompanied by some conspicuously anonymous crew members. It is clear that these crew members, the ultimate followers, are destined to perish. The central characters, having learned about the perils facing the *Enterprise* through the sacrifice of their subordinates, now are prepared to carry out their mission.

A World That Is Satisfied with the Status Quo

A number of factors contribute to the reinforcement of the status quo in media programming. Advertising instructs audiences about success through adherence to the system. More than merely selling a product, ads often sell a successful lifestyle. These ads feature models who are young, attractive, and the center of attention. They are beneficiaries of the system who have found happiness through the acquisition of the product.

Media programs reinforce the status quo by romanticizing the established order. *Gone with the Wind* (1939) represents an idealized vision of the antebellum South, in which slaves and masters lived in harmony. In the film, the slaves regarded the outbreak of the Civil War as an unwelcome disruption of the harmonious plantation life rather than as an opportunity to end the institution of slavery.

Entertainment programs reinforce the class system through their depictions of rulers and those who serve. The world depicted in the media is predominately populated by members of the dominant stratum. The featured characters in films and television epitomize standards of success. They are in control of their environment and have the freedom to act in their best interests. In contrast, members of subcultures are underrepresented on American television, reflecting their relative powerlessness in society: When members of these subgroups do appear in television narratives, these characters experience a lower success rate in the programs than their more mainstream counterparts (this indicator was determined by the characters' ability to achieve their goals). Thus, one of the chief measures of success in the world of entertainment programming is simply being a member of the dominant stratum.

Members of subcultures who appear as media stereotypes often are presented as powerless, marginalized members of society. When African Americans appear as characters on TV programs, they generally are found in one of the following categories:

- Exceptions (e.g., the one black face in an otherwise all-white cast)
- Extras (part of the background that provides the contrast for the successful protagonists)
- Villains who are threats to the system
- Victims of violence (and of the system)

Media stereotypes send the message that it is futile for members of minority groups to overcome their prescribed roles and capabilities. Recently, some prime-time programs featuring African Americans have moved beyond these traditional stereotypes. But, as mentioned earlier, these shows often fall into the trap of denying that race is even an issue in America and suggest that overcoming racism is simply a result of individual effort.

These cumulative messages contribute to an ideology of apathy, cynicism, and lack of connectedness, ultimately discouraging active participation in the community. This sensibility feeds into the ideology of the dominant culture, leaving major decisions in the hands of those currently holding positions of power.

Historical Context

Examining a media program from a different era also can furnish perspective into the ideology of the period in which it was made. Media programs are influenced by historical events. For example, the long-running series of Godzilla films serves as an allegory about Japan's relationship with the United States and, later, with the Soviet Union. On March 1, 1954, as the United States conducted a test of its new hydrogen bomb in the South Pacific, a small Japanese fishing boat, the *Lucky Dragon,* was exposed to the nuclear fallout. But despite public anguish, the Japanese government maintained a strict code of silence about the incident, fearful about upsetting its delicate relationship with the United States in the post–World War II era. Historian Michael Schaller observes that "the monster's trail stretches back to a time of fear and mistrust in Japan":

> Against this backdrop, *Godzilla: King of the Monsters* was released in late 1954, the first of more than 20 *Godzilla* features from Japan. The horror genre gave the filmmakers the cover they needed to skirt the Government's policy of silence. Appearing only a few months after the Lucky Dragon incident, *Godzilla* opens with an ominous explosion and series of flashes that sink Japanese fishing boats. Moving along an island-hopping route like that of both America's wartime aerial attacks and the Lucky Dragon, Godzilla inflicts burns and carnage that are described in the same terms used by the Japanese press for the war's bombing victims.[69]

During the 1970s, the focus of the films shifted, with the monster representing the emerging threat of the Soviet Union. In these versions, Godzilla emerged from the Arctic Ocean and first attacked the northern Japanese island of Hokkaido—"just as the Soviets might."[70] In one film, the Japanese enlisted the help of King Kong, an American creation who embodied the alliance between Japan and the United States.

At the same time, an analysis of a media presentation can help us to understand historical events. Thus, a media presentation can operate as an allegory commenting on current events and conditions. For example, *The Manchurian Candidate* (2005), a remake of a 1962 original, was released immediately after the 2004 Democratic National Convention—the beginning of the general election. Director Jonathan Demme explains, "I am haunted by notions of things like the military-industrial complex. But it's only in the last couple of years that this terrain is making its way into magazines and newspapers."[71] Sharon Waxman explains, "In the new film, a sinister corporation, Manchurian Global, profits from America's wars and plots to put in power—through an Election Night surprise—a vice presidential candidate it controls. The filmmakers acknowledge that the company is a virtual stand-in for Halliburton, the multinational formerly run by Vice President Dick Cheney, though the script was written before Halliburton became a focus of criticism."[72]

Point of View

Examining point of view is a way of identifying the prevailing ideology of a media presentation. Point of view refers to the source of information—who tells the story. Point of view has an impact on how a story is told and what information is conveyed, including (1) who or what is important; (2) what is included and excluded; and (3) commentary on what is being presented. In that way, point of view influences the audience's attitudes toward the content. We are directed to see the world in a particular way and base our responses to characters on the point of view of the narrative.

The audience naturally assumes that information is being presented in a truthful, straightforward manner. However, the perspective of narrators (or reporters) may not be reliable, for a variety of reasons:

- Media communicators may have agendas or conflicts of interest that affect the presentation of media content.
- Media communicators may be influenced by their personal background, experiences, or belief systems.
- Media communicators may have an insufficient command of the information to prepare a thorough and balanced presentation.
- Media communicators may include inaccuracies by mistake.

Media presentations generally assume the point of view of members of the dominant culture. According to media scholar Michael Parenti, historical dramas typically assume the point of view of the aristocracy. For example, *The Private Lives of Elizabeth and Essex* (1939), starring Bette Davis and Errol Flynn, takes a very sympathetic view of the burdens of rule facing Queen Elizabeth. In another Flynn film, *The Adventures of Robin Hood* (1938), the revolt incited by Robin's merry band is not intended to install democracy but rather to restore the rightful, benevolent ruler to the throne of England. Indeed, in the course of the film Robin Hood gently rebukes King Richard for having deserted his subjects to join the crusades, which necessitated that the lower classes (led by Robin) fight to restore him to the throne.[73]

Even when the manifest (or surface) point of view offers an alternative perspective, the latent (under the surface) point of view often remains the dominant culture. For example, children's programming appears to be presented from a kid's perspective. However, commercials for children feature actors who are slightly older than the target audience. Young audiences are influenced by how "cool" these performers are; consequently, they either "take their word" for the quality of the product or associate the positive qualities of the actors with the quality of the product. Ultimately, the "actual" media communicators—the producer, writer, and advertising executive—are typically white, male adults whose interest in the audience extends only to profit margin. An interesting exercise, then, is to show a television ad and ask children who is *really* speaking—and why.

A related line of inquiry involving point of view involves focusing on the *visual field* that is encompassed by the gaze of the protagonist. This field of vision consists of a world that operates according to certain principles, and these principles affect members of this world differently. Frequently, the protagonist (and audience) sees an imperfect world, in which members of a subculture are the source of the problems in the story. This depiction serves as the ideological foundation of the media presentation—the need for restoration of order (as defined at the conclusion of the presentation).

Oppositional Interpretation

Oppositional interpretation is an approach that furnishes perspective into the ideological point of view of a media presentation. Even though media presentations offer a *preferred reading,* all texts are open to alternative interpretations. In this approach, individuals assume the point of view of one of the secondary characters in the narrative.

These subordinate characters are often members of the underclass (e.g., African Americans, females, or Latinos). These characters literally play "supporting roles," serving the stars, who are generally members of the dominant culture. In that way, media presentations serve as microcosms of the social systems that operate in the world outside of these fictional narratives.

Conducting an oppositional interpretation can provide insight into the ideology of the media presentation, in several respects:

- Providing insight into the operation and impact of the dominant ideology presented in the text

- Enhancing the audience's sensitivity to the ideology of subcultures that exist within the dominant culture
- Disclosing the dynamics between the dominant ideology and subcultures

The film *Gunga Din* (1939), starring Cary Grant, Douglas Fairbanks Jr., Victor McLaglen, and Sam Jaffe as Gunga Din, lends itself to oppositional interpretation. Based loosely on the poem by Rudyard Kipling, the film takes place in India during the Thuggee uprising against the occupation of their country by the British. Within the context of the film (i.e., the preferred reading), the British are the heroes who are faced with the task of putting down the revolt and bringing civilization to India. Grant, Fairbanks, and McLaglen are three fun-loving sergeants who take on Gunga Din as an unofficial company mascot. They allow him to hang around the barracks and pretend to be a "real soldier," but his actual duties consist of attending to the sergeants' personal needs.

During the course of the film, the Indian natives mount an insurrection against the British forces. Shot in close-ups, with the lighting coming from below, the Thuggee natives look unnatural and demonic. Individually, the natives are no match for the heroes, a sign of their physical and spiritual inferiority to the British. In one scene, a band of natives pounces on McLaglen, but he shakes them off with ease. These natives are atrocious marksmen; try as they might, they can never hit our British heroes. In contrast, every shot fired by the sergeants seems to find a native target. Our heroes consider themselves morally superior, referring to the non-Christian natives as "savages," "heathens," "fiends," and "apes."

These unscrupulous fanatics manage to lure the British troops into an ambush. However, Gunga Din saves the day by climbing to the top of a tower and blowing his bugle, alerting the oncoming British reinforcements to the impending ambush. Gunga Din is killed in mid-toot, a martyr to the British cause. For Din's act of selfless heroism, the British award him a posthumous medal, finally accepting him as a bona fide British soldier.

However, an oppositional interpretation from the perspective of the subculture (the native Indians) results in a far different reading of the film. Within the context of this alternative reading, the British are the aggressors who have invaded India and, armed with superior weaponry, imposed their way of life on the natives. The three heroes are drunken mercenaries whose interests are confined to fighting, carousing with one another, and plundering the country for gold. In contrast, the insurgents

Gunga Din

Oppositional interpretation is a technique that furnishes perspective on the ideological point of view of a media presentation. A film that lends itself to oppositional interpretation is *Gunga Din* (1939). Within the context of the film (i.e., the preferred reading), the British are the heroes who are faced with the task of bringing civilization to India. The production value of this shot of the leader of the insurrection reinforces the dominant ideology by emphasizing the dark skin of the villain. In addition, the lighting makes the native look satanic. (*RKO Radio Pictures, 1939*)

are patriots, committed to resisting the British takeover. According to *this* interpretation, Gunga Din is a traitor who has betrayed his country. The conclusion of the film is hardly a celebration but, instead, is a chilling commentary about the forces of colonial imperialism on the sovereignty of a people.

The oppositional approach can furnish perspective into the operational ideology in news articles as well. For example, in May 2007, Simon Romero of the *New York Times* wrote an article entitled "Chávez Takes Over Foreign-Controlled Oil Projects in Venezuela":

San Felipe, Venezuela, May 1—President Hugo Chávez on Tuesday seized control of the last remaining oil projects in Venezuela controlled by large

American and European energy companies. The move to take over the projects, announced in January, is the centerpiece of recent actions aimed at consolidating his government's control over the economy. . . .

Venezuela's control over the oil-production projects, which are in the Orinoco region in the country's interior and worth an estimated $30 billion, will weaken companies like Exxon Mobil, Chevron and ConocoPhillips in one of the world's most promising oil exploration regions.[74]

Rewritten from the point of view of the native-born peasant class in Venezuela, the article might look like this:

San Felipe, Venezuela, May 1—President Hugo Chávez on Tuesday reclaimed the last remaining oil projects in Venezuela controlled by large American and European energy companies. . . .

Venezuela's control over the oil-production projects, which are in the Orinoco region in the country's interior and worth an estimated $30 billion, will strengthen the national oil industry, which distributes its profits among the nation's poor.

This exercise serves as an indication of how the mainstream media continue to reinforce the dominant culture. By assuming the perspective of the Venezuelan working-class natives, the article makes clear that the international oil companies have been the beneficiaries of the previous oil agreements, while the indigenous natives were exploited.

Rhetorical Techniques

Rhetorical devices refer to the manipulation of information to influence how the public responds to issues and candidates. It is important for the public to recognize these tactics, so that they will be in a position to form independent judgments about candidates and issues. Richard Paul and Linda Elder, authors of *The Thinker's Guide to Fallacies: The Art of Mental Trickery and Manipulation,* observe, "[The public's] goal should be to recognize fallacies for what they are—the dirty tricks of those who want to gain an advantage. You will withstand their impact more effectively when you know these fallacies inside and out. When you are inoculated against fallacies, your response to them is transformed. You ask key questions. You probe behind the masks, the fronts, the fostered images, the impressive pomp and ceremony. You take charge of your own mind and emotions. You become [increasingly] your own person."[75]

Politicians rely heavily on the following rhetorical devices to position their ideas in ways that reinforce the dominant ideology of the culture:

Spin

Spin is a rhetorical strategy in which communicators present their particular interpretation, or spin, on a story in order to shape how information is presented, reported, and received by the public. The objectives of spin control are to (1) establish the agenda (what is important about the event or issue); (2) influence the public's attitude toward the event or issue; and (3) in cases of negative news, deflect responsibility for the event or issue in another direction. For example, media consultants and political cronies typically circulate among the press after presidential debates, announcing that their candidate has "won" the debate.

Spin also is used outside of the political arena to shape attitudes. The Ku Klux Klan has begun to employ spin techniques as a way of influencing public attitude toward this extremist organization. Christopher Goodwin notes:

> It is a challenge that would tax the most devious political spin doctor: the Ku Klux Klan (KKK), founded to enforce white supremacy . . . is launching a recruitment drive and claims that it wants to become more respectable. The racist language has been toned down and the organization, founded in 1866, is now more likely to hold coffee mornings than cross burnings as it tries to attract new recruits. The KKK fears it is losing many extremists to America's burgeoning militia movement and so it is trying to edge closer to mainstream American politics by encouraging more young professionals to join its ranks.
>
> This new image was in danger of being jeopardized last week after two Klansmen pleaded guilty to burning down churches in rural southern states, the traditional stronghold of the KKK. More than 70 churches with black congregations have been destroyed in fires since the beginning of last year. However, Thom Robb, the grand wizard of the Klan, dismisses allegations of KKK violence: "We have a long-standing position against violence," he insisted at the Klan's remote headquarters just outside the half-abandoned mining town of Zinc, in the Ozark mountains of northwestern Arkansas.
>
> It is Robb, 48, who is seeking to broaden the Klan's appeal, trying to attract middle-class supporters by recasting the Klan as a "civil rights group for whites." . . . Robb is even planning to abandon his own title

of grand wizard soon in favor of the blander and more technocratic "national director" and his underlings will no longer be known as grand dragons . . . [Robb] insists that "we don't hate blacks; we just love whites . . ."[76]

Redirection

Redirection occurs when a media communicator uses language that shifts the audience's attention from one ideological sphere to a more innocuous or acceptable ideology. An example can be found in the ad campaign for Nike, the ubiquitous shoe empire. In the early 1990s, Nike moved its manufacturing operations from the United States to countries in Asia as a cost-saving measure. The labor abuses for the company have been well documented. In Vietnam, young women are paid twenty cents an hour to make Nike athletic products. An internal audit of a Vietnamese Nike factory found that the electric ventilation system and natural-air booths at the plant were insufficient to reduce the dust from harmful chemical powders. Prolonged exposure to this chemical can cause severe damage to the liver, kidneys, and nervous system.[77] Consequently, as many as 77 percent of the workers there suffered from respiratory problems. The chemical solvent toluene was measured at levels of between six and 177 times the amount allowed by Vietnamese law.[78]

This level of worker exploitation has contributed to huge profits for the company and its ownership. Nike's CEO Mark Parker's combined compensation in 2007 (salary, bonus, and stock options) was $21,399,456.[79] Nike has become a $17 billion global business, selling shoes, sports apparel, and equipment.[80]

However, the advertising campaign for Nike substitutes an altogether different ideology for its oppressive company policy. The message of Nike ads is one of empowerment: "Just do it." This prosocial message promotes the athletic accomplishments of women ("Play like a girl") and celebrates the achievements of African Americans ("Thank you, Jackie Robinson"). In 1997, Nike introduced a new variation of this ideological theme: "I can."

One 1997 Nike ad featuring Michael Jordon offers the ultimate empowerment message. In this commercial, Jordon leaves a basketball game during halftime to tend to his business. As a Nike corporate executive, Jordon sits at his desk inspecting a pile of shoes. In this fantasy, labor has merged with management, and workers have been given a raise—from 20 cents per hour to $34 million per year. Nike's ideology has been redirected back onto itself, so that it promotes the empowerment of the labor movement, even while it continues its unfair labor practices abroad.

Misrepresenting a Person's Position and Presenting It in a Form That People Will Reject

During the 2004 U.S. presidential campaign, George W. Bush characterized opponent John Kerry's health care plan as a government program that would lead to rationing. Despite Kerry's denials, Bush persisted in repeating this mischaracterization.

Taking Your Opponent's Words out of Context

Political campaign staffs include "opposition research" teams that comb through the backgrounds of their opponents to find comments that can be damaging when taken out of context. For example, at one point during the 2004 campaign, Kerry declared, "I believe I can fight a more effective, more thoughtful, more strategic, more proactive, more *sensitive* war on terror." Vice President Dick Cheney then lifted the word "sensitive" out of this statement, declaring, "President Lincoln and General Grant did not wage sensitive warfare, nor did President Roosevelt, nor Generals Eisenhower and MacArthur."[81] By taking Kerry's statement out of context, Cheney was able to depict Kerry as unmanly (in contrast with Bush's macho persona).

Using the Three-Card Monte

The three-card monte is a sophisticated rhetorical technique, used in the following way: Bush would make a false statement. He then qualifies it by admitting its falsehood, but then reiterates the first statement, reinforcing the idea in the mind of the public. Columnist Paul Krugman provides the following example in reference to how Bush linked terrorism to the Iraq war: "Speeches about Iraq invariably included references to 9/11, leading much of the public to believe that invading Iraq somehow meant taking the war to the terrorists. When pressed, war supporters would admit that they lacked evidence of any significant links between Iraq and Al Qaeda, let alone any Iraqi role in 9/11—yet in the next sentence it would be 9/11 and Saddam, together again."[82]

Krugman points out that the Bush administration used this same rhetorical technique as part of its plan to overhaul Social Security: "Calls for privatization invariably begin with ominous warnings about Social Security's financial future. When pressed, administration officials admit that private accounts would do nothing to improve that financial future. Yet in the next sentence, they once again link privatization to the problems posed by an aging population."[83]

Shifting the Burden of Proof

The "burden of proof" is a legalistic-sounding term, but it simply means that a party in a dispute has the responsibility to prove what he or she asserts. This concept is also tied to the notion of whether a person is presumed innocent or guilty. A prime example of shifting the burden of proof occurred when the United States invaded Iraq. Richard Paul and Linda Elder explain, "'Wait a minute. Before I have to prove that the invasion of Iraq was justified, you need to prove that it wasn't.' In point of fact any country that invades another needs to have powerful evidence to justify that act. No country has the obligation to prove that it ought not to be invaded. By international law, the burden of proof is on the other side, the side that initiates violence."[84]

Shifting the Argument

Media communicators have learned to seamlessly change the rationale for a policy if the given reason falls flat. This rhetorical technique depends on: (1) the limited attention span of the audience; (2) the convincing nature of the media communicator; and (3) media support. For example, the rationale for the war in Iraq has shifted several times since the invasion in 2002:

- Iraq, under Saddam Hussein, possessed weapons of mass destruction.
- Saddam was complicit in the attack of 9/11.
- The Iraq war was designed to "bring democracy" to the people of Iraq.
- We're fighting the enemy over there so that they won't follow us over here.

Ignoring/Downplaying Evidence

When faced with incriminating evidence, one approach is to *ignore* it. In his 2004 campaign speeches, Bush simply overlooked the evidence to paint a rosy scenario about Iraq and the economy.

A related rhetorical technique occurred when the Bush team *downplayed* potentially damaging evidence. For example, in October 2004, there were news reports that after the American invasion of Baghdad, a cache of explosives was discovered to have been missing (See discussion, Tactic #5). These explosives were powerful enough to shatter airplanes or tear apart buildings. However, Bush spokesperson Scott McClellen minimized their significance, saying that the stockpile contained "no nuclear materials."

A third approach occurred when Bush used incriminating evidence to support his own position. In 2007, a U.S. intelligence finding was released, reporting that Iran had halted its nuclear weapons program in 2003. However, the Bush camp argued that the report vindicated their policy and, in fact, supported the value of imposing new sanctions, since Iran could renew its nuclear program in the future.

In this case, the Bush campaign made the following assumptions that proved correct: (1) people won't read the document in its entirety; (2) the right-wing media would trumpet Bush's positive spin; (3) in the interest of "fairness," the nonideological media would give equal attention to the Bush administration's statement, legitimizing this false assertion.

Substituting Fact for Truth

Political rhetoric is often designed to confuse the public by presenting isolated facts as truth. For instance, in December 2007, Rudolph Giuliani accused Mitt Romney of having a bad record on crime while governor of Massachusetts: "Violent crime and murder went up when he was governor," Giuliani said of his Republican rival. Romney's response was that violent crime, which includes murder, actually went down. Both were correct. In the four years Romney was governor, murders increased in Massachusetts, from 173 in 2002, the year before he took office, to 186 in 2006. However, *violent crime,* a broader category made up of murder, rape, robbery, and assault, decreased in the Romney era, from 31,137 to 28,775.[85]

Indeed, statistics can be employed to confuse rather than clarify the truth. In January 2005, the administration defended the legitimacy of the upcoming

Iraqi elections, since only four of the eighteen provinces in the country were deemed too unsafe to conduct the vote. But although this may be factually accurate, the larger truth is that approximately 50 percent of the population lives in these four provinces. As economics reporter David Leonhardt explains, "Numbers without context, especially large ones with many zeros trailing behind, are about as intelligible as vowels without consonants."[86]

In other cases, facts are distorted or omitted entirely. For example, Republican presidential candidate Rudy Giuliani ran ads in Iowa, claiming that as mayor of New York, he "turned a $2.3 billion deficit into a multibillion dollar surplus." In fact, Giuliani left the city with a bigger deficit than the one he had to deal with when he arrived in 1994. "He inherited a gap, and he left a gap for his successor," said Ronnie Lowenstein, the director of the city's Independent Budget Office. But the Giuliani campaign defended the advertisement, noting that it merely states that Mr. Giuliani created a multibillion-dollar surplus, not that he passed one on to his successor.[87]

Indeed, politicians do not hesitate to rewrite history when it is to their advantage. For instance, in the past, Republicans were highly critical of budget deficits, arguing that they were detrimental to the economic well-being of the country. However, during the 2004 campaign, George W. Bush reversed course, contending that the deficits accrued during his first term would have a minimal impact.

In the face of this bewildering array of information, facts become meaningless. Truth has become reduced to a matter of *faith*—whose facts the public chooses to believe.

Using Evasive Rhetorical Techniques

The following rhetorical techniques are designed to avoid difficult or embarrassing questions.

- *Jokes.* This technique involves answering a hard question with a joke that deflects the query.
- *Truistic answers.* These answers may be true, but they do not answer the question. For instance, in response to the question, "How long will the troops have to remain in Iraq?" Bush answered, "As long as it is necessary and not one day longer."[88]
- *Diversions.* This technique involves providing an answer so long and detailed that the speaker manages to avoid answering the thrust of the question.

- *Talking in vague generalities.* Paul and Elder explain, "It is hard to prove people wrong when they can't be pinned down. So instead of focusing on particulars, manipulators talk in the most-vague terms they can get away with."[89]
- *Ignoring the main point.* Politicians typically appear in venues in which their statements go unchallenged, such as debates or press conferences in which the journalist asks only one question. As a result, they can simply ignore the question and provide an answer to a different topic. For instance, during the third debate of the 2004 election, Bush was asked a question about minimum wage. Bush immediately moved the question to a discussion on education.

Word Choice

Linguist Kenneth Burke once remarked that "language precedes thought." By this, he meant that until a child acquires the tools of language, he or she can only experience a stream of impressions. Language is used to recall experiences, to catalog these impressions, and put them in the context of other experiences. Language can also be used to shape an individual's understanding of the world and influence the individual's belief system. For example, in February 2003, U.S. secretary of state Colin Powell made a presentation to the United Nations Security Council, making the American case for going to war against Iraq. As evidence, Powell presented satellite photographs of a cluster of buildings that he described as a poisons and explosives factory that is supported by both Baghdad and Al Qaeda. The next day, the Iraqis invited twenty journalists to enter the compound. The reporters found a cluster of buildings that lacked plumbing and had only the limited electricity supplied by a generator. In response, a senior State Department official explained, "A poison factory is a 'term of art,' and it doesn't necessarily mean that people are pumping out thousands of gallons a year." A more accurate term, however, would be *lie* or *deception.*

Other uses of language include the following:

Newspeak

Newspeak, a term that originated in George Orwell's novel *Nineteen Eighty-Four,* refers to words that mean the opposite of their original meaning. In the totalitarian world of Orwell's novel, newspeak was employed to control people's thoughts and behaviors: "The purpose of Newspeak was not only to provide a medium of expression . . . but to make all other modes of thought impossible. It was intended that when Newspeak had been adopted once and for all, . . . [divergent thoughts]— should be literally unthinkable."[90]

The George W. Bush administration used newspeak to shape attitudes toward their controversial policies. For example, the Bush administration employed the term "Clear Skies" to describe its environmental policy—which, in fact, relaxes many federal protections against air and water pollution.

Connotative Words

A *connotative word* assumes associated meanings beyond its literal dictionary definition. Synonyms have very distinct connotative meanings that can color and define an individual's understanding. *Connotation* refers to the meaning associated with a word beyond its *denotative* (dictionary) definition. The meaning of a connotative word is universally understood and agreed upon. For example, two terms that are used interchangeably to describe the president of the United States are *Commander in Chief* and *Chief Executive.*

The term *commander in chief* was used only occasionally to describe the president of the United States until the administration of George W. Bush. However, the reliance on this term by the Bush administration can be traced back to May 1, 2003, when President Bush, in pilot gear, landed in a fighter jet on the USS *Abraham Lincoln* to announce "Mission Accomplished" in Iraq. The exterior of the plane was marked with "Navy 1" in the back and "George W. Bush Commander-in-Chief" just below the cockpit window. A Google search of "Bush" *and* "Commander in Chief" conducted on February 15, 2007, found 1.2 million references in various publications.

The media instantly picked up on this term. For instance, CNN.com's coverage of the event began with the headline "Commander in Chief Lands on USS *Lincoln.*"

The term *commander* suggests unlimited authority and power. The root of the term *commander* is *to command,* suggesting autocratic authority. According to the *American Heritage Dictionary,* the definition of command is "to have control or authority over; to dominate; to demand obedience on the part of the person or group addressed." This characterization of the presidency was also reinforced by the invention of another term by Bush, when he said, "I'm the *decider.*"

The use of this term has an ideological context rooted in Vice President Dick Cheney's expressed belief in a strong executive branch of government. In contrast, *Chief Executive* is derived from the word *execute,* which means "to carry out, or put into effect." Thus, instead of Bush being an administrator who carries out the law of the land, he is a commander who exercises authority and control. Further, the use of *Commander in Chief* by the Bush administration also is designed to remind the public that the United States is at war, which gives the president wide-ranging authority.

Euphemism

A *euphemism* is an inoffensive term that tempers, or softens, the meaning of an explicit, harsh, or distasteful idea or concept. The derivation of *euphemism* comes from the Greek word *euphonos,* or sweet-voiced, suggesting that this discourse device can make harsh concepts or ideas sweeter, or more palatable. For example, defending itself against charges of torture against enemy combatants held in prison at Guantánamo, the Bush administration used the neutral term *enhanced interrogation techniques.* William Lutz offers other examples of euphemisms used in war:

- Preemptive counterattack: an invasion where we strike first
- Predawn vertical insertion: we strike first, and when it's still dark
- Collateral damage: civilian casualties
- Traumatic amputation: arms and legs blown off soldiers
- Special weapon: atomic bomb
- Aluminum transfer containers: temporary coffins
- Misspoke: lied
- Energetic disassemblies: nuclear explosions
- Radiation enhancement devices: nuclear weapons[91]

Special interest organizations often assume euphemistic titles to conceal their mission, ideology, and sponsorship. Jim Drinkard refers to this phenomenon as "Astroturf," in that the names of these organizations suggest grassroots activism.[92] For instance, the Information Council on the Environment, which sounds like a pro-environmental group, is actually an organization formed by the oil and coal lobbies to discourage the establishment of global-warming policies. The late Molly Irvins reported, "The public relations firm hired to do its bidding frankly stated its mission: 'to reposition global warming as theory rather than fact.' According to [Ross Gelbspan, author of *The Heat Is On*], 'Big oil and big coal have successfully created the general perception that climate scientists are sharply divided over the extent and the likely impacts of climate change—and even over whether it is taking place at all.'"[93]

Other examples of "Astroturf" lobbying groups, whose names don't always reflect their financial backing or true agenda, include:

- *Californians for Statewide Smoking Restrictions:* This group was formed in 1994 by tobacco companies in an effort to head off strict new rules on workplace smoking.
- *Coalition for Energy and Economic Revitalization:* Formed by a Roanoke, Virginia, public relations consultant, this organization is pushing for a new 115-mile power line for American Electrical Power Co., which is paying its expenses.
- *Coalition for Vehicle Choice:* In arguing against stricter auto fuel-economy standards, this group has cited police needs for large cruisers, the need for full-sized vans for the disabled, and the safety of big cars. Its money comes from Detroit automakers.[94]

Narrative Analysis

Popular media narratives frequently rely on unquestioned acceptance on the part of the audience. However, examining the narrative can uncover the ideological principles that underlie these assumptions.

Illogical Premise

Premise refers to the central idea of a story, which answers the question, "What is this program about?" Many fictional narratives call for the willing suspension of disbelief, in which the audience is asked to accept, without question, the basic premise of the program: Bugs Bunny can talk, the Rock can run and fight for hours without getting tired, and using Head and Shoulders shampoo will get you a girlfriend and a role on Broadway. Once the premise has been accepted, however, the remainder of the narrative progresses logically.

In some cases, the audience accepts, without question, a premise with ideological overtones. For example, the animated feature film *Anastasia* (1997) is a romantic tale about a beautiful young princess who has become separated from her family, and then orphaned, during the fall of the Romanov monarchy in Russia. She meets a young Russian boy and, together, they set off for Paris to find her true identity. In the process, they must contend with Rasputin and his minions, who try to bring about her demise. At the conclusion, she reclaims her birthright, including the royal jewels to which she was entitled.

The premise of the film assumes the following: (1) that the fall of the czar was a result of a magical spell by "the evil sorcerer" Rasputin; (2) that toppling the monarchy caused a sense of loss among the people; (3) that the masses suffered more after the revolution than before; and (4) that the people longed for the restoration of the monarchy. However, Russian historian Nikolai Zlobin disputes these assumptions:

> March 2, 1917, was a very mystical moment in Russian history, when Nicholas II signed his resignation decree and abdicated the throne. It was mystical because one of the strongest European monarchies disappeared peacefully (the Romanov family came to the throne in 1613). The Russian monarchy fell like the leaves from a dead tree. Everyone saw the fall as inevitable. Nobody supported Nicholas II, and nobody asked him to keep the throne. Even more, the people who came to him with the draft of the Resignation Act were members of the monarchy party. People were surprisingly indifferent to the dissolution of the monarchy, and they certainly weren't nostalgic about the royalty after they were gone. Even many who disagreed with communism were interested in a constitutional republic—there was no place for a czar in the system anymore.
>
> Rasputin was hardly involved in state business, was unknown outside of the circle of nobility, and was killed in December 1916, before the fall of the monarchy.
>
> Regarding the condition of the people, any kind of reform brings some instability to society. But we must remember that most people suffered under the czars, and that revolution brought them, at least, the hope that the majority of society would have a better life. People were prepared for hardship in the wake of the revolution. And the communist system did raise the standard of living for the masses, within a very few years. Only a very few people who had prospered under the czars longed for the return of the Romanovs.
>
> Finally, the jewels were not the private property of the Romanov family but were national property, which were taken out of the country illegally.[95]

Illogical Conclusion

The last segment that an audience is exposed to influences how the audience responds to the narrative as a whole. The conclusion of a narrative should be a logical extension of the ideology of the premise, characters, and worldview.

In the 1930s, the Hollywood's Motion Picture Production Code asserted that "no picture shall be produced that will lower the moral standards of those who see it. Hence the sympathy of the audience should never be thrown to the side of crime, wrongdoing, evil or sin."[96] Thus, the "Hollywood ending" was characterized by tidy resolutions that reinforced the moral belief system, in which good prevails over evil. Film critic Joe Williams explains, "As a result, most American movies in the first half of the twentieth century are characterized by happy—or at least hopeful—endings. With God on their side, the Yanks win the war. With Pee Wee in the hospital, the home team wins the big game. With a ring on her finger, the bedridden matchstick girl learns to walk again."[97]

Significantly however, the conclusion of many media programs are illogical, confused, or simply implausible when considered within the flow of the program. Given the ideology of the program, a happy ending requires the "divine" intervention of a scriptwriter and director. Although the main characters may be struggling throughout the course of the program (often because of flaws in the system), the resolution of the narrative finds them at peace.

For example, *Pretty Woman* (1990) is a modern fairy tale involving corporate executive Edward Lewis (Richard Gere) and a prostitute, Vivian Ward (Julia Roberts). The promo for the film announces, "She walked off of the street, into his life, and stole his heart."[98] Although it is unlikely that Vivian could really have adapted to Edward's world, and even more unlikely that Edward would have accepted Vivian into his world, the two characters parade off at the end of the film.

A critical question, then, is: Given its premise, characters, and worldview, how should the film end? While the film clearly is a romance, it is also a story about class differences. The logical flow of the narrative leads to the conclusion that socioeconomic constraints put people in completely different worlds that affect how they look at the world and relationships. The movie dismisses these issues with a romantic (but false) ending, in which love renders class differences meaningless. But the logical conclusion of the film dictates that the two lovers part ways or that Edward continues to "employ" Vivian.

Characterization also sends ideological messages. Characters can be considered embodiments of ideological positions, based on whose interests they represent. In a narrative, plot conflicts are ideological oppositions, as represented by the characters in the program. Heroes and heroines epitomize those qualities that society considers admirable and thus generally reflect the values of dominant culture. Henry A. Murray notes, "The forces that are aligned with the group's welfare, with its hopes for the future, being beneficent in direction, are exalted as the good powers. The opposing and hence maleficent forces are portrayed as evil."[99] Thus, the character of Edward Lewis in *Pretty Woman* represents several ideological positions that support the dominant culture: (1) male; (2) white; (3) rich; (4) handsome; (5) exclusive; (6) insider.

The triumph of good over evil generally is dependent on the characters' adherence to the values and goals of dominant culture. In the *Spider-Man* series, the hero complies with the code of law and order. Despite this apparent disadvantage, Spider-Man's adherence to the rules gives him the strength to defeat his adversaries. The triumph of the hero at the conclusion of the program, therefore, reinforces the ideology of the dominant culture. Daniel Chandler declares, "The structure of the text works to position the reader to 'privilege one set of values and meanings over the other.'"[100]

Significantly, in many contemporary programs the hero cheats a bit or exhibits behavior that falls outside of the law. For instance, in the television series *House,* renegade Dr. House continually violates hospital policies in the interest of patient care. This behavior reflects a more complex and subjective sense of ethics than the bureaucratic hospital culture normally permits. Ultimately, however, House's attitude of "doing what it takes," in fact coalesces with the basic corporate ideology of using free enterprise and initiative to achieve one's goals.

The heroes of media presentations always enjoy the benefits of a material world. In the classic sitcom *Friends,* the characters lived in expensive apartments in New York City, although Joey and Phoebe did not have jobs that would have enabled them to pay their rent and other expenses.

Characterization in media programming also sends messages about the value of conformity to the system. Heroes epitomize conformity; they are like everyone else—only more so. As an example, Tom Cruise embodies normal, all-American good looks. Conversely, characters who are too different are objects of ridicule or scorn. In this sense, there is a suspicion of difference and fear of change. Thus, many programs offer the illusion of the hero-as-rebel. In the series of *Lethal Weapon* films, Mel Gibson plays nonconformist cop Martin Riggs, who doesn't dress in uniform like his peers; instead, Riggs wears fashionable clothing and drives expensive, high-speed cars. However, Riggs's rebellious persona is only cosmetic; despite his long hair and jeans, Riggs remains an agent of the establishment, eradicating crimes without questioning the conditions that contribute to these situations.

Conversely, villains generally represent negative values that threaten the established worldview. However, villains are not bound by the moral constraints to which heroes must adhere. They are free to draw first, lie, and cheat. However, these momentary advantages are not powerful enough to contest the moral order of the universe. They are inevitably brought to justice—for their crime and, in a broader sense, for their transgressions against the system.

Genre Analysis

A genre is a type, class, or category of artistic work, featuring a standardized narrative format, such as horror films, romances, sci-fi, situation comedies, westerns, and the evening news. Each genre is distinctive and readily identifiable, regardless of time or place of composition, author, or subject matter. Moreover, genre is not confined to one medium. For instance, at one time or another, superhero tales have appeared in print, on radio, on television, and in film.

Every genre contains patterns in plot and structure, characteristic conventions or devices (such as the horses, characters, and outfits found in westerns), and stylistic similarities. Individual programs generally conform to a clear formula of the genre. As John Cawelti observes, "Individual works are ephemeral, but the formula lingers on, evolving and changing with time, yet still basically recognizable."[101]

There are many ways to study genre. One approach that is useful for our purposes is to consider the *shared ideological orientation* of a particular genre. Each genre frames the action within a particular worldview and set of expectations with respect to the following features:

- What culture or cultures populate this world
- Definitions of success
- Whether people are in control of their own destinies

For example, the ideology of the *action drama* is essentially conservative, in that the central focus of each program is a return to the status quo. The conventional plot operates according to the formula of order-chaos-order. Initially, the world exists in a state of harmony. However, almost immediately some problem (e.g., a troublemaker or natural disaster) disrupts this initial tranquility. The remainder of the plot focuses on the restoration of order, which is achieved at the conclusion. Thus, this world is reactionary; it does not require change but changing *back*.

The population of this world (and by extension, the audience) longs for some form of authoritarianism—either a more efficient law enforcement system or a protector who goes outside the system to punish wrongdoers. According to George Gerbner, the striking amount of violence in action dramas is an instrument of the status quo. Violence teaches lessons about the exercise of power: who can impose their will on whom. Action dramas therefore create a Darwinian environment, in which audience members value protection and security, often at the expense of an individual's civil liberties.[102]

At the same time, the social issues facing the characters are trivialized as simply personal problems or individual choices. Thus, in action dramas, street hoods deal drugs because they are inherently evil or because they have made a personal, conscious choice, leaving out any mention of the social context that might furnish perspective into this type of behavior. The *horror* genre focuses on issues about good and evil. In some horror presentations, the characters are victims of external supernatural forces (e.g., ghosts, monsters, Satan, Dracula). In other contemporary programs, the evil originates *within* human beings. Slasher movies depict a world in which *we* are the monsters; human nature is bestial, wicked, and corrupt. In this Darwinian world, the weak (usually women characters) are preyed upon and brutalized by the strong.

In addition, the horror genre conveys ideological messages about the uncertainty posed by threats, or perceived threats, to the system. According to Douglas Kellner, during periods in which people feel a loss of control in their lives, there is a resurgence of occult horror films. Thus, the escalation of cold war tensions in the 1950s was accompanied by a wave of horror films.[103]

The *gangster* genre presents conflicting ideological messages, as reflected in the rise and fall of the protagonist. The beginning of the film typically focuses on the spectacular success of the young gangster, who epitomizes the American ideology of hard work, initiative, and free enterprise. But at a critical point in the narrative, the protagonist typically crosses a moral line and is punished for his violation of the social order. This stage of the plot sends the message that individuals must obey the law and conform to the system.

However, the initial ascension of the gangster often is the most glamorous and memorable part of the narrative. In the popular HBO television series *The Sopranos,* the performance of Tony (James Gandolfini) as a brutal mobster living in suburbia was so mesmerizing that creator David Chase was compelled to add an additional season. Significantly, however, the controversial ending of the series eliminated the ideological message about the consequences of criminal behavior. In the final scene, the family gathers in a restaurant. A man hovers ominously at the bar as Tony's daughter, Meadow, hurriedly crosses the street to join her family. These production cues signal a final denouement—but at that moment, the action is frozen, and the episode (and series) ends, reinforcing a world without consequence.

The ideological orientation of *situation comedies* focuses on the satisfaction of personal needs. Sitcoms concentrate on the small problems facing the major characters (e.g., Larry David gets a haircut or Homer Simpson enrolls the family dog in obedience school). Sitcoms often focus on the travails of relationships. Much of the confusion or plot conflict results from dishonesty or poor communication (e.g., mistaken identity). In that regard, success is measured purely in terms of personal gratification. Values such as communication, loyalty, and honesty are rewarded at the conclusion of each episode.

In sitcoms, the concept of community is limited to members of the immediate cast. The theme song to the sitcom *Cheers* reminded us that the world of the sitcom is a small place "where everybody knows your name." When the primary characters do think beyond their own needs, they focus only on the well-being of the other characters in the program. Hence, social activism is reduced to taking care of one's own immediate community.

Increasingly, situation comedies are becoming vehicles for the ideology of consumer culture. Although *Seinfeld* proudly promoted itself as a show "about nothing," this description is only half accurate: The series was about nothing of *substance.* Instead, the episodes focused on an empty world, devoid of meaning. Jerry, George, Elaine, and Kramer are shallow, self-absorbed characters who are incapable of sustaining relationships. What meaning there is in the world of *Seinfeld*—and what constitutes the plot of each program—consists of consumer behavior. Characters spent their time engaged in diversions, such as going to the movies, shopping, or hanging out at the coffee shop. Life consists of small pleasures—a cup of soup, Junior Mints—which can be purchased, consumed, and thrown away.

Musicals present an ideology that moves people away from the consideration of societal or political concerns. James M. Collins notes that musicals present "dance as the only viable alternative to despair (financial or otherwise) . . . or [as the] solution to problems."

> One finds in this depiction of "life in the streets" the central ideological tensions of these early Warner musicals, perhaps best illustrated by the opening and closing numbers of *Gold Diggers of 1933*. In the opening, assembled chorus girls are clad in giant coins as they sing "We're in the Money," a scene which is surely one of the most preposterously optimistic reflections on the Depression in film history. Here the Hollywood musical offers the viewer a saccharine alternative to economic hard times outside the confines of the movie theater.[104]

"Backstage" musicals such as *There's No Business Like Show Business* (1954) revolve around the inner workings of show business. In the backstage musical, the central *metaphorical concept* is that "life is a show." As Ethel Merman sang most emphatically in the title song, even though life is full of disappointments and setbacks, you must "go on with the show"—that is, put the best face on your situation and perform as though you are satisfied.

In other musicals, song and dance are incorporated into the narrative, so that life *itself* becomes a musical. Collins observes, "The shift from day-to-day life to musical life appears completely natural, the distinctions purposely blurred—life is not *like* a song, it *is* a song."[105] For instance, in *Meet Me in St. Louis* (1944), Judy Garland casually launches into "The Trolley Song" as she is riding around St. Louis. The cumulative message is that, although there may be nothing that we can do about the injustices in society, we can at least control our *attitudes* toward these conditions. Keeping a song in our hearts keeps alive the possibility of personal redemption.

Perhaps more than any other genre, the *science fiction* genre is distinctly ideological in nature, offering a range of commentaries on the present and future condition of society. One subgenre consists of invasion films, in which some foreign element threatens our current system. Often in invasion films, the outside threat brings out the best in the prevailing system. In *Independence Day* (1997), people of all nationalities work together (under American leadership) to defeat the forces of evil who are trying to conquer the earth.

Another subcategory of science fiction consists of allegories that are set in the future but comment on present conditions. The genre of science fiction has long focused on this theme of a world in which the machines have transcended the capabilities of humankind. Films such as *Forbidden Planet* (1956), *2001, A Space Odyssey* (1968), *Blade Runner* (1982), *The Terminator* (1984), and *The Matrix* (1999) share a common premise: "The machines" have taken over and punish human beings for their hubris in thinking that they can play God by creating these omnipotent computers.

A derivative category of *utopian* science fiction programs alerts the audience to societal possibilities by offering a glimpse into a world that is superior to our own. In *Contact* (1997), scientist Ellie Arroway (Jodie Foster) discovers a highly evolved civilization that has transcended many of the limitations that plague contemporary earthlings (exemplified by the petty bickering and shortsighted thinking that nearly sabotage the space expedition). In this way, the film extends hope to a world that has become corrupt and self-absorbed.

Other genres, such as westerns, quiz shows, news programs, tabloid talk shows, spy programs, and sports programming, also possess distinctive ideological orientations that send messages about what life is and what life ought to be. Examining the ideological underpinnings of these genres can provide insight into ways in which a genre shapes the audience's expectations and understanding of the content.

In like fashion, radio stations are organized around particular formats, such as rap, classic rock, or talk radio. These formats sometimes have an ideological point of origin. For instance, country music is generally conservative in tone, in that it is rooted in traditional American values. Longtime Nashville songwriter Bobby Braddock explains, "Something political will not get played on country radio unless it's on the conservative side. If you show both sides, it's not good enough. It's got to be just on the right."[106] Indeed, the Republican Party commonly uses country music at political events, particularly patriotic songs like Toby Keith's "Courtesy of the Red, White and Blue (the Angry American)" and Darryl Worley's "Have You Forgotten?"

When the lead singer of the Dixie Chicks, Natalie Maines, said at a concert in London in March 2003, "We're ashamed the president of the United States is from Texas," the reaction was fierce and swift. Country stations stopped playing the group's songs. Talk-radio hosts urged listeners to complain about Maines's remarks. Other progressive country musicians expressed hesitation to express political views, for fear of being "Dixie Chicked."[107]

Upon close examination, a genre may contain a *latent ideology.* For instance, the worldview of reality programs such as *Survivor* presents a community that, on the surface, is supportive, with members working together. However, the rules of these shows are designed to undermine and ultimately destroy the community, all in the name of drama. In *Big Brother,* one house member is voted out each week, with viewers participating by phone and Internet. Jordan Levin, president of entertainment at the WB Network, declares, "A lot of the reality programming . . . just shows [the bad] side of human behavior."[108]

Production Elements

Analysis of production elements can be a useful tool in uncovering ideological messages in media presentations. Production elements such as color, shape, and movement convey ideological messages by affecting our way of seeing, attributing meaning, and understanding social relationships within a program. (For a more comprehensive discussion of production elements, see Chapter 5.)

Production elements operate on an *affective,* or emotional, level, so that ideology is introduced on a subtle, unconscious level. *Warm colors,* such as red, orange, and yellow, tend to make us feel happy, secure, positive, and intensely involved. *Dead colors,* such as gray or black, make us feel sad, alone, or uncomfortable. For example, the most common background colors employed in American politics are red, white, and blue. In addition to their patriotic connotation, these warm, uplifting colors evoke positive feelings in the audience. Bright colors are also common in positive political ads. In contrast, dark colors are frequently employed to send negative messages.

The media communicator makes choices with regard to production elements that signal approval or disapproval. These production elements nurture desires and interests that reinforce the interests of dominant culture. Through the choice of production elements, the ideology of the program simply may *feel* right to the audience. In contrast, the production values used to depict an alternative ideological worldview may trigger feelings of discomfort or antagonism. Production elements frequently work in combination to convey a message. Media literacy teacher Darlene Wagner observes, "*The Titanic* (1997) contains a scene in which Rose DeWitt Bukater (Kate Winslet) reunites with Jack Dawson (Leonardo DiCaprio) after telling him earlier that day that she no longer wanted to see him. Rose finds Jack overlooking the sea at the forefront of the ship. All is still—the ocean, the serenity of the music and lighting. Jack asks Rose to step up onto the railing that overlooks the front of the ship. While the two embrace, a rush of romantic music, combined with dark, dramatic lighting, underscores the significance of the moment."[109]

In addition, recurrences of production elements may signal approval or disapproval. The appearance of villains may be accompanied by a distinctive discordant musical theme throughout the narrative, so that the audience learns to associate their appearance with something disagreeable.

Editing

In film and television, the *sequencing of information* can convey ideological messages. Although a news broadcast may contain a number of separate reports, the flow of segments has a powerful tendency to merge contents, sending unintended (or intentional) messages. Jane Caputi observes that the sequencing of messages can work together to (1) emphasize a political meaning of the primary text; (2) undercut, defuse, or mock a political meaning of the primary text; or (3) create an explicit political significance that otherwise would be absent from any of the segments taken singly.[110]

For example, a CNN segment, *News from Medicine,* aired a report on the beneficial effects of aspirin in preventing heart attacks. Immediately following the segment, a tag line appeared: "*News from Medicine* is brought to you by Bristol-Meyers Squibb, makers of Bayer Aspirin," followed by commercial for Bayer aspirin. This sequence conveys the message that not simply aspirin, but *Bayer* aspirin will reduce heart attacks.[111]

The inclusion and omission of information convey messages about the relative importance of a story. For example, between January 2007 and January 2008, the top Sunday morning political talk show hosts (i.e., Tim Russert of NBC's *Meet the Press* and George Stephanopoulos of

ABC's *This Week*) asked a total of 2,938 questions. However, only six of these questions pertained to the issue of global warming, signaling that this issue is relatively unimportant.[112]

Moreover, stories that are considered leading news stories in one publication are sometimes skipped altogether in other presentations. For example, on December 22, 2007, the front page of the *Washington Post* carried the following story: "FBI Prepares Vast Database of Biometrics; $1 Billion Project to Include Images of Irises and Faces." The article disclosed that the FBI has established the world's largest computer database of people's physical characteristics (e.g., digital images of faces, fingerprints, iris patterns, face-shape data, and scars). This program gives the U.S. government the unprecedented ability to identify individuals, both at home and abroad. Although this story was published on the front page of the *Post* and the Albany *Times Union,* a search on Lexis-Nexis disclosed that this story did not appear at all in the *New York Times.* Thus, while some news organizations believed that this story was of major significance, the *New York Times* felt that it had absolutely no news value.

Lighting

Lighting can convey ideological messages by manipulating the emotions of audience members. A brightly lit photograph evokes feelings of security and happiness. In contrast, a dark picture filled with shadows creates a mysterious atmosphere or arouses fear and apprehension. Dim lighting can also trigger a sense of powerlessness and loss of control, as viewers must struggle to grasp a clear visual understanding of the environment.

Relative Position

Relative position refers to where a character or object appears on the screen (or page). Objects appearing toward the front attract immediate attention, whereas things in the background are generally considered of secondary importance. The upper portion of the page or screen connotes positive messages, so that people who appear on the upper portion of the page or screen display power, dominance, importance, happiness, control, enlightenment, health, prosperity, status, virtue, and reason. Conversely, people appearing off-center on the screen are marginalized. Individu-

Tommy Hilfiger

Relative position can convey ideological messages. This photograph stimulates the composition and arrangement of an advertisement for Tommy Hilfiger Fragrance. On the surface, the photograph of six young people appearing in the ad represents a multicultural society. However, a closer examination of relative position reveals that the members of subcultures are marginalized in the ad. The males assume the dominant (upper) position in the north-south corridor, so that the white models occupy the center. Thus, although the manifest message of the ad is that differences appear to be acceptable, the latent message of this arrangement is that white males remain the center of power. *Photo by Aaron Mednick.*

als positioned on the lower echelon reflect positions of powerlessness, subordination, unimportance, sadness, lack of control, unconsciousness, illness, poverty, lack of status, wickedness, and emotion.

An advertisement for Tommy Hilfiger Fragrance provides an example of how relative position discloses ideology. On the surface, the photograph of six young people appearing in the ad represents a multicultural society (the photo contains four men and two women—three Caucasians and three African Americans). However, as graduate student Angela Rollins observes, a closer examination of relative position reveals that the subgroups are marginalized in the ad: "The white members of the ad are squarely in the center, reflecting their status within the group. The African Americans are off to both sides. . . . At the same time, the female is far below where the men appear, indicating a subordinate position. The message seems to be that differences appear to be acceptable, it is still the mainstream (white males) who are the center of power. This juxtaposition of diversity and conformity sends a conflicting message to the audience."[113]

Movement

The direction of movement also has distinct ideological properties. Movement directed toward the audience can either be friendly (e.g., an invitation or sign of intimacy), or aggressive, or menacing, depending on the context. Movement directed away from the audience can signal abandonment, retreat, avoidance, or resolution. Movement directed upward often is a positive sign (something going to heaven or, perhaps, outer space). Movement directed downward often is a negative sign (e.g., crashes or fights), or signals defeat.

Angle

Angle refers to the level at which the camera is shooting in relation to the subject. A person filmed from a high angle looks small, weak, frightened, or vulnerable. In contrast, a person filmed from a low angle appears larger, important, and powerful. Thus, in political ads, the camera is often tilted up at candidates, which conveys messages about his or her competence and generates feelings of respect for the candidate among members of the audience.

Connotative Image

According Bill Nichols, the use of images can serve an ideological function, influencing how we think about our world: "Images . . . contribute to our sense of who we are and to our everyday engagement with the world around us. What these signs never announce is that they are most fundamentally the signifiers of ideology. . . . After all, seeing is believing, and how we see ourselves and the world around us is often how we believe ourselves and the world to be."[114]

Transmutation of symbols occurs when an image takes on a symbolic meaning that supports the dominant ideology. Images of violence like the Magnum symbolize economic dominance, power, and control. Sexual images are also transformed into symbols that support the system. Ads commonly employ images of sexy women with automobiles to draw attention. Through the continued use of sexual imagery, the consumer is conditioned to associate the automobile with sexual desire. We buy cars as an expression of our sexuality. Indeed, we learn to see the cars themselves as sexy.

The diamond industry has been successful in positioning its product as a symbol of eternal love. Media programs contain countless images of men giving diamonds as tangible evidence of their love—to the point that *not* giving a diamond is regarded as a lack of devotion. A diamond declares that love will be permanent, and that the couple will live happily ever after. An ad for the American Gem Society asks the question, "The diamond engagement ring. Is two month's salary too much for something that lasts forever?" Given what the diamond represents (eternal love), "only two month's salary" represents quite a bargain.

Other products are positioned as symbols of affluence. Jose Cuervo is marketing a brand of tequila for $1,000 (far in excess of the standard $16 bottle of Cuervo Gold). Frank J. Prial asks, "It must be good, but, but then again, how good can tequila get?" The answer is that customers are purchasing the status that is associated with the expensive brand through packaging and advertising. Prial adds, "As Cuervo representatives readily acknowledge, half the price is in the package: a bottle made of Belgian crystal, trimmed in pewter and served up in a suede and leather case."[115] The tequila becomes a symbol of status, which, for some, is worth the inflated price tag. Indeed, the extraordinary cost of the product reinforces its image of opulence and prosperity.

In contrast, *masking images* conceal inequities of the system by presenting a worldview that reframes how we think about our experience under the existing system. Nichols explains, "Ideology seeks to mask contradictions and paradox inherent in a given historical situation."[116] For instance, Visa commercials depict a world in which debt is presented as freedom. Ads for gambling boats show everyday citizens striking it rich, masking the reality that the big winners ultimately always are the owners of the casinos. Consequently, despite their personal experiences, people are conditioned to participate in a system without questioning its basic assumptions.

Imagistic layering is a production technique in which two images are juxtaposed to form a third meaning. The fusion of two images operates on humans' gestalt, or predisposition to order, so that the audience naturally constructs a third, distinct meaning from the two disparate images (described by the equation $A + B = C$). This production technique enables a media communicator to comment on the relationship between objects and events. For example, an ad for American Express juxtaposes images of the Greek Parthenon with an American Express card, associating the power, stability, and wealth of the ancient Greek temple with American Express. On another level, the idea of the sacredness of the temple is transferred to the credit card, sanctifying the power of wealth.

In the first film version of *Dracula* (1931), imagistic layering attaches a vicious anti-Semitic meaning to the vampire tale. As part of his attire, Bela Lugosi wore a medallion around his neck, consisting of a star with six points—the Jewish Star of David. The anti-Semitic subtext of the film hearkens back to the nineteenth-century author of the novel, Bram Stoker, who was a member of several anti-Semitic organizations.

As the embodiment of the stereotypes, misconceptions, and superstitions that formed the basis of the persecution of the Jews, Dracula is a figure to be dreaded. Dracula is of dark Eastern European descent, of unknown origin. At the beginning of the film, the count is cast out of his country and has purchased an estate in the richest area of London. The problems in the film stem from the count's unwanted intrusion into British aristocratic society.

Dracula is "undead," meaning that he has no hope for the salvation of the soul that comes through acceptance of Christ. This "prince of darkness" has a strange, hypnotic power that can seduce people to his way of life if they are not vigilant. Dracula cannot bear to behold a crucifix, reflecting his state of damnation as an enemy of Christ.

Vampires live by taking the blood from young innocents; this echoes tales of Jews kidnapping Christian children and using their blood in the making of the Passover meal. An article entitled, "Blood Libel, Host

American Express

The juxtaposition of images can be used to construct a separate, discrete meaning. This American Express ad juxtaposes images of the Greek Parthenon with an American Express card, connecting the power, stability, and wealth of the ancient Greek temple with American Express. *Copyright © American Express TRS Inc. Reprinted by permission.*

Dracula

In this example of imagistic layering from the film *Dracula* (1931), Count Dracula is wearing the Jewish Star of David. This combination of images attaches an anti-Semitic perspective to the vampire story. (*Universal Studios*)

Desecration, Ritual Murder, and Other Largely Anti-Semitic Fables" provides perspective into the Dracula myth:

> In 1144 CE, an unfounded rumor began in eastern England, that Jews had kidnapped a Christian child, tied him to a cross, stabbed his head to simulate Jesus' crown of thorns, killed him, drained his body completely of blood, and mixed the blood into matzohs (unleavened bread) at time of Passover. The rumor arose from a former Jew, Theobald, who had become a Christian monk. He said that Jewish representatives gathered each year in Narbonne, France. They decided in which city a Christian child would be sacrificed. The boy became known as St. William of Norwich. Many people made pilgrimages to his tomb and claimed that miracles had resulted from appeals to St. William. The myth shows a complete lack of understanding of Judaism. Aside from the prohibition of killing innocent persons, the Torah specifically forbids the drinking or eating of any form of blood in any quantity. However, reality never has had much of an impact on blood libel myths. This rumor lasted for many centuries; even today it has not completely disappeared.[117]

Further, imagistic layering is a technique that is often used in political communications to send subtle messages to the audience. For example, in August 2002, President George W. Bush gave a speech at the site of Mount Rushmore. In the photograph of the speech, the president is shown off center (which is highly unusual), capturing his likeness as part of the row of America's most beloved presidents. This instance of imagistic layering is designed to convey the message that Bush is part of the tradition of great American presidents.

Music

Music elicits an affective response in the audience, arousing feelings of excitement, tension, drama, or romance that can be used to reinforce ideological messages. Music often works in conjunction with visual messages, to signal approval or disapproval. For instance, negative political commercials often include ominous-sounding music to reinforce the attack on the opponent.

Ideological Analysis: Cinderella

A close examination of Walt Disney's classic cartoon *Cinderella* furnishes surprising perspective into its underlying ideology. First released in 1950, *Cinderella* was a celebration of the romantic ideal (see discussion, Chapter 4, "American Cultural Myths"). In this world, the values of love, beauty, truth, faith, and justice are absolute and interchangeable. Cinderella is a young woman whose beauty is a reflection of her inner goodness, Although she suffered at the hands of her cruel stepmother, she is finally united with her prince, justifying her faith in a just and harmonious world, in which goodness prevails over evil. Cinderella and the prince's kiss at the conclusion is a promise that they will live "happily ever after."

In 2002, Disney released *Cinderella II: Dreams Come True* (2002) followed by *Cinderella III: A Twist in Time* (2007). These sequels introduce a series of challenges facing the new royal couple. A review of *Cinderella II* by "Britney" on the Internet Movie Database provides the following plot summary: "The movie explores Cinderella's 'happily ever after' life as a princess in three stories, with help from the Fairy Godmother. First, Cinderella's awkward first days at the palace, when she tried so hard to fit in that she forgot to be herself. Second, how Jaq felt so left out that he wished to be a human. Third, how Cinderella taught one of her nasty step-sisters how to smile which leads to her own true love."[118]

Cinderella

Walt Disney's *Cinderella* (1950) has long been a favorite cartoon of children, in large measure because of its celebration of the romantic ideal. However, the 2002 release of *Cinderella II: Dreams Come True* followed by *Cinderella III: A Twist in Time* in 2007, are sequels that undermine the original message that the couple will "live happily ever after," replaced by the message that the "bottom line (profit) conquers all."

Ironically, these sequels impose a new layer beyond the original conclusion that undermines the romantic ideal of the original Cinderella. The characters do not live happily ever after. Cinderella and the prince encounter a series of new troubles. Love is not triumphant, and absolute justice does not prevail—at least, until the new conclusion.

Thus, the cumulative message of these sequels is that to the Disney Corporation, *Cinderella* is simply a product that can be repackaged to generate profits for its stockholders. Indeed, within the context of the romantic ideal, the Disney Corporation is the stereotypical "bad guy" (not unlike the wicked stepmother) who is willing to exploit the idealism of the audience to make a dollar.

Summary: Approaches to Ideological Analysis

The objectives of ideological analysis include:

- Examining media text as a way to identify its prevailing ideology
- Enabling the audience to become more sensitive to the impact of ideology on content
- Enabling people to see the impact of media content as a vehicle that shapes, reflects, and reinforces ideology within a culture
- Broadening the public's exposure to the unique experience and contributions of subcultures in society
- Identifying ideological shifts within the culture
- Encouraging an ideological detoxification, that is, a healthy skepticism toward ideologically based explanations of the world conveyed through media presentations by challenging the media's representations of culture

Theoretical Framework: Approaches to Ideological Analysis

I. Organizational analysis: What are the ownership patterns within the media industry? How do these ownership patterns affect media content?
   A. What are the ownership patterns within the particular media system you are examining (e.g., television, film, radio)?
   B. Who owns the production company that has produced the presentation you are examining (e.g., television station, newspaper, film company)?
   C. How is the media industry regulated? How does government regulation affect media messages?
   D. What is the internal structure of the media organization responsible for producing the media presentation? How does this internal structure influence content?
      1. What are the resources of the production company?
      2. What is the organizational framework of the production company?
      3. What is the process of decision making in the production company?
II. Worldview: What is the prevailing ideological worldview in the media presentation?

    A. What culture or cultures populate this world?
        1. What kinds of people populate this world?
        2. What is the ideology of this culture?
    B. What do we know about the people who populate this world?
        1. Are characters presented in a stereotypical manner?
        2. What does this tell us about the cultural stereotype of this group?
    C. Does this world present an optimistic or pessimistic view of life?
        1. Are the characters in the presentation happy?
        2. Do the characters have a chance to be happy?
    D. Are people in control of their own destinies?
        1. Is there a supernatural presence in this world?
        2. Are the characters under the influence of other people?
    E. What does it mean to be a success in this world?
        1. How does a person succeed in this world?
        2. What kinds of behavior are rewarded in this world?
III. Historical context: In what ways has the media presentation been influenced by the events of the day?
    A. When was this media production first presented?
        1. What prior events led to the climate in which this media presentation was produced?
        2. How did people react to the production when it was first presented? Why?
           a. How do people react to the production today?
           b. How do you account for any differences in reaction?
           c. In what ways does an understanding of the historical context provide insight into the ideological messages contained in the presentation?
    B. What does the media production tell us about the ideology of the period in which it was produced?
    C. What can be learned about shifts in cultural ideology by contrasting past and present media presentations?
IV. Point of view: oppositional interpretation—Does an alternative reading furnish perspective on the operation and impact of the dominant ideology reflected in the text?
    A. What is the ideology of the subcultures that exist within the dominant culture in the program?

    B. What does the oppositional interpretation reveal about the dynamics between the dominant ideology and subcultures?

V. Rhetorical techniques: Are any of the following rhetorical devices used to position ideas in ways that reinforce the dominant ideology of the culture?

    A. Euphemisms

    B. Labels

    C. Metaphors

    D. Obfuscation

    E. Spin

    F. Redirection

VI. Narrative analysis: Does analysis of the narrative structure uncover the ideology of the media presentation? Examine the following:

    A. Illogical premise

    B. Illogical conclusion

    C. Characterization

VII. Genre analysis: Examine a genre. What is its shared ideological orientation?

VIII. Production elements: What do the following production elements disclose about the ideological subtext in the media production?

    A. Color

    B. Lighting

    C. Relative position

    D. Scale

    E. Movement

    F. Angle

    G. Music

    H. Images

        1. Juxtaposition of images

        2. Imagistic layering

        3. Transmutation of symbols

        4. Masking images

        5. Sequence of Images

2

Autobiographical Analysis

Overview

Autobiographical analysis is an approach that investigates media content as a way to promote personal discovery and growth. This framework provides opportunities for individuals to examine the impact of the media on their attitudes, values, lifestyles, and personal decisions. The autobiographical approach is *audience driven;* that is, the individual uses his or her own experience with the media as a springboard for analysis. This approach emphasizes process and exploration—ways of looking at media content—rather than set answers. At the same time, analyzing media presentations within the context of one's own personal experiences can furnish insight into the text, including characterization, plot conventions, worldview, and messages regarding success and violence.

The autobiographical approach broadens the scope of media literacy education. Because discussion and analysis begin with personal response to media content, autobiographical analysis is an excellent way to approach media literacy in the classroom. In addition, this approach can be particularly effective in nonacademic settings such as community groups, older adults, church organizations, and at-risk children. For instance, while people in retirement centers may not have the capability or inclination to apply themselves to the academic rigor of media literacy analysis, the autobiographical approach becomes educational in a broader sense—that is, providing a way to promote personal reflection and understanding. The autobiographical approach also offers an accessible way for parents to generate discussion with their children.

The autobiographical approach can also help bridge the disconnect between generations. Parents and teachers can use media to understand the language, culture, preoccupations, and concerns of younger generations. Moreover, this approach can bridge the gap between ethnic and racial groups, as well as other cultural schisms, such as rural/urban, rich/poor, and educated/uneducated.

Audience Interpretation of Media Content

Understanding the role of the audience in the interpretation of media content is critical to autobiographical analysis. Two schools of thought exist with respect to the role of the audience. According to the *hegemonic model,* the audience's interpretation of text generally is aligned with the values and beliefs of the dominant culture. Although a mass media text may be open to several interpretations, the text dictates a "preferred reading," from the perspective of the media communicator. Within this construct, the audience assumes a passive role in the communications process. (For further discussion on the hegemonic model, see Chapter 1, "Ideological Analysis.")

The autobiographical approach is based on the *reception theory,* which maintains that individuals assume an active role in interpreting the information they receive through mass media. The Ontario Ministry of Education states that audience members *negotiate* their own meaning as they encounter media messages:

> Basic to an understanding of media is an awareness of how we interact with media texts. When we look at any media text, each of us finds meaning through a wide variety of factors: personal needs and anxieties, the pleasures or troubles of the day, racial and sexual attitudes, family and cultural background. All of these have a bearing on how we process information. For example, the way in which two students respond to a telephone situation comedy (sitcom) depends on what each brings to that text. In short, each of us finds or "negotiates" meaning in different ways. Media teachers, therefore, have to be open to the ways in which students have individually experienced the text with which they are dealing.[1]

Consequently, audiences may negotiate a meaning that is entirely different from the "preferred" reading dictated by the media communicator.

Individuals may use one of several processes to assimilate the information they receive through the media.

- *Selective exposure* is a process in which individuals choose what to watch and listen to, based on their personal values and interests.

If a person has an aversion to horror movies, he or she will avoid these types of programs.

- *Selective perception* occurs when a person's interpretation of content is colored by his or her predispositions and opinions. We hear what we want to hear and see what we want to see. For example, audiences at political debates tend to think that their candidate "won" the debate.
- *Selective retention* occurs when individuals remember (or forget) information, based on their interest level and attitudes toward the topic. For instance, we have all been cornered by a person who insists on talking at us about a subject we know (or care) little about. In these situations, we tend to tune the person out, waiting for an appropriate moment to escape to a more rewarding conversation.

A number of factors can influence how an individual responds to media programming.

Stage of Development

In general, younger children are more attuned to external characteristics (e.g., strength, beauty) than older children, who are more likely to use internal descriptors, such as motivational and personality characteristics.[2] A person's stage of development can also affect his or her particular frame of reference. In one study, adults who were asked to interpret the title of Olivia Newton-John's popular single "Let's Get Physical" said that the song was about sex. In contrast, teenagers thought that the song was about exercise.[3]

Psychological Disposition of the Individual

Some studies suggest that aggressive children may be attracted to media violence, which causes them to be even more aggressive.[4] Other personality variables that influence response to violent programming include:

- Introversion or extroversion
- Stability or instability
- Tenderness or tough-mindedness[5]

Social Context

The social context of a media presentation can have a significant bearing on how individuals respond to the content. For instance, watching a comedy in an empty movie theater is an entirely different experience from seeing the film in a filled house, with everyone laughing.

Media scholar David Buckingham has found that children often engage in "social performance" in group settings—expressive or dramatic displays such as crying or hugging in response to (or for the benefit of) others in the group.[6] However, in some cases, social context can actually *inhibit* behavior. For example, boys may feel uncomfortable crying in front of others during poignant points of a film.

At other times, the social context of a media presentation can be distracting. Is someone sitting directly in front of you in the movie theater, blocking your view? Are kids running up and down the aisles? Can you hear the dialogue in the film? These distractions can affect the way you react to the media presentation.

Content Attributes

Content attributes of a media presentation can affect behaviors and attitudes. A program with a solid script, fine performances, and skillful direction can elicit particular reactions in the audience. Conversely, a program that lacks these qualities can evoke an unintended response— laughter instead of fear—or, worse yet, no response whatsoever.

Another content attribute is the *verisimilitude* of the program—how "real" the program appears to be. Barry Gunter found that children are more disturbed by realistic depictions of violence, such as news broadcasts, as opposed to similar acts in fictional entertainment genres, such as westerns, science fiction, or cartoons.[7]

An individual may also be affected when the situation depicted in a program is reminiscent of an occurrence in the life of the audience member. This *psychological proximity* can also arise when a character resembles someone with whom the audience member has been involved. An anecdote by one of the authors may illustrate this point. In the early days of television, Jimmy Durante hosted a weekly variety program. Each episode featured the same conclusion: "The set darkened, except for a series of spotlights on the floor. Durante would walk away from the camera; as he moved from one spotlight to the next, the circle of light he had occupied faded. Durante then would turn to the camera and wave, calling, 'Good night, Mrs. Calabash (his pet name for his departed wife)—wherever you are.'" At the end of each show, the author (then a small child) would burst into tears, hysterical. The little boy's bewildered parents would explain that Jimmy would return the next week—but to no avail.

Unbeknownst to his parents, this rather innocuous program segment had assumed a personal significance for the youngster. At that time, the author's grandfather (an elderly man who resembled Durante) had suffered a debilitating stroke. Durante's finale served as an enactment of death for the boy, triggering feelings of fear and grief. Thus, regardless of the intentions of the media communicator, a presentation may strike a responsive chord within the audience member.

Gender

Gender can also be a factor in the negotiation of meaning. For example, communication professor Byron Reeves found that children tend to respond most favorably toward same-sex characters.[8] Further, because of expectations and conditioning, boys in Western culture are attracted to characters high in activity and strength dimensions, while girls are drawn to attractive characters.[9] These gender-inspired responses may also serve as an indication of the relative positions of men and women in society. For example, many women respond intensely to a horror film depicting the victimization of females, whereas males are not as sensitive to this particular depiction of violence in media presentations.

Ethnic, Racial, and Class Identity

Members of different subcultures (e.g., racial or ethnic groups, social classes) have distinct, identifiable interests and, consequently, look for specific objectives or gratifications in media programming. When media content is generally congruent with the real-life experience of the audience, the result is a marked amplification in the response to the media presentation. Richard Frost and John Stauffer found that a sample of inner-city subjects responded more intensely to violent programming than a sample of college students. These researchers concluded that since the environment of the inner-city residents is indeed more violent than that of the college students, the formers' significantly higher arousal levels to violent stimuli may be connected to their real-life surroundings.[10]

Affective Response Analysis

This line of inquiry asks audience members to focus on their emotional responses to a media presentation as a springboard to critical analysis. Visual and aural media are particularly well suited to emotional appeals. Unlike print, which is processed at a cognitive level, photography, film, television, and radio are directed at the heart; we first react emotionally, and then translate these feelings into words. One of the primary reasons for attending movies is to provide the audience with an intense emotional experience; indeed, the "feel-good" movie has emerged as a new genre. Because the response to visual and aural media content is largely emotional, discourse about media content is often reduced to a "Beavis and Butthead" sensibility: Either a program is "cool" or it "sucks." Although this type of response initially discourages conversation, affective response offers an excellent springboard for systematic investigation of media content, beginning with *why* a program engenders a particular response in an individual.

Affective Response and Personal Belief Systems

Affective response analysis furnishes a framework for the systematic exploration of personal belief systems and can serve as the basis for critical self-analysis. Media programs give us an opportunity to "try out" emotions in a safe environment. There is little risk involved, since the media experience is private, and the individual's emotional involvement is limited to the duration of the program. This emotional outlet is particularly healthy in cultures in which many people—particularly men—are removed from their emotions.

Indeed, different genres put audience members in touch with a range of primal feelings.

- The horror genre targets our most basic fears.
- Melodramas touch feelings of sadness, pathos, and regret.
- Comedies make us laugh.
- Action films tap into feelings of rage.
- Romances evoke feelings of passion, longing, and regret.

Affective response analysis can be especially instructive for children, by putting them in touch with their feelings. David Buckingham observes,

"Children are also 'learning how to feel'—they are discovering what counts as an acceptable or appropriate emotional response, and the ways in which such responses serve to define them as individuals, both for themselves and for others."[11]

For example, Disney films are distinctive in their ability to introduce their young audiences to an array of emotional experiences. For instance, during the course of watching *The Lion King* (1994), children *grieve* for the loss of Simba's father, are *outraged* by Simba's subsequent humiliation and exile, and *rejoice* at Simba's newly found resolve to reclaim his throne.

Moreover, affective responses to media programs can contribute to the formation of self-concept. Buckingham cites the example of Jenny, a fifteen-year-old girl who describes herself in terms of her responses to media programs—she is the type of person who would "cry at anything."[12] People learn to react to media programs in ways that correspond to culturally acceptable gender roles: women cry; men rage. Moreover, individuals' affective responses to media programs often change as they move into new stages of life. Young people who wish to "act like adults" learn to tone down their responses to media programs.

Asking individuals to talk about how they feel during particular parts of a narrative can provide insight into the audience member's personal belief system. Examining affective responses to media presentations can also furnish insight into the *origin* and *source* of a person's emotional reactions. Buckingham explains, "The things that make us cry in films also make us cry in real life."[13] Buckingham has found that children tend to identify themes in media programs that resonate in their everyday lives, such as disruption of the family, the impossible romance, pity toward those who are presumed to be vulnerable or innocent (e.g., animals), or body violation.[14]

Follow-up questions can then focus on whether the emotional responses they experience while watching a program carry over into their everyday interactions, and what these responses may indicate about their personal belief systems.

An extension of this approach is the *pleasure perspective,* which is based on the assumption that media programs are often the source of genuine enjoyment. It can be revealing, therefore, to discover what kinds of activities depicted in a media presentation generate a pleasurable response from audience members. Particular elements of a program such as sex, violence, or romantic tension may evoke consistent reactions from an audience member; these same elements trigger a pleasurable response when they appear in other programs as well. The appearance of particular actors may serve as the source of continual pleasure. Particular programs or genres (e.g., musicals or romantic comedies) may elicit a positive response. Consequently, examining pleasurable responses to media programming can serve as a starting point for self-analysis, by examining what these responses reveal about the individual's interests, attitudes, and values.

Programs may also elicit pleasurable *secondary* emotions; for example, being frightened in a horror film can be followed by a sensation of excitement. It can be useful, then, to backtrack, focusing attention on the initial reaction that leads to the secondary response.

However, it should be noted that when using this mode of analysis in a group setting, facilitators are faced with the challenge of encouraging students to be open and honest in their responses, while maintaining a mutually respectful classroom environment. Because the mode of analysis is rooted in personal experience, a student's responses may diverge with others in the class, especially the teacher's. Len Masterman explains, "Some people may be disturbed, worried or offended by the very things in a text which others find pleasurable."[15] A pleasurable response can be tied to "dubious or oppressive purposes," such as violence or acts of racism.[16]

Coping Strategies

The study of affective response can furnish perspective into the *coping strategies* that individuals commonly use to deal with emotional distress. From birth, people learn to develop strategies to distance themselves from sources of emotional trauma. Once established, these coping strategies become a habitual response that helps individuals keep their feelings under control.

The media have emerged as a principal arena in which people learn coping mechanisms. Buckingham has identified the following coping strategies that children use in response to disturbing media content:

- *Denial.* Some children disown their emotions by refusing to acknowledge their feelings, either to themselves or to others. For instance, they may be scared by a scary movie but wouldn't admit it.[17]

- *Challenge.* This coping mechanism establishes the media experience as a personal challenge: "I *should* be able to watch." In this case, the audience member's ability to persevere through this uncomfortable experience is looked upon as a rite of passage that moves the person to the next stage of personal development, toward adulthood.
- *Mockery.* Some audience members maintain a safe distance from the media experience by installing an emotional filter—mockery or irony—between themselves and their feelings. For instance, during a horror movie, some members of the audience may laugh, electing to see the program as comical. By making fun of the presentation, they are able to regain control of the situation. *Overreaction* is a related coping strategy, in which audience members turn their emotions into a safe burlesque by exaggerating their responses. For instance, at a horror movie audience members may scream or try to scare one another during tense points in a narrative.
- *Comfort devices.* In response to disturbing content, some individuals seek physical comfort in the form of pillows, toys, or people to hug.
- *Partial or total avoidance.* Some people simply avoid material that they feel incapable of dealing with by hiding their faces at pivotal moments or leaving the screening area.
- *Reality checking.* Others cope by consciously reminding themselves that the media presentation isn't real. For instance, fearful viewers may force themselves to think of a horror film as "only a movie." Another reality check is to look for flaws in the program, (e.g., artistic mistakes, poor acting performances, or logical inconsistencies in the plot).
- *Distraction.* Audience members who are uncomfortable may try to distract themselves by thinking of "happy thoughts" or aspects of their everyday lives (e.g., errands they have to run after the film) as a way to regain control and perspective.
- *Repetition.* Some audience members respond to disturbing content by seeing the program repeatedly. By becoming familiar with the material, audience members regain the control they relinquished on the first viewing. Because they are no longer surprised or shocked by the content, they become immune to the effects of the content.
- *Alibi.* Some children in Buckingham's study dealt with the embarrassment caused by their responses by attributing their reactions to other factors. Some excuses were physical (e.g., "something in

my eye"), while others manufactured alternate reasons for their response (e.g., "My sister left town.")
- *Changing the context.* Watching at another time, with other people, can help people put a troubling media experience into perspective.

Understanding the ways that audience members cope with emotional tensions generated by the media can furnish perspective into the coping mechanisms they use elsewhere in their lives. After identifying an individual's coping strategies, it is then possible to focus on the *source* of these defensive mechanisms. And, if appropriate, this self-knowledge provides the individual with an opportunity to change these coping behaviors.

Affective Analysis: Function

Examining the *function,* or purpose, of affective response asks audience members to think along with the media communicator:

- What objective is served when the media communicator elicits a particular reaction from the audience?
- How does the media communicator want you to be feeling at particular points in the plot? Sad? Happy? Scared? Insecure? Envious?
- *Why* does the media communicator attempt to elicit that intended emotional response from the audience.

Media artists often strive to spark an emotional reaction from the audience for dramatic purposes. "*Show,* don't *tell*" is an adage that can be applied to media presentations. Rather than simply talking about a subject, it is always more effective to evoke the same emotions from the audience that the characters in the presentation are experiencing. The effective media communicator is able to anticipate how the audience should react at each point of the presentation and then strives to elicit that particular response. For instance, Hollywood director George Cukor was not known for his technical expertise. Instead, he surrounded himself with the best available cast and crew and, stationing himself by the camera, acted as his *own* audience while the action unfolded. If Cukor was moved by the scene, he was satisfied. If not, he would gather his experts around him to discuss strategies that would produce the intended response.

Advertisers manipulate the emotions of their audience to persuade them to buy their products. Ads often are directed at one of a number of *intrinsic psychological motivations,* including: guilt, love, need for approval, nostalgia, and fixation with death (including need for control, promises of immortality, fears of failure and of the unknown). For instance, in a television commercial for Tide detergent, a woman confesses her shame about her own experience as the youngest of several sisters who had to endure the embarrassment of wearing discolored hand-me-downs. As a mother of several girls, she is determined to spare her youngest daughter from this trauma. Thus, Tide has been transformed into a product that cleanses not only laundry but one's stained emotional past as well.

In contrast, advertisements that display animals or babies evoke a warm response, which the media communicator hopes the audience will transfer to the product. Advertisers may also use humor, snappy music, or celebrities to make viewing commercials enjoyable and memorable.

Affective response can serve an *ideological* function as well. Cultural studies scholar Douglas Kellner declares that a positive reaction to content is often associated with power and knowledge:

> We often are conditioned about what to enjoy and what we should avoid. We learn when to laugh and when to cheer (and laugh tracks on TV sitcoms and entertainment cue us in case we don't get it ourselves). A system of power and privilege thus conditions our pleasures so that we seek certain socially sanctioned pleasures and avoid others. Some people learn to laugh at racist jokes and other learn to feel pleasure at the brutal use of violence. . . . Pleasures are often, therefore, a conditioned response to certain stimuli and should thus be problematized, along with other forms of experience and behavior, and interrogated as to whether they contribute to the production of a better life and society, or help trap us into modes of everyday life that ultimately oppress and degrade us.[18]

Thus, media communicators maneuver the audience into emotional reactions that reinforce the prevailing ideology of the program. For instance, when violent action is accompanied by a laugh track or silly music, the violence is discounted as a humorous activity and the audience tends to discount the violence. Further, media educator Len Masterman contends that making media messages pleasurable is an effective way to "sell" objectionable ideas: "A narrative seeks to enlist our sympathies for a cause, a character or an idea that we might repudiate given the time for more mature reflection."[19] (For further discussion of ideology, see Chapter 1.)

Identification Analysis

Identification analysis is an approach in which individuals contrast media presentations with their own personal experience. Viewing a media presentation affords individuals the opportunity to project their personal experience onto the characters, enabling them to view their situations from a safe distance. Analyzing the characters in a media presentation can serve as a springboard to an examination of an individual's own life and social environment. Linguist Kenneth Burke suggests that literature (and by extension media presentations) can be understood as "equipment for living": "[Within narratives] are strategies for selecting enemies and allies, for socializing loses, for warding off the evil eye, for purification, propitiation and desanctification, consolation and vengeance, admonition, and exhortation, implicit commands for instructions of one sort or another. Art forms like 'tragedy' or 'comedy' or 'satire' . . . size up situations in various ways in keeping with correspondingly various attitudes."[20] In addition, media presentations can introduce clients to ideas they may not be ready or willing to hear directly. Therapists John and Jan Hesley strategically assign the viewing of certain films they feel will be beneficial to the therapeutic process of their clients. In addition, the narratives provide both the therapists and clients with metaphors for reflection and discussion.[21]

In her essay "Premature Burial," writer Jane Anne Phillips vividly recounts the mirroring between the B-grade horror films of Roger Corman and her own life growing up in a coal town in West Virginia. Corman's gothic sets and frequent gothic burials, she says, "were haunting, inverted metaphors of things that were true, things too frightening to think about as a child. . . ." What about my own life, how shaky things seem. . . ." "What does it mean buried? The frequent, gothic burials in Corman's films are relatively speedy events; here in our town, there's daily life—along slow process."[22]

Identification analysis can serve as a particularly effective counseling tool with young people who have difficulty talking about themselves. Identification fulfills a critical role in the formation of self-concept. Psychologist Gloria Johnson Powell explains that children discover personality traits in themselves by recognizing them in others: "After the early differentiation of self from the animate and inanimate worlds, the process of self-concept development becomes more social in nature. It begins to involve identification with others, introjection from others, and expansion into interpersonal relationships."[23] Thus, talking about the characters in a media presentation and discussing questions about the narrative can help to bridge this "disconnect" and disclose information about their own values, attitudes, behaviors, preoccupations, and concerns.

Character Identification

Character identification can furnish perspective into individuals' interests, aspirations, and values. Audience members' identification with particular characters can be a valuable source of information about what people consider attractive or engaging behaviors, values, or attributes.

Audience members frequently identify with media figures and the worlds they inhabit, measuring their own lives in relation to what is happening to their favorite characters on-screen. For example, after Jerry Seinfeld decided to discontinue his hit sitcom, fans made a pilgrimage to Tom's Restaurant, the site of the exterior shots used for the coffee-shop scenes in the program (although all of the interior scenes were shot in a studio in Los Angeles). "Where else could we go?" asked Denise Jones, a secretary from Queens who made the sojourn with two friends to have a tuna sandwich (one of the staples of the show's characters).

For Donna Stephen, a visitor from Houston, the version of New York City portrayed in *Seinfeld* served as her tour guide during her trip to the city: "Everything we know about New York City is from *Seinfeld*. Like how to bootleg a movie, how to smuggle cafe latte into the movies in your pants, how to fight for a parking space, how to follow the protocol at the Soup Nazi."[24]

Fans were in mourning, seeing the end of the series as a form of death for the characters, who had become very real to them. Teri Goldberg remarked, "I wish I was friends with Elaine . . . I love her. She's so funny. I feel like I use her expressions all the time." Lynly Stephen, a speech therapist from Dallas, said she would miss Kramer, also known by his elusive first name Cosmo: "What a bad way to wake up, and me even here in New York. I just worry, what will happen to Cosmo."[25]

The character-identification process operates in one of the following ways:

- Audience members identify with characters they feel are similar to them.

Seinfeld

Character identification can furnish perspective into individuals' interests, aspirations, and values. To illustrate, many fans of *Seinfeld* measured their own lives in relation to what happened to their favorite characters of the popular sitcom. (*Getty Images; photographer: Bob Riha, Jr.*)

- Audience member identify with those they aspire to be like.
- Audience members adopt the point of view of the person with whom they identify.
- Audience members react to what is happening to the character as if it was happening to them.
- Audience members identify with the situation in which the characters find themselves.
- Audience members emulate behaviors exhibited by the characters with whom they identify.

Some critics have expressed concern that identification with media personalities can lead directly to imitative behavior. However, it should be noted that modeling behavior can be a positive, instructive stage of personality formation. Moreover, although identification is a *precondition* of imitation, it is not a *guarantee* that people will adopt the modeling behavior.

Identification is a widespread and normal part of the formation of identity, and people have always looked to external sources (e.g., parents, actors, actresses, sports figures) as role models. This process enables individuals to "try on" aspects of personality that they admire in a media figure. Children sometimes engage in *fantasy participation,* in which they insert themselves into the program. Fantasy participation can help children prepare for the world off screen, as they picture what they would do in those circumstances to alter the situation.[26]

In like fashion, identifying with a media figure can serve as a public declaration of self. For instance, a young man who wears a T-shirt with the likeness of Bono on it is displaying his taste in music. Moreover, wearing the shirt is making a statement about his lifestyle, attitudes, and positions on political and social issues.

Character identification can be a valuable source of information about what people consider attractive or engaging behaviors, values, or attributes. In that sense, examining an individual's responses to characters in a media presentation can provide insight into his or her belief system. This mode of analysis includes the following steps:

- Identify favorite characters and explain what you liked and disliked about them.
- Clarify the nature of the character identification: *likeness* (in which the individual sees a resemblance with the character) or *aspiration* (in which the individual would like to emulate the character). This strategy can provide insight into the individual's perceived gender, ethnic, racial, and class identification, as well as information about what the individual considers attractive or engaging behaviors, values, and attributes.
- Name additional attributes that the individual did *not* include in his or her original list of character traits. This may lead to discussion about qualities that may not be readily apparent but are nevertheless essential to the overall positive portrait of the character. This also can serve as a useful springboard for discussion about cultural values, in cases where individuals identify with "negative" attributes (such as violent tendencies) depicted in the media presentation.
- Discuss the role that the attributes of the character play in the successful outcome of the story. For example, a violent temperament often is key to resolving problems in media programs. At the same time, other attributes may help the individual succeed within the

context of the narrative—some of which, perhaps, the audience member does not identify with or immediately think about. From this point, individuals can examine the role that these attributes play in the outcome of their own life "narratives." Does being tough or violent guarantee success?

- Discuss whether there are *missing* attributes in some characters that prevent them from succeeding within the context of the narrative.
- Name characters to whom individuals *cannot* relate. This can stimulate discussion about expectations: what can be regarded as unrealistic or "too perfect" characters, or characters with attributes that the individual may regard as unobtainable in his or her own life.
- Oppositional identification is a particularly useful approach, in which individuals identify with a character other than the protagonist: a member of a subculture, a member of the opposite sex, or a supporting character (see discussion of this technique in Chapter 1, "Ideological Analysis"). The analysis could, then, pursue the following line of questioning:

  - What could you accomplish as one of *these* characters?
  - What opportunities would be available to you?
  - What advantages would you have?
  - What could you "get away with" because of your position?
  - What conclusions can you draw from this analysis?

- Discuss how the individual relates to villains in the media presentation. This tactic often reveals that individuals are attracted to some of the character traits of the antagonists and find the heroes to be less appealing. One way to account for this phenomenon is that audience members identify with some of the flaws of the antagonists. Moreover, there could be appealing aspects to the villainous character—in that sense, characterization (and human nature) is more complex than the absolute distinctions presented in the media. In fact, villainous characters may display an energy, creativity, and sexuality that can be seen as attractive.

Unfortunately, media portrayals of minority groups offer limited opportunities for character identification. Aimee Dorr observes, "If minority children look for models of the same ethnicity as themselves, they find few to choose from on television. Those they do find have a limited range of personality characteristics, occupations, and social circumstances to emulate. If, on the other hand, they look for role models who are powerful and successful, then they would probably emulate white characters."[27] Dorr observes that the cumulative media messages about social class suggest that in order to become successful, one must relinquish one's identification with these subcultures. "If [minority children] look to minority characters as role models, then they might learn to be less knowledgeable, wealthy, assertive, or dominant than would white children, to defer to whites, or to accept largely white versions of their minority culture. If they look to white characters as role models, then they might learn white values and behaviors vis-à-vis work, money, aggression, competition, cooperation, family life, and so on. All of which may require giving up some distinctive elements of one's own ethnic culture."[28]

Character identification can also provide insight into the *ideology* of a narrative. The media text encourages the audience member to identify with the primary protagonists, who are the sources of power in the presentation and aligned with its prevalent ideology (for further discussion, see Chapter 1, "Ideological Analysis"). By imagining themselves in the role of the primary figure in the program, individuals gain insight into the sources of power and assumptions about what constitutes "the good life," within the context of the media presentation. Questions to consider include:

- As the lead character, what could *you* accomplish?
- What opportunities would be available to you?
- What advantages would you have? What could you "get away with"?

Another useful line of inquiry involves examining an individual's initial emotional response to characters "making an entrance." The first impression an actor makes sets the emotional tone for the entire program and establishes a relationship between the character and the audience. Consequently, it can be beneficial to ask audience members to describe their affective (emotional) responses at that moment and what generated their initial impression. For example, the selection of clothing can elicit a reaction, including admiration or sexual attraction. Or the character may be involved in an activity or engaged in dialogue that moves the audience. Often the character displays an intense emotion that shocks or impresses the audience.

The next area of exploration is whether the audience maintains or changes this initial impression, and what (if anything) causes this change. Finally, based on their subsequent behavior in the story, do the characters deserve that particular initial response from the audience?

Narrative Analysis

Narrative analysis is a line of inquiry in which a story serves as a springboard for personal reflection and discussion. Two approaches involving narrative analysis are particularly useful: narrative reconstruction and narrative forecasting.

Narrative Reconstruction

Narrative reconstruction refers to a process in which individuals recount a story they have seen, heard, or read in the media. Narrative reconstruction is rooted in the experience of the individual, providing insight into how individuals make sense of the programming they have watched, heard, or read. Thus, asking an individual to reconstruct the essential elements of a narrative can be an excellent way to learn about his or her interests and preoccupations.

The first step involves focusing on the *explicit content* of a media presentation. Explicit content refers to the essential events and activities in a story that are displayed through visible action. The audience constructs meaning by selecting the essential pieces of explicit information in the story that answer the question, "What was the program about?" For example, consider the following scenario: A man bops another fellow over the head with a brickbat, takes his money, and flees. Later in the program he is caught and carted off to jail. The audience constructs meaning by selecting the essential pieces of explicit information in the story. In this example, five distinct actions are described: (1) the clubbing; (2) the theft; (3) the flight; (4) the apprehension; and (5) the incarceration.

In his study of children's comprehension of television content, psychology professor W. Andrew Collins found that children typically have difficulty remembering explicit details and identifying important scenes:

- Eighth graders recalled 92 percent of the scenes that adults had judged as essential to the plot.

- Fifth graders recalled 84 percent of the scenes that adults had judged as essential to the plot.
- Second graders recalled an average of only 66 percent of the scenes that adults had judged as essential to the plot.[29]

According to Collins, young children's limited grasp of explicit story material impairs their ability to interpret media content: "Young children fail to comprehend observed actions and events in an adult-like way because they arrive at different interpretations of the various actors' plans or intentions. . . . Thus, it is possible that second and third graders take away not only a less complete understanding of the program than fifth and eighth graders do, they may also be perceiving the content of the program somewhat *differently* because they retain (and work off of) a different set of cues."[30] In retelling stories, young children often have difficulty deciding on the essential points in the narrative. They may omit parts of the story that adults judge to be essential content and may include pieces of the story deemed nonessential.

Young children often embellish a story with their own experiences, sometimes inserting themselves into the narrative. In addition, they may include or emphasize what they regard as important and omit or de-emphasize what they see as unimportant. For example, in describing a James Bond movie, a young child may devote an extraordinary amount of attention describing the Austin Healy driven by the British agent, reflecting his or her interest in cars. In recounting a media narrative, individuals may also add their editorial commentary (e.g., "This was neat").

Reconstructing the narrative also provides insight into an individual's understanding of *implicit content.* Implicit content refers to those elements of a narrative that remain under the surface:

- Motives (why did the characters behave as they did?)
- The relationship between events
- The relationship between characters
- The consequences of earlier action

According to Collins, young children have even more difficulty identifying implicit than explicit content. In their narrative reconstruction of plots, second-grade boys operate on a "chance" level, meaning that they are developmentally incapable of recognizing the implicit elements in a plot.[31] Therefore, as part of narrative reconstruction, it is useful to ask the following:

- Why do you think that an event occurred?
- What is the relationship between events in the story?
- What is the relationship between characters in the story?
- Were the consequences of characters' actions made clear?

Narrative Forecasting

Narrative forecasting refers to a process in which individuals put themselves in the situation depicted in the media program and respond to the following questions:

- What is the significance of (or meaning behind) the events in the narrative?
- How would you feel about being in that situation?
- What do you think will happen next? Why?
- How will the characters be affected? Why?
- How would you react if it happened to you?
- Does the situation remind you of your own life?

For example, a team of educators, college students, and staff members used identification analysis with some success at the Hogan Street Regional Youth Center, a juvenile offender facility in the state of Missouri. Judy McMillan, a teacher at Hogan, described these adolescents, some of whom have committed serious crimes, as a strange anomaly: "None of the teenagers have been off of their block, but all of them have been to Hollywood."[32] In this case, movies serve as a primary source of information about gender roles, as well as definitions and strategies for success.

The teaching team presented a series of film clips from *Boyz n the Hood* (1991) as a vehicle for discussion about behavior and personal choice. The first clip depicts a confrontation between two groups of African American teenagers: Verbal exchanges between the groups become heated, and challenges are issued. The narrative then cuts to a shot of Darin "Doughboy" Baker (Ice Cube), who reaches inside his coat pocket. At that point, the video was paused. The teenagers talked about what principles were at stake: In a world of diminished prospects and expectations, conducting oneself with honor, personal dignity, and concern for reputation was magnified in importance.

The students were then asked to speculate about what was going to occur next in the narrative. All of the students agreed that Doughboy was reaching for a gun and was going to shoot members of the rival gang. The discussion then turned to "why" this was a "logical" next step in the narrative: The students explained that in a world of diminished expectations, this behavior was equated with conducting oneself with honor, personal dignity, and concern for reputation.

The teenagers were then asked to draw connections between the fictional narrative and their own lives. The members of the group generally agreed that the worldview depicted in the film was reminiscent of their own experience and that the values delineated in the narrative were an important part of their own lives as well.

A question was then raised that focused on *consequences:* What do you think will happen to Doughboy if, indeed, he does pull a gun and shoot a rival gang member? Significantly, the answer was universally, "Nothing bad will happen to him." As one student explained, no harm could possibly come to him because Doughboy was the star of the movie.

Once again, the discussion moved from discussion of the narrative to their *own* experiences: What do you think would happen if *you* had fired the gun? If you shot someone, would you get caught? What would the punishment be?

The subsequent discussion focused on the *consequences* of the code of conduct displayed in the film: Are there other options available that would have enabled the characters to retain their dignity and self-respect?

Then the team played the rest of the scene. Significantly, Doughboy fired his gun into the air.

De-identification

A related mode of analysis focuses attention on the *limits* of identification. Although film, television, and other media may appear to reflect the audience's experience, the media construct a reality that is impossible to emulate in real life. Production elements such as editing present selected moments that make the world depicted in the media appear exciting. The addition of a musical score makes even pedestrian acts like crossing the street appear dramatic. Special effects and stunt specialists enable characters to perform astonishing acts of strength and daring. And because the action is scripted, our heroes and heroines never miss a line, accidentally spill their food, or die in the middle of the story.

Moreover, through the use of makeup, editing, lighting, and digital manipulation, actors always look perfect. The members of the audience cannot possibly measure up to these idealized figures. Ironically, even the stars *themselves* cannot measure up to their own idealized standard of beauty. For example, actress Isabella Rossellini was asked about the secret of her unlined looks, captured on the cover of *Vogue* magazine when she was forty-five: "Well, you can't go by the photo. Because obviously, the photo is an enhanced version of me, you know. It generally takes hours of makeup and fantastic lighting, a great photographer. So I don't think I look as good in life as in my photos."[33] Examining these production and performance elements can provide insight into how efforts to identify with media characters can create unrealistic expectations on the part of the audience.

Media Chronicles

The mass media have emerged as a pervasive influence in American culture. We continually receive information through the channels of mass communication whether we are at home, in the car, or in the supermarket. Through technological advances, media programming accompanies us everywhere. In the 1950s, thanks to the invention of the transistor, the radio became a constant companion—on the beach, on family vacations, and at parties. More recently, iPods and BlackBerries provide us with universal access to music, information, and access to the Web.

Because of the repetitive nature of commercial media programming, the public is inundated with the same messages, delivered over a relatively brief time span. Radio stations play their most popular tunes once per hour. Reruns and spin-offs abound on television. Further, the advertising industry bombards the consumer with the same images and slogans in order to establish audience recognition and patronage. Indeed, much of the information that we receive is involuntary. Members of the family may have programs blaring in another room that we cannot avoid hearing.

Consequently, mass communications has assumed a very personal role in the lives of its audience. Watching old films, TV shows, or listening to radio programs can spark personal recollections of otherwise forgotten pieces of the past. Indeed, media programming often assumes a personal significance that transcends its aesthetic or entertainment value. Instead, the media program has become internalized as a part of our personal experience, and we may feel nostalgic about a program because it has put us in touch with ourselves and our pasts. Hearing an old song on the radio may awaken memories of a summer long ago, perhaps, or of old friends, or a first romance. In that sense, it may not be the song that we are reacting to (in fact, we may dislike the particular tune).

In the 1970s, scholars began to conduct *oral histories,* in which they recorded the personal reminiscences of older citizens as a means of studying personal and cultural history. In like fashion, a media chronicle project consists of presenting clips of popular media programs from a particular era to the audience. The facilitator then records individuals' personal recollections that have been stimulated by the program. For instance, playing the tune "Take Me Out to the Ball Game" to a group at a retirement center in St. Louis, Missouri, reminded one old gentleman of his youth, when he would skip school and take the streetcar to Sportsman's Park to watch the Gas House Gang—the St. Louis Cardinals baseball club, featuring Dizzy Dean, Pepper Martin, and Frankie Frisch. He even recalled watching the St. Louis Browns playing the New York Yankees and seeing Babe Ruth hit a home run.

In addition to stimulating personal recollections, media chronicles furnish insight into historical events. For instance, many songs, films, and radio programs of the Depression era commented on this period of American history (e.g., the popular tune that began, "We ain't got a barrel of money"). Presenting snippets of these programs may trigger personal memories about this historical period. Media can also be associated with social movements. For instance, the cult film *Easy Rider* (1969) assumes a significance for members of the sixties counterculture. Seeing this film many years later may evoke memories about the social and political experiences of this social group.

Media programs also kindle personal recollections about stages of life. For instance, people may embrace films, songs, and television programs that they associate with their adolescence. Media programs may also be associated with seasonal activities. For example, Christmas music and movies often evoke memories of family and past holiday seasons.

A freshman seminar at Webster University participated in a media chronicles exercise in which the students brought CDs to class and played songs that had personal significance for them. The students then were invited to share any of their personal recollections triggered by the song. The following is an edited transcript of their recollections:

Song: "Fight for Your Right," Beastie Boys
Angie Kilber:
It just completely reminds me of my entire four years in high school. Because it talked about, first of all, "I don't want to go to school. Mom, please don't make me go." But I had to go anyway, because she was one of those, really "into school" parents. And then the second verse is like smoking and you can't do that. And I started smoking when I was sixteen and my parents hated it and now they finally understand now that I'm a . . . It was just this big ordeal throughout high school that I could not smoke. It was just bad. And my dad was just being a hypocrite and it says that in the song too.

And it also reminds me of the summer after my senior year. Because finally, it was all over. This past summer I was like, "Wow, I love the song. Now I'm not in high school anymore. I don't have to do this anymore. I don't have to put up with it. My parents don't care that I smoke." And I was so happy. And I brought it to a friend of mine's house where we used to go all the time. He was one of my best friends. He had a really big party here. And we played this song. And everyone there screamed through the entire song really, really, really loud. And I will never forget it. Because we were all sitting in . . . thinking of this song.

Other students were then invited to discuss any of their own personal recollections that were evoked by "Fight for Your Right."

Plesah Mayo:
This reminds me of the beginning of my senior year. Because my dad was living in Colorado Springs. He'd got stationed there. It was just me and my mom alone here together. And she was driving me up the wall. . . . And she'd make me come home at 10 o'clock during the summer and stuff like that. Even on weekends. And I was getting really upset with this because all my friends stayed out late. I was sixteen but I was going into my senior year. And my friend Tracy used to take her brother's car all the time and it had a CD in there. And what happened is I start getting so sick of my mom, and I'd sneak out at night. And there were times when Tracy would come and pick me up at night and this song would be playing and I'd be like yeah, rebellion. But then it just kind of reminds me of all the stuff I did . . . in the school year. I did irritate my mom. I'd go to parties really late at night. . . . But now I really feel bad.

Shay Malone:
This song reminds me of my freshman year in high school. . . . We couldn't have our prom because the principal stole our money. So, I remember

all the ninth graders trying to figure out what they were going to do. And this guy stood up and he had on a cowboy hat and he just started singing this song. And the whole auditorium started singing this song. Because we wanted our prom.

Callie Pitt:
This is not one of those happy associations memories. Like a senior's last day or a bunch of people getting together listening to this. This was possibly one of the worst first-date songs. My best friend's boyfriend fixed me up with his brother. And I met his brother before. And we got along fine. But apparently, some rumors had reached his school about me that were not true. . . . He went over called his friend and said come get me there's somebody here I don't want to be around. This song was playing in the background. So every time I hear that I think Bryan was really a jerk.

Song: "Crash into Me," Dave Matthews Band
Bernard Cummings:
This song reminds me of the last show in high school. It was *The Boys Next Door.* I remember the entire cast being in the dressing room just listening to . . . It felt sad. . . . We said how much we love each other, how much we'll miss each other. . . . We started thinking about how the theater department would survive without us. And we were, "Oh, well, we have this guy here, this girl here, she can do it."

Gretchen Olson:
It was from this past summer. Right before I left for college, I had to make some money. So, I got a job at a video store in my hometown. And there was this guy who worked there who was my age but he'd gone to another high school. . . . And I got just this massive crush on him. . . . We'd close the store at night and he put Dave Matthews in the tape deck. So, while we were cleaning up the store, all the lights off in the store, and this song would be playing. And our boss would be like, "Hey, you guys want a beer?" And we all would sit up front, sit on the counter drinking our beer just listening to this song and, like, wow, these are the best days. And I'd go yeah, these are the best days . . . so much. And I always think about that when I hear that song.

Angie Kilber:
Mine isn't a sappy, happy memory at all. This song reminds me of the day I got fired. Cause it was playing when I left. . . . And I loved that job.

I'd been there for two years. And I knew everything about it. I trained people because I worked there for so long. Then one day they the district manager . . . told me that someone had said that I had stolen something. And it was really a big misunderstanding because I would have never stolen from the company or anything like that. And I was trying to tell them that and it just made them more mad because they felt I was lying to them. . . . It made me very angry. And listening to that song makes very angry. Because when I left the store there was that song on a stupid tape they play over and over again. And I had to leave. . . . Just hearing that song makes me very, very angry. As if you can't tell. . . . I didn't know I could get this angry just hearing a song. I didn't know that just hearing something could make me that emotional.

Song: "The Time Warp, from The Rocky Horror Picture Show"
Lisa Pavia:
I was involved in a youth group. Every year we have three hundred teenagers crowding in this theater for a skit night on Thursday night. And it's a very long night because we have a lot of kids . . . and they all do skits. The leaders are all together and they are all the same age. And they have as much time as they want. So, they did a medley of songs. And my very first year there, I'm like, who are these weird people? And they're dancing around to this song. It was very, very cramped. And a lot of people were sweating. And we just want to get out of here. But that [song] kind of took us away from that. And we were all, like, singing and having a good time. And we all got to jump onto the stage and do the *Rocky Horror Picture Show* at the end.

This set of media chronicles demonstrates why individuals have such a passionate attachment to popular music. Clearly, the songs triggered deeply emotional memories. As Angie recalled an unhappy memory associated with the song, she actually re-experienced the anger that she had felt at the time. She observed in amazement, "I didn't know that just hearing something could make me that emotional." Further, popular music put the students in touch with a range of emotions. Gretchen associated "Crash into Me" with romantic feelings, while Callie began, "This is not one of those happy associations memories."

Recalling popular media programming can bring past experiences into the present. Gretchen treasured "Crash into Me" because it froze a moment in time and space. ("We all would sit up front . . . just listening to this song and, like, wow, these are the best days.") Indeed, at one point in Lisa Pavian's recollection, she moves between past and present tense ("It was very, very cramped. And a lot of people were sweating. And we just want to get out of here"). For Lisa, hearing the music triggered other senses as well, such as sight and smell, making the memory even more real.

Some students associated songs with significant moments in their lives. Shay's recollection focused on an incident in which "Fight for Your Right" emerged as an anthem for her high school class, expressing their indignation and sense of betrayal when her principal absconded with their prom funds. Some students linked popular songs to rites of passage commemorating significant personal changes, such as proms or graduation. A song may remind an individual of a broad time span ("entire four years of high school") or embody a general attitude toward the world. For Angie, the Beastie Boys song articulated her general distaste for her high school years. Song lyrics may articulate the precise feelings and experiences of the listener. (Angie declares, "And then the second verse is like smoking and you can't do that. And I started smoking when I was sixteen and my parents hated it.")

Popular music also helps to forge meaningful connections between people. Whether the students in the class hailed from Madison, Wisconsin, or Crestwood, Missouri, sharing the same musical interests served as a unifying experience for the members of the class. Taste in music also provided significant information about classmates, serving as an indication of other interests and personality traits. As Angie commented during the debriefing session, "I think that it's a good thing because [Shay] had kind of the same thing going on about [the Beastie Boys] song. Because that was my whole rebellion. I hated school so it was kind of the same for her. And just the fact that she liked it. I don't know, I get along good with people who like the same music I do, for some reason."

Media Production Analysis

Media technology provides tools that can help promote personal discovery and growth. The digital domain offers teenagers an opportunity to experiment with new ideas, ways to relate to others, and experience different sides of self. Psychologist Camille Sweeney explains:

> Herein lies the thrill of the on-line self: its malleability, its plasticity, the fact that it can be made up entirely of your own imagination. You can take your old self, or don a fresh one, and hang out in a group of jocks for a post game chat, argue the banality of Britney Spears with an international posse of pop connoisseurs, post a note to a cool-sounding guy from

Detroit—all without ever having to leave your bedroom. Maybe this is the Internet's greatest asset to teendom: access, and the confidence to slip in and out of personalities, the ability to try on identities, the adolescent equivalent of playing dress-up in the attic, standing before the mirror in heels and lipstick long before you own your own.[34]

The choice of a blogger's alias can provide clues into his or her character, as well as insight into the personal significance of the naming process. For instance, Tony Pierro observes,

> Jim McKay of Huntington blogs under his real name on his blog "Wabi-Sabi" (www.inblogs.net/jimmckay). Although the name of his blog might not be familiar to most surfing the World Wide Web, it reflects McKay's personal style and view of blogging.
>
> "Wabi-Sabi is described as: 'The beauty of things imperfect, impermanent, and incomplete. The beauty of things modest and humble. The beauty of things unconventional,'" McKay said.[35]

However, the anonymity of the Internet can also mask the identity of people who, for various reasons, are engaged in some form of deception. As with any relationship, you should develop a relationship gradually; trust should be earned, not assumed.

Web arenas such as blogs and MySpace can serve as personal diaries that give individuals the opportunity to reflect on issues that affect their sense of identity. A poll conducted in 2007 found that the average teenager spends four and a half hours a week blogging or visiting social-sharing sites on the Internet such as MySpace and YouTube, with 22 percent of teenagers blogging five times a week or more.[36]

In contemporary mass culture, in which people must compete for attention, these virtual arenas give individuals an opportunity to express themselves—to be heard by others as well as to "hear" their own views, thoughts, and attitudes. Ironically, while the Internet technology may be rather sophisticated, it provides a means for an ancient, primitive form of expression—the diary or journal. However, one key difference between traditional diaries and blogs is that while diaries are intensely private, blogs are meant to be shared with a select audience. Individuals are invited to read and respond to the author's comments.

Blogs can also serve as social networks. Several different configurations of blogs have emerged:

- An *aggregation* is a collection in which different bloggers contribute to a body of work on a particular topic.
- A *cloud* of blogs is an informal network, in which bloggers post their thoughts, followed by other bloggers' comments
- *Resyndicated* blogs refer to blogs from around the virtual universe that are republished on one site.
- *Carnival* blogs consist of one blog compiling the most up-to-date information on a topic each week. These posts are either submitted by individual bloggers or are collected by a designated person.
- *Group blogs* are composed of a community of people with a common purpose, values, and goals. John Tropea observes, "It's within a community that has a leader, moderator, members, forum, etc . . . ; basically a community of practice with a social network feature."[37]
- *Branded blogs* are a formal network in which the blogger formally "registers" the topic, making it easier for individuals to locate it or contribute to the community of bloggers.

Blog sites can also serve as vehicles to both record and learn about local history. For instance, History Matters, a British organization, established a campaign in 2006 to raise awareness of the importance of history in the everyday lives of individuals and to encourage involvement in heritage, by creating the world's biggest blog. On October 17, as many people as possible uploaded their own blog entries, contributing to a "national blog" housed in the British Library as a record of national life. October 17 was selected at random, as a day to record national life.

Another technological avenue for self-examination is the *video diary,* a form of personal storytelling in which videographers use the conventions of the medium—narrative structure, plot, and character—to tell their stories to a broad-based audience. These diaries record the artists' personal experiences. At the same time, these videos also reflect broader individual and cultural issues. Ellen Schneider, a video diarist explains,

> Why, we asked, were [the video diarists] willing to make private moments public? "To use my reunion with a grown sister I've never known as a kind of emblem for the black family experience in America today," answered Meredith Woods in St. Paul. "A personal search for justice," said Jeffrey Tuchman in Los Angeles, who shot 20 hours of tape when

he accompanied his father back to Germany to confront the Nazi officer who killed his grandmother. "We wanted to offer unscripted glimpse into our lives," replied Herbert Peck in New York, whose diary documents his wife's normal pregnancy through the birth of a son with Down's Syndrome. "Video diarists are taking risks . . . but also showing the power of what TV can be.'"[38]

Programs featuring video diarists have been presented on public television stations in New York; St. Paul, Minnesota; Los Angeles; and San Francisco.

Empowerment Strategies

After having gone through an extensive experience in media literacy, you are left with what may be termed the *quintessential so-what?:* that is, what steps can you take to act on your knowledge and understanding of the media and media content? The Aspen Institute National Leadership Conference on Media Literacy raises this critical issue of possible applications of this body of knowledge: "Is media literacy important only to the extent that it enables one to be a better citizen in society? What is the role of ideology in the process? To what extent is an individual 'media literate' if she just appreciates the aesthetics of a message without going further with it?"[39]

Empowerment strategies encourage audience members to assume an active role in determining media content. Rather than expect that the media industry will protect citizens from irresponsible images and messages, the empowerment view holds that individuals must assume responsibility for understanding the political, social, and economic influence of the media. Thus, empowerment strategies enable audience members to change the way in which they respond to and interact with the media.

Empowerment Circle

Eddie Dick and Elizabeth Thoman advocate a four-step approach by which media literacy can effect social change, which they refer to as the *empowerment circle:*

- *Awareness.* Use the tools of media literacy to examine and understand the impact of media messages, including: (1) becoming

well-informed in matters of media coverage; (2) discussing media
programming with friends, colleagues, and children.

- *Analysis.* Examine the political, economic, social, and cultural
  factors that shape media messages. This may involve the following steps: (1) developing a sensitivity to programming trends as a
  way of learning about the culture; (2) keeping abreast of patterns
  in ownership and government regulations that affect the media
  industry.
- *Reflection.* Consider the role of the media in individual decision
  making, lifestyle, attitudes, and values.
- *Action.* Decide on appropriate strategies on the basis of the first
  three steps. These strategies can include: (1) discussing media content with friends, colleagues, and children; (2) exercising critical
  choices in personal use of media; (3) writing letters to the editor
  or to a TV station; (4) meeting with the staff of the newspaper, TV,
  or radio station; (5) boycotting the advertisers of the program or
  newspaper; (6) promoting the instruction of media literacy throughout the school system (K–12) by contacting members of the local
  board of education, PTA, and principals; (7) joining media literacy
  organizations.[40]

Emancipatory Media Programming

Another action step consists of the production of *emancipatory media
programming*—programs that challenge the institutions and values of
the dominant culture. Popular television programs such as *The Daily
Show* and *The Colbert Report* raise questions about the underlying assumptions of the dominant culture.

Yet another empowerment action step involves the development of
public response strategies for media policy legislation. The Center for
Media Education has proposed a twelve-step action plan that citizens
can adopt to help ensure that the public interest is made a part of media
and telecommunications policy:

Concentration and Control

1. *Media mergers.* Public interest groups need political support to
   help make the case against current and future media mergers.
2. *Ownership limits.* Citizens can write letters to FCC commis-

The Daily Show

The Daily Show is an example of emancipatory media programming, which challenges the institutions and values of the dominant culture by raising questions about the underlying assumptions of the dominant culture. (*Getty Images; photographer: Peter Kramer*)

sioners and congressional representatives supporting strong ownership safeguards.

3. *Broadcaster accountability.* Citizens and community groups can file petitions with the FCC to deny transfer of licenses. They can challenge new owners to live up to their public interest obligations, as well as participate in broadcast license renewals. Also, citizens should fight the proposal at the FCC to extend license renewals from five to eight years.

4. *Cable accountability.* Citizens can urge local officials to demand public interest obligations and safeguards in return for the cable companies' use of public rights-of-way.

5. *Crucial appointments.* Citizens can write to the appropriate government office to support appointments of officials truly independent of the telecommunications industry.

Access and Affordability

6. *Universal service.* Citizens can file and organize in support of access for the poor, and for community institutions, at the FCC and state regulatory agencies, making sure that information-highway access is meaningful and rates truly affordable.

7. *Consumer pricing for broadband service.* Citizens can file petitions with the local public utility commission calling for a consumer-oriented, low-cost, flat-rate tariff for ISDN service.

8. *Competition and consumer protection.* Citizens can join coalitions of national public-interest groups and state public advocates to file at these regulatory agencies, giving them the necessary political support to take on local monopolies by denying them unfair advantages in the marketplace.

9. *Children's television.* Citizens can write to the FCC to urge that it require broadcasters to air a minimum amount of educational programming for children as part of their public service obligation.

10. *Spectrum auctions.* Citizens can tell their representatives and the FCC that the spectrum should be auctioned off, and that the proceeds reinvested for public use.

11. *Open access for video programming.* Citizens can support non-discriminatory access for independent video providers on the new open video systems platforms created for phone companies in the Telecommunications Act. Citizens can also support advocates who are fighting at the FCC for a low rate of programmers on cable companies' leased access channels. Special provisions and rates for educational programming on telephone and cable systems are also needed.

12. *Intellectual property.* Citizens can support the Digital Future Coalition, which is fighting for policies that ensure accessible, affordable, and noncommercial information for the public.[41]

Empowerment Strategies in the Classroom

One of the fundamental objectives of media education is the development of critical autonomy, so that students learn to develop an independence from the messages being conveyed through the media. In order to achieve this objective, Len Masterman argues that media education must avoid the hierarchical, authoritative structure that is characteristic of most classroom environments:

> This approach follows closely that practiced by Brazilian educator Paulo Freir, who argued for a pedagogy which would liberate rather than oppress or domesticate. His approach rests firmly on a belief in our human potential to reflect critically upon our experience, to discover what, within our own and others' experiences, oppresses and limits our thinking and our actions, and finally to act in order to transform those debilitating factors in the interests of all human beings and of the ecological systems of which we are a part.
>
> First and foremost, Freir *trusts* the potentiality and inclination of human beings to move in these directions. Secondly, he also recognizes that most of what passes for education mitigates against this movement for liberation.[42]

Media literacy scholar Barry Duncan has identified the following strategies designed to promote empowerment in the classroom:

- Try to encourage students to transfer their insights into other areas: schooling, the family, the world of work; otherwise, much of our endeavor will have limited impact.
- Model a variety of individual response to media texts . . . so that students can be introduced to the notions of consent, negotiation and resistance to popular culture texts. Explore the connections between knowledge, pleasure and power.
- Make media studies inquiry centered, and investigative. There should be plenty of room for independent study.[43]

Autobiographical Analysis

"I'm No Superman: An Autobiographical Analysis of *Scrubs*"
Dana Keeven, May 2006

According to Webster University graduate student Dana Keeven, much of the humor of the popular TV sitcom *Scrubs* stems from the characters' coping mechanisms—the ways in which they deal with the pain, suffering, chaos, and unfairness in the world.

Coping strategies enable individuals to deal with the source of their emotional responses as a way of keeping their feelings under control.

Significantly, all of the characters in *Scrubs* use coping strategies to some extent during each and every show, which seems to work very well for them. Some of these coping strategies are quite funny and bizarre, which makes the content pleasurable to watch, but it is important to remember that they are still coping strategies and that some degree of emotional distress is involved.

The *Scrubs* theme song, "Superman," by Lazlo Bane, carries a message about how doctors feel the pressure of trying to live up to their Superman-like title:

*Well, I know what I've been told
You gotta work to feel the soul
But I can't do this all on my own
No, I know I'm no Superman
I'm no Superman*

*Well, I know what I've been told
You gotta know just when to fold
But I can't do this all on my own
No, I know I'm no Superman
I'm no Superman*

The characters on the show are faced with all of the same problems and dilemmas as other doctors and hospital staff, but they just react a little differently. For example, in one episode, J.D. (Zach Braff) has a cancer patient who is undergoing chemotherapy treatment. This woman's immediate family decides to shave their heads to show their support and understanding to her as she loses her hair. Because J.D. is such a great doctor to her, the family asks him to please participate in the "shaving of the heads" too. J.D. is hesitant at first because he is dating a new girl who loves his hair, but he finally decides to do the right thing and shave his head. This is the kind of humorous spin that is put on a serious situation to make it a little more lighthearted. I think that this reaction from J.D. helps everyone involved cope with the situation a little better; the patient, the family, and J.D. And even though it is kind of bizarre, it still has a realness about it, which makes it funny.

Another example of this occurs in a different episode when a favorite patient is in a serious coma, and each member of the staff employs variations of the coping strategy of *diversion.* Dr. Cox (John C. McGinley) and the janitor (Neil Flynn) bond over drinks at the bar and Nurse Carla (Judy Reyes) makes it her mission to make the hospital's gym female friendly. Meanwhile, Dr. Turk (Donald Faison) suggests that J.D. and Elliot find themselves "booty calls." Seeing the "doctors" on the series use this common coping strategy legitimizes the practice.

Individual characters are defined by their unique coping strategies. J.D. often relies on the coping strategy of *envisioning,* in which scenarios play out in an exaggerated (and humorous) fashion that plays out the consequences of his decisions. Since he is the main character of the show, we see things mostly from his point of view, so every thought of his—however inappropriate it may be—becomes literal and materializes onscreen. For example, in an episode during the second season, J.D. once again exercised his bad habit of running his mouth after Dr. Cox scolds him for making a minor mistake. Of course Dr. Cox overhears his snide comment, and as he turns around to let J.D. have it, we can hear (and see) exactly what is running through J.D.'s head. He is thinking, "I wish I had a guy in my life that would stop me before I did something stupid." And as he is thinking this, the scene plays out right before our eyes. We see J.D. in a bar about to kiss a beautiful girl, when all of the sudden this man appears and rips the wig off of her head to reveal that she is in fact a man! To make matters even funnier (and a little strange), the man is an opera singer and he belts out "Mistaaaaake," in an opera-esque fashion right before J.D. is about to make his stupid move.

Another example of a coping strategy exemplified by a character is *partial avoidance.* In an episode from the second season, the topic of conversation around the hospital is chief of medicine Dr. Kelso's wedding anniversary. This is a celebrated holiday at Sacred Heart for one reason, and one reason only: Dr. Kelso is in a good mood on this day, and it is the only day of the year that everyone can fearlessly ask him for things. The surgeons give Turk the task of asking for a new piece of equipment that they need, but Turk forgets and is forced to ask him the following day. Turk fills J.D. in on his awful mistake and the two become distracted by their imaginations as they consider the difference a day can make in the behavior of Dr. Kelso. They envision him head butting a nurse, kicking a man in a wheelchair, and punching a few other nurses and doctors on his path of rage. Because of this far-fetched fear, Turk decides to just avoid asking him for the time being.

Other coping strategies displayed by characters include Dr. Cox's constant behavior of *ridicule,* which tends to be his most dominant coping strategy. J.D. and Turk also share a "one hug a day" rule, which acts as a *comfort mechanism* that enables each of them to cope with the stress of their jobs.

Thus, the coping strategies displayed by the characters of *Scrubs* mirror the techniques commonly employed by viewers. Presenting these coping strategies in the media has a pro-social function, by legitimizing the behavior. Further, this helps to explain the popularity of the series—audience members recognize their own coping strategies in the behaviors of the characters.

Theoretical Framework: Autobiographical Approach to Media Literacy Analysis

Applying the following Lines of Inquiry related to Autobiographical Analysis offers ways to approach the analysis of media and media presentations.

I. Affective response analysis
   A. Affective response and personal belief systems
      1. The origins or causes of affective response
         a. Describe your emotional responses to the media presentation.
         b. How do you feel at various points of the program?
            1). What in particular made you feel that way? Describe or recall specific incidents in detail.
         c. How does your emotional reaction to the media presentation carry over into your everyday lives?
            1) Do you react in the same way to events *outside* of the media?
            2) What do these responses reveal about your personal values system?
      2. Pleasure perspective
         a. What aspects of a media program generate a pleasurable response?
            1) What is your favorite program, and why do you enjoy it?
            2) Describe your reaction to the program (e.g., Why is it funny? What is the source of the humor?). Be specific.
         b. What does this exercise reveal about the program?
         c. Do these same elements trigger a pleasurable response when they appear in other programs?
         d. What does this reveal about your interests, attitudes, and values?
      3. Coping mechanisms
         a. Reconstruct the media presentation, focusing on your emotional and physical responses.
         b. What coping mechanisms did you employ? At what points in the presentation?
         c. Do you use any of the coping mechanisms elsewhere in your life?

        1) Are there similarities to the events or themes in the media presentation and to events or themes in your own life?

        2) Do you use these coping mechanisms in response to other events or themes in your own life?

        3) Is the use of the coping mechanisms effective? Explain.

  B. Affective response analysis: media content

    1. The entrance

      a. How did you feel about the character when you first saw him or her?

      b. What accounts for your emotional response?

        1) What was the character doing?

        2) What was he or she wearing?

        3) What did the character say?

      c. Did the media communicator intend to elicit this response?

        1) If so, how does making this emotional connection between character and audience support the themes and worldview of the narrative?

      d. Did you maintain this initial impression?

        1) If not, why? What (if anything) caused this change?

        2) Based on his or her actions in the remainder of the story, did the character deserve the emotional response that he or she elicited from you?

  C. Affective analysis: function

    1. How did you to feel at particular points in the narrative?

    2. Why does the media communicator want you to feel this way?

    3. Do your affective responses provide insight into the media messages? Explain.

    4. Do your affective responses provide insight into your personal belief system?

II. Identification analysis

  A. Character identification

    1. Imagine yourself in the role of the primary figure in a media presentation. What insights does this provide into the

sources of power and assumptions about what constitutes "the good life"?

    a. As the lead character, what could you accomplish?

    b. What opportunities would be available to you?

    c. What advantages would you have? What could you "get away with" because of your position?

2. Identify favorite characters and explain what you liked and disliked about the characters.

    a. Clarify the nature of the character identification:

        1) Likeness: Do you see a resemblance with the character?

        2) Aspiration: Would you like to emulate the character?

    b. Which attributes of the character make you choose the character as a model?

        1) Are these attributes generally regarded as positive or negative? Explain.

        2) Is this character a hero or villain in the narrative?

    c. Name additional attributes of the character that you did *not* include in your original list of attributes.

    d. Discuss the role that the attributes of the character play in the successful outcome of the story.

    e. Were there *missing* attributes in some characters that prevented them from succeeding within the context of the narrative?

    f. Are there characters in the narrative whom you may like or admire but cannot relate to? Explain.

3. Oppositional identification: Identify with another character in the media presentation (e.g., a villain, a member of a subculture, a person of the opposite gender, or a supporting character).

    a. What could you accomplish (as one of *these* characters)?

    b. What opportunities would be available to you?

    c. What advantages would you have?

    d. What could you "get away with" because of your position?

4. How do you relate to the villains in the narrative?

B. Narrative analysis
1. Narrative reconstruction
    a. Explicit content: In detail, relate the story of the media program you just saw (read, heard, etc.). What was the story about?
        1) What were the significant events in the story?
        2) What is the primary story of the plot?
        3) What are the subplots, if any?
    b. Implicit content
        1) What are the characters' motives for their actions? Why did the characters behave in the ways that they did?
        2) What is the relationship between the significant events in the narrative?
        3) What is the relationship between the characters in the narrative?
        4) Are the consequences to specific behaviors defined? Explain.
2. Narrative forecasting
    a. Discuss the role that the admirable character attributes you have identified play in the successful outcome of the story.
        1) What role do these attributes play in the outcome of your own lives?
        2) Are there other attributes that you haven't identified that play a role in the outcome of the narrative? Explain.
    b. Put yourselves in the situation depicted in the media presentation.
        1) How would you feel about being in that situation?
        2) How would you react?
        3) Does the situation remind you of your own experience? How?
    c. Compare the narrative to your own personal experience.
        1) Does the situation remind you of your own life? How?
        2) How would the characters handle your situation?
        3) Would it work? Why or why not?

    C. Examine the *limits* of identification (de-identification)
        1. In what ways does the media presentation construct a reality which is different from your everyday experience? Be specific.
        2. What production elements are used to construct this reality?
        3. Are the actions of the characters unrealistic? Explain.

III. Media chronicles: Questions to ask when conducting a media chronicles interview
    A. What does this program remind you of? Be specific, detailed.
    B. How old were you when the program was popular?
    C. What were you doing when it was popular?
    D. Can you describe the environment in which you watched the program?
        1. With whom did you watch the program?
        2. Where did you watch the program?
        3. What were you doing while you were watching the program?
    E. Can you recall the first time you saw or heard the program?
    F. Can you recall how you felt (scared, amused) while you watched or listened to the program?
    G. Does the program remind you of any people or experiences?
    H. Are there any cultural artifacts (e.g., cars, dress) or behaviors appearing on the program that had personal significance in your own life? Explain.
    I. Do you remember any of the characters?
        1. Which characters did you like? Dislike? Why?
        2. Did you identify with any of the characters? Why?

IV. Production elements

V. Empowerment strategies
    A. Empowerment cycle
    B. Emancipatory media programming
    C. Public response strategies

3

Nonverbal Communication Analysis

When body language and words are in conflict, people
believe body language.
—Daryl Perkins, Mark S. Norman & Associates

Overview

The most conspicuous and direct vehicle of expression in interpersonal communication is the verbal exchange. At the same time, nonverbal communication is a surprisingly sophisticated and efficient system for conveying meaning. According to communications scholar J.S. Philpott, more than two-thirds of the total impact of a message is the result of nonverbal factors.[1] Moreover, political consultant Bill Carrick maintains that the subtle nonverbal cues of gesture, posture, syntax, and tone of voice account for as much as 75 percent of a viewer's judgment about the electability of a candidate.[2]

The field of nonverbal analysis is defined by the following research findings:

- Subtle and implicit information is conveyed through nonverbal channels in a few seconds or even a fraction of a second.[3]
- People are quite accurate in decoding these brief instances of non-verbal communication.[4]
- Specific nonverbal behaviors accompany certain feelings.[5]
- Nonverbal cues are especially adept at communicating information about emotions and mood.[6]

Although nonverbal communication behavior generally has been linked to the study of interpersonal communication, it is applicable to the critical analysis of mass communications as well.

- Nonverbal communications analysis provides insight into the ways in which nonverbal communication behaviors reinforce verbal messages in media presentations. In visual media (photographs, film, and television), actors employ nonverbal behaviors such as body posture, accents, or subtle facial expressions and eye movements to reinforce messages. In the 1950 film Sunset Boulevard, Norma Desmond (Gloria Swanson), a reclusive silent film diva, declared, "We didn't need dialogue [in those days]. We had faces." Even in radio, which relies only on sound, vocal modulation, rhythm, and pitch have an enormous impact on the impressions received by the audience.

- Nonverbal communications analysis examines ways in which media communicators use "scripted" nonverbal strategies to create a particular image or impression. People who are interviewed on camera often follow a "script" devised by impression formation managers. These professionals carefully orchestrate the nonverbal behaviors of their clients to make their verbal messages more convincing. For example, in 2007, Senator Larry Craig (R-ID) was arrested for sexual misconduct in the restroom of the Minneapolis airport. Craig then held a news conference to announce his innocence. As he approached the podium, he was holding hands with his wife, Suzanne. Asked about this carefully scripted nonverbal behavior, a class of college students responded that the gesture sent a series of messages declaring Craig's innocence. Holding hands is "wholesome," a "romantic and platonic gesture which counterbalances the more sordid sexual aspects of the accusation." In addition, holding Craig's hand is "both a physical and emotional expression of support by Craig's wife."

- *Nonverbal communications analysis furnishes individuals with tools to detect behaviors that are at variance with the "scripted" verbal message.* As discussed earlier, people who are interviewed on camera often follow a "script" devised by their media handlers. For instance, during the 2007 Republican primary race for president, TV footage captured challenger Mike Huckabee throwing snowballs in Michigan before its primary. Commentators leaped on this image, declaring that this was evidence that the former governor of Arkansas was "just like regular folks."

Larry Craig and Wife

Media communicators often rely on "scripted" nonverbal behaviors to create a particular image or impression. For example, after Senator Larry Craig (R-ID) was arrested for sexual misconduct in the restroom of the Minneapolis airport in 2007, Craig held a news conference to announce his innocence. As he approached the podium, he was holding hands with his wife Suzanne, which conveyed the message that he was innocent. (*AP Images/Troy Maben*)

However, at the same time, their nonverbal behaviors may reveal their actual thoughts and feelings. In 2007, Democrat Hillary Clinton, running in the New Hampshire presidential primary election, was asked by a prospective voter how she managed to persevere, despite all of the hardships involved in running for president. Obviously fatigued, Clinton responded with what appeared to be a spontaneous display of emotional nonverbal behavior. With tears welling up in her eyes, Clinton replied in a shaky voice that although her task was difficult, she cared about the country and didn't want it to "go backward." Clinton's win in New Hampshire defied the polls, which had predicted that Barack Obama would win by a wide margin. Postelection polls confirmed that a significant number of women voters were influenced by this genuine emotional declaration to change their vote to support Clinton.

Today, the media—and particularly the Internet—have blurred the distinction between private and public activities. Media scholar Joshua Meyrowitz observes that modern political candidates are always onstage and consequently must maintain a steady state of performance. Before the advent of the Internet, politicians could retain some semblance of privacy. Today, however, political figures no longer have the luxury of "backstage activities"—areas of privacy hidden from public viewing.[7]

A striking demonstration of the potency of unintended gestures in the media occurred during the third 1992 presidential debate between Bill Clinton and George Bush. The town-meeting format was more favorable to Clinton's public performance style. During the debate, Clinton employed a series of carefully crafted gestures designed to add a personal dimension to his performance. At one point, Marissa Hall asked a question about the economy. Clinton approached Hall, smiled, and made it a one-to-one conversation. His scripted open hand gestures were synchronized perfectly with his words and conveyed an emotional aura of warmth and openness. While Clinton was answering the question, Bush clearly was visible in the background. As Clinton spoke, Bush glanced down and, turning his wrist slightly, peeked at his watch. This gesture spoke volumes about Bush's lack of engagement in this debate. In a broader sense, the gesture served as a metaphor for Bush's lackluster campaign and his diminished chances at reelection; clearly, his "time was up."

Today, nearly everyone carries video technology (in a tool as simple as a cell phone); consequently, public figures should assume that they are always being recorded. News organizations such as CBS and Fox News now employ "embeds"—freelance reporters who record public figures and send the footage to the networks—but private citizens can also post their videos on Internet sites such as YouTube.

Meyrowitz contends that this backstage visibility has led to a decline in the prestige of political leaders. The opening up of traditional back-stage behavior means that citizens now know, in intimate detail, about the private behavior of those in authority. The scrutiny of politicians' private behavior has challenged our public conception of "appropriate behavior." For instance, in the days leading up to the 2006 midterm elections, Barbara Cubin, a Republican candidate for the House of Representatives from the state of Wyoming, was caught on camera

George H. W. Bush

Nonverbal communications analysis furnishes individuals with tools to detect unscripted behaviors that are at variance with the verbal message. In this 1992 presidential debate, the camera captures George H.W. Bush as he is glancing at his watch, signaling lack of interest in the proceedings. *AP/Wide World Photo.*

telling opponent Thomas Rankin, who has multiple sclerosis and uses a wheelchair, "If you weren't sitting in that chair, I'd slap you across the face."[8] The incident was distributed on YouTube, playing a role in the election (despite a usually dominant Republican edge in conservative Wyoming, Cubin won by only 1,000 votes, one of the closest margins in the state's history).

These candid glimpses into a candidate's behavior can provide perspective into a candidate's qualifications. However, it can also be argued that this media scrutiny has inhibited the ability of our elected officials to govern effectively. Politicians must monitor every action and reaction to maintain the desired image they wish to project and to prevent any damage to this image.

Nonverbal communication furnishes perspective into cultural attitudes, values, behaviors, preoccupations, and myths that define a culture.

For example, sociologist Erving Goffman has identified patterns of nonverbal behaviors in advertisements that provide insight into gender relations in American culture. Goffman discovered a preponderance of *function-ranking* images in ads: "In our society when a man and a woman collaborate face-to-face in an undertaking, the man . . . is likely to perform the executive role."[9] The principle of function ranking also extends to instruction; in advertising, men are depicted instructing women more than the reverse, which "involves some sort of subordination of the instructed and deference for the instructor."[10] When females are depicted as engaged in a "traditionally" male task, such as fixing a car, a male is present to "parenthesize the activity, looking on appraisingly, condescendingly, or with wonder."[11]

Goffman also found that ads often depict women as victims of "ritualistic humiliation" at the hands of men. For example, in Newport Cigarette ads, male models dunk females in water, pour water on their heads, and hold them aloft in precarious positions. The women in these ads are smiling; they are not threatened but, rather, appear impressed by this display of dominance. Although the mock assault games are set within a comedic context, Goffman declares, "Underneath this show a man may be engaged in a deeper one, the suggestion of what he could do if he got serious about it."[12]

Moreover, male models in ads are frequently depicted encircling the female model with their arms. This gesture establishes the male as protector from outside attack. However, at the same time, the encircling arm prevents the female from withdrawing from the male. Goffman notes that "the extended arm, in effect, marks the boundary of his social property."[13]

Nonverbal communications analysis provides insight into the role of nonverbal communication cues in the depiction of media stereotypes.

Media communicators rely on nonverbal communications cues in presenting stereotypes in programs. For instance, body type plays a role in the casting of parts in films. Characters with athletic frames (mesomorphic body types) are often cast as the heroic figures, who are highly confident, task oriented, energetic, talkative, aggressive, and dominant. In contrast, people with heavy builds (endomorphic body types) are frequently cast as characters who are lazy, warmhearted, sympathetic, good-natured, dependent, passive, sloppy, and indolent. Characters with thin, fragile frames (ectomorphic body types) often play the role of characters who are tense, fussy, critical, suspicious, tense, nervous, pessimistic, anxious, self-conscious, and reticent.

Characters also are stereotyped in terms of age. Media consultant Jane Squier Bruns relates a story in which her son Mark Squier, who is also a political media consultant, produced a TV spot for the Democratic Party designed to raise concerns about the Republicans' Medicare policy. The commercial consisted of visuals of a grandmother tending her infant grandson, while the voice-over declared that Republican initiatives would jeopardize the health care of young and old alike. Squiers's infant daughter Emma was cast as the baby in the campaign spot. Bruns, a vibrant, attractive woman who is also an actress, suggested that she play the role of the grandmother. However, she was told that she was not "right" for the part because she did not fit the stereotypical image of a grandmother—even though she is Emma's actual grandma. Instead, the role of the grandmother was given to an elderly, frumpy woman who wore a frumpy housedress.[14]

Height is frequently associated with stereotypes of males that appear in the media. Leading men are generally cast with females who are shorter. When women do appear with shorter men, the male characters generally appear in comedic roles. Consequently, when diminutive leading man Alan Ladd was cast with taller actresses, the crew dug trenches for the women to walk in to even out the height differential.

This nonverbal cue reflects, reinforces, and shapes cultural attitudes with regard to height. A 2007 study found that taller immigrants to the United States earned more than shorter ones, with an extra inch of height associated with a 1 percent increase in income.[15]

A Cautionary Note

Nonverbal cues can serve as a springboard to further analysis of media messages. However, several mitigating factors must be taken into consideration when conducting a nonverbal communications analysis. First, the culture to which a person belongs can influence the meaning ascribed to nonverbal communications behaviors. For instance, greeting people with a kiss is common in Mediterranean countries, whereas people in Northern European countries are less inclined to greet relative strangers with a kiss. Further, individual countries may have their own protocol with regard to a nonverbal behavior. For instance, in France, people greet each other with a kiss on both cheeks—one kiss each—although in a few regions it is the double-double kiss, with two on each cheek. The Belgians, the Dutch, and the Swiss go for the triple kiss. Indeed, these behaviors can be so confusing that the lip balm company Blistex has included a catalogue of kissing customs on its Web site.[16]

In addition, nonverbal behaviors may have innocent explanations. For instance, a person may assume a particular posture because her back hurts. As Groucho Marx commented, "Sometimes a cigar is only a cigar." Thus, although a nonverbal analysis can identify patterns of nonverbal behaviors, it cannot identify the *intention* behind a nonverbal act. However, a nonverbal study can provide insight into scripted nonverbal communications and can serve as a point of origin for further examination of the meanings conveyed by unscripted nonverbal communications.

Finally, in conducting nonverbal analysis, it is essential to develop consistency in the identification of nonverbal communication through orientation, training, and pretesting.

Functions of Nonverbal Communication

Despite different cultural expressions, people share common communication functions. For example, *openness gestures* (e.g., unbuttoning coats, uncrossing legs, moving toward the edge of the chair) convey a sense of confidence, encouraging interaction. In contrast, fidgeting, tugging at clothing, and playing with objects are *nervousness gestures.*

Identifying the *function,* or purpose, of nonverbal communication behaviors in media presentations can provide considerable insight into messages:

- *Clarification.* Nonverbal behaviors may emphasize points or dramatize the verbal content in pantomime. For example, hand gestures punctuate the verbal content, indicating which points are of vital importance.
- *Persuasion.* Nonverbal behaviors may be used to enlist the agreement or cooperation of the listener. An earnest look or slap on the back may serve as an appeal to support the verbal message.
- *Facilitating the communication process.* Nonverbal cues regulate the process of communication. For instance, a puzzled expression asks the communicator for clarification, whereas a fixed gaze can reassure the communicator that the listener is interested and paying attention.
- *Expression of emotion.* Nonverbal cues can express a range of emotions, including anger, nervousness, sadness, happiness, sympathy, satisfaction, fear, love, and jealousy. Nonverbal cues also can furnish information about the communicator's attitude toward the subject matter. Posture or eye contact can disclose how the person *feels* about what is being said. Nonverbal behavior also can reveal the speaker's attitude toward the other person(s) involved in the conversation. Finally, nonverbal cues can express the communicator's feelings about the environment, context, or circumstances in which the conversation is taking place.
- *Expression of intimacy.* Nonverbal behaviors can signify the level of intimacy that exists between the parties engaged in conversation. Touch, eye contact, and proximity convey attentiveness, interest, and emotional engagement between the people engaged in communication. Nonverbal cues (such as an icy stare) also can be used to maintain a distance between the communicators. Moreover, lovers often position themselves in close proximity to one another and may touch (e.g., hold hands, kiss) while conversing.
- *Social control.* Nonverbal cues can furnish perspective into disparities in social status and power. During the course of a conversation, a relationship, however brief, is formed, based on a shared interest—the topic of conversation. As in all positive relationships, the two parties must adhere to unwritten rules of decorum that govern a

communication exchange, including the length of time that two people look each other in the eye, the distance between two people engaged in conversation, and the proper (or improper) boundaries for touching. Significantly, the rules of nonverbal communication are often dictated by the party who enjoys higher status. For example, at a ceremony in January 2007, New York mayor Michael R. Bloomberg planted a double kiss on Chief Judge Judith S. Kaye of New York State.[17]

Indeed, the person who assumes a dominant role in the relationship is free to violate the conventional rules of conduct. In 2006, U.S. president George W. Bush greeted German chancellor Angela Merkel by squeezing her shoulders and neck. Merkel winced in surprise and pain. Larry Sabato, professor of politics at the University of Virginia, criticized Bush's behavior as inappropriate: "Almost any male alive today knows that you don't offer uninvited massages to any female, much less the chancellor of Germany."[18]

Moreover, reporter Joan Vennoch questioned whether this was an imposition of power, given that the recipient of this squeeze was the only female in the room: "This interaction between two heads of state put an international spotlight on a fact of life for working women. You can spend a career perfecting your handshake and still be startled by a man who suddenly invades your personal space with unexpected intimacy in a professional setting. Is it a mostly innocent, if socially boorish, version of the male-to-male, locker room towel snap? Or, is it a way to demean and patronize, to change the equation by neutralizing the woman's power so it is no longer a case of two professional equals?"[19]

Indeed, the formula of tabloid talk shows often revolves around the violation of the accepted rules of nonverbal communications conduct. For example, in 2004, *The Jerry Springer Show* surpassed *The Oprah Winfrey Show* as the highest-rated daytime talk show, in large measure because of the fisticuffs between guests. The formula of Springer shows consisted of a confrontation between guests who delivered shocking news (e.g., a husband telling his wife on national television that he is a female impersonator and is sleeping with her best friend). Much of the "excitement" of the program then involved the guests pummeling each other—clearly a violation of the rules of decorum for daytime talk shows.

President Bush and German Chancellor Merkel

Nonverbal behaviors can reveal the dynamics of a relationship. In 2006, U.S. president George W. Bush greeted German chancellor Merkel by squeezing her shoulders and neck. Merkel winced in surprise and pain at this demonstration of male dominance.

However, in 2004, it was disclosed that these fights were scripted. Guests were given instructions such as "We want four fights" and threatened with lawsuits if they didn't deliver.[20] As a result of pressure from politicians, including Senator Joseph I. Lieberman and former secretary of education William Bennett, Springer Studios USA announced a new policy that would prohibit fighting on the show. Significantly, the ratings for the show immediately plummeted.

Nonverbal communication cues may fulfill more than one function simultaneously. For instance, a gesture may express intimacy and at the same time have a persuasive purpose. In addition, nonverbal communication behaviors may serve both a *manifest* and a *latent* function. Manifest functions are direct and clear to the audience. We may have little trouble recognizing these messages when we are paying full attention to a media presentation. Latent functions refer to instances in which the media communicator's intention may not be immediately obvious to the audience. Latent functions are indirect and beneath the surface and, consequently, escape our immediate attention. Indeed, it is surprising to discover how frequently the manifest function is irrelevant—or at least subordinate—to other, latent purposes, like impressing the audience, nurturing relationships, or expressing emotion. For instance, it is not uncommon to become involved in an information exchange in which it becomes clear that the other person is not really interested in your opinions but instead is intent on converting you to his or her point of view. In this case, the latent function is *persuasion.*

Types of Nonverbal Behaviors

Examining specific nonverbal behaviors can provide insight into the message, the communicator, and the dynamics of a communication exchange.

Facial Expressions

Facial expressions are a reliable source of emotional information. According to psychology professor Dr. Paul Ekman, seven basic human emotions have very clear facial signals—anger, sadness, fear, surprise, disgust, contempt, and happiness.[21] In addition, the face can register a range of responses, including evaluative judgments (e.g., pain, pleasure, superiority, determination, surprise, attention, and bewilderment), degree of interest or disinterest in the subject, and level of understanding.

People tend to attribute positive characteristics to individuals who smile, including intelligence, a good personality, and being a "pleasant person."[22] Smiling also assumes gender-based meanings. Women tend to smile more often than males, perhaps reflecting a desire to please as a subordinate member of society. However, because smiling can be a social construction for women, their behavior may be scripted (i.e., covering other emotions) and, consequently, more difficult to interpret.

People in the public eye, such as political figures, high-profile corporate executives, and broadcast journalists, are trained to develop their *presentational* facial expressions as part of an overall "impression management" strategy. Media relations consultant Tripp Frohlichstein trains his clients to maintain an "open face" while in front of the camera: "Keep your eyebrows up and smile when appropriate. This helps you better convey your pride, as well as intensity. When the eyebrows are flat, so are your voice and feelings. When your eyebrows are down, so is the interview, and you may be perceived as angry or negative."[23]

A person's immediate facial reaction is often an accurate measure of his or her genuine feelings; however, this expression quickly is replaced by a presentational expression. Some facial cues to be alert for include the following:

- Raised eyebrows indicate surprise.
- A set jaw reveals anger, determination, tension, resolve, or decision.
- A chin retraction is a protective action or a signal that something is scary or frightening.
- Flared nostrils express anger.
- A nose wrinkle signifies dislike, disapproval, or disgust.

Eye Behaviors

The eyes have a mystical quality that defies rational explanation. Look in the mirror, covering your face with your hands and leaving only your eyes exposed. Think of something sad, then something funny, and finally something that makes you angry. It is uncanny how these simple orbs can express powerful emotions: eyes narrow with anger, grin with joy, fill with tears of sorrow, and widen with surprise.

Modern politicians employ media advisers to assist them in the best ways to make eye contact with as many voters as possible when giving campaign speeches. Direct eye contact with the camera, reporter, or audience heightens the candidate's credibility. For example, during the famous Kennedy-Nixon debates, the majority of voters listening on the radio felt that Nixon won the debate. However, the majority of the television audience believed that Kennedy won. This disparity can be attributed to Nixon's shifty eye behavior on camera, which undermined his honesty and trustworthiness.

The length and direction of eye contact also can be an expression of dominance and control. In the film *Death and the Maiden* (1994), Paulina Escobar (Sigourney Weaver) becomes reacquainted with Dr. Miranda (Ben Kingsley), a sadistic character who had repeatedly tortured and sexually abused her while she was his political prisoner. (Miranda had been in a position of power in an unnamed totalitarian country.) During their meetings, Miranda attempts to extend his control over her. In

Richard M. Nixon

Eye behavior can be regarded as a barometer of a person's character and intentions. During the famous Kennedy-Nixon debates, the majority of radio listeners felt that Nixon won the debate. However, most of the television audience believed that Kennedy had won. This disparity can be attributed to Nixon's shifty eye behavior on camera, which made him appear dishonest and untrustworthy. *AP/Wide World Photo.*

the final sequence of the film, both characters are seated at a concert listening to Schubert's "Death and the Maiden." Miranda is positioned diagonally above Paulina. The camera circles slowly from the orchestra to a close-up of Paulina seated in the lower orchestra section with her husband. The camera guides us as she slowly turns her head and looks directly up toward the box circle, where Miranda is seated with his family. At this point, the camera closes in on Miranda staring down at Paulina. Briefly he turns toward his son, smiles, and pats him on the head, and then turns back, resuming his fixed stare down at Paulina. The camera then returns slowly to focus on Paulina again. She avoids Miranda's stare, sitting rigidly, with a tense, fixed, forward gaze. This eye interaction reinforces the hierarchical relationship between the two characters. Further, the elliptical circle formed by the camera movement from Paulina to Miranda and back to Paulina informs us that the issue is closed. Dr. Miranda will remain in his position of power and will never be punished for his abuses.

Posture

Posture refers to a stance or positioning of the body or body part. Postures can convey a range of personal information about a communicator's character. An upright posture communicates a message of confidence and integrity. A slumping posture conveys a sense of cowardice, meekness, sadness, or depression.[24] Having good posture—standing tall—is an indication of empowerment, authority, and rank in society. In contrast, slouching conveys a passive attitude, sloppiness, and incompetence. Crossing one's arms and legs is a defensive posture that suggests that the communicator is inaccessible and angry.

Examining posture in media presentations provides insight into the relative positions of power and authority. Erving Goffman points out that in many advertisements, females pose in a cant position, in which the head or body is bowed. The latent message of this body language is deference, submission, and subordination.[25] For example, a recent Nike ad featured nude portraits of five male and three female athletes. The posture of the athletes reflects a hierarchy in which the men are deemed more powerful. The male athletes are standing erect, their figures filling most of the page. In contrast, the three women are diminished in both body position and in relation to the size of the page. One woman is stooped on the lower left side of a two-page spread. The second is crouched at the bottom of the page, and the third appears in a sexually receptive position, semireclining on her back with her legs in the air.

Posture may also indicate the speaker's attitude toward the subject matter or the audience. Leaning toward a person is a receptive position, while slumping communicates a negative attitude. In a commercial for *Sports Illustrated,* a man standing behind the bar in his rec room leans forward (toward the camera) to tell us about a special offer to subscribe to the magazine. This posture conveys a sense of intimacy and informality, which in turn suggests friendship, honesty, and trustworthiness. This fellow is not trying to "sell us anything" (actually, he is); instead, he just wants to let us in on a good thing.

Posture

Posture can express thought, reveal character, or reflect attitudes. Examples include the following. *Photos by Jamie Clark.*

A pensive attitude

A defensive posture

An active, assertive position

A relaxed, confident demeanor

An assertive stance

A thoughtful attitude

Gestures

Gestures refer to the act of moving the limbs or body as an expression of thought or emphasis. The meaning of gestures may vary enormously in different cultures. For instance, in the United States, an individual beckons someone to come by holding the palm up and moving the fingers toward his or her body. In Thailand, a person moves his or her fingers back and forth with the palm down to signal another person to come near. The Tongans sit down in the presence of superiors; in the West, people stand up.

However, some nonverbal gestures have a universal meaning. According to Desmond Morris, the palm punch, in which the fist of one hand is punched rhythmically several times against the palm of the other, is an angry gesture that has a primal, symbolic significance: "This has a common meaning of a mimed blow against an enemy, redirected onto the palm of the gesturer. In such cases the gesture indicates a state of barely controlled rage."[26] Other universal gestures include the chin stroke (pensiveness, concentration), chin rub (dubiousness, questioning), and the chest beat (strength, power).

Hand gestures are often used to enhance a speaker's credibility. The hand gestures of political candidates are carefully synchronized with rhetorical devices to emphasize points as well as direct audience response—either encouraging or halting applause.

Another positive hand gesture is the "steeple," in which the tips of all five fingers of each hand are touching to simulate a church steeple. Because the fingertips are pointed toward heaven, this is a very positive gesture, signaling confidence, integrity, contemplation and sincerity. The meaning of gestures may vary enormously in different cultures. For instance, in the United States, the sign in which the thumb and index finger are joined in a circle means "A-OK." However, this gesture has a variety of connotations in other cultures: In Latin America, this gesture is regarded as obscene and insulting, with associations with excretory functions. In France, this gesture means "zero" or "worthless." In Japan, the thumb and forefinger making a circle is used as symbol for money.

Proxemic Communication

Proxemic communication refers to the way that space configurations convey meaning. The use of space falls into three distinct categories:

- *Personal space* consists of the space immediately encircling our bodies, which each of us considers our own territory. Personal space is the area we maintain between ourselves and others. The boundaries of personal space may be culturally determined. For example, members of Arab nations typically stand closer when conversing than do Europeans. Moreover, the boundaries of personal space also vary *within* a culture. In the United States, women tend to stand closer together than men.

  When communicating, individuals negotiate a comfort zone for interaction. Any violation of this space creates feelings of discomfort and apprehension. As mentioned earlier, close proximity between people often is regarded as a sign of intimacy. Thus, trespassing on an individual's personal space may signify an imposition of control, reflecting (and reinforcing) status or power differences. According to Professor Ann E. Fuehrer, "The more powerful person is the one who determines the amount of physical space. They are taking the initiative to determine the degree of proximity."[27]

- *Group formation* refers to how people are positioned in relation to one another. The arrangement of people within a group often reveals the *attitudinal position* that an individual assumes with regard to the activity. For instance, students frequently sit in the same place in the classroom, even if the seats aren't assigned. To be sure, habit plays a role in students' seat selections, but where students decide to sit may also be an indication of whether they are comfortable participating in class discussions or prefer to take a less active role.

  Group formations may also indicate relative status. People in control often assume a place in the center of the group, with marginal members on the fringe. This hierarchical principle also applies to seating arrangements. In America, people at the head of the table are in control, whereas the individual seated to the left of the head of the table has the least status in the group.[28] In Japan, however, the most important person sits at one end of the rectangular table, with those nearest in rank at the right and left of this senior position. The lowliest member of the group sits at the opposite end of the table from the person with the most authority and is nearest to the door.[29]

  Group formation also indicates whether the assemblage of people forms an open or closed society. People standing in a closed formation are excluding others from joining the group, while groups in an open formation are more inclusive.

  Contact (1997) is a film in which group interactions send messages of inclusion and exclusion. Dr. Ellie Arroway (Jodie Foster) is an astronomer who finds herself in a subservient position to her male colleagues despite her considerable knowledge and expertise in the field. In one scene, Ellie stands at the end of a table in front of the door giving a presentation, while her former boss Drumlin (Tom Skerritt) sits, relaxed, in the middle of a group of peers. The group arrangement requires that Ellie confront the entire group, mostly males, while Drumlin receives their nonverbal support. In the final scene, Ellie finally is positioned in the center of a group—this time, teaching science to young children. Within the context of the film, she has assumed her "rightful" place in society—not as a scientist but as a caretaker or teacher.

- *Fixed space* refers to the characteristics associated with particular locations. In media programs, certain activities are associated with particular rooms. For instance, scenes depicting informal socializing often take place in the kitchen. In contrast, embarrassing moments often occur in scenes taking place in the more formal setting of the dining room.

    Locations may also serve as metaphors for aspects of characters' psyches. For instance, *Gaslight* (1944) is a film in which the attic represents the subconscious. Mattias Thuresson provides the following plot synopsis:

> Young Paula Alquist (Ingrid Bergman) marries the charming Gregory Anton (Charles Boyer). An elderly aunt of Paula's was murdered a few years ago in her home at Tresvenor Square. Paula inherited the apartment which the newlyweds make their home. Slowly but methodically Gregory convinces Paula that she always forgets things, is nervous, and unwell. He also makes sure that she does not get out much and has only minimal contact with other people.[30]

Gregory's ruse enables him to dig around in the attic for the aunt's hidden jewels without attracting attention. Paula remains oblivious to the nefarious intentions of her husband and does not fully remember (or understand) the events leading to her aunt's death—until she finally makes the journey up to the attic and confronts her husband, as well as her own subconscious fears and buried memories. It is in the attic that Paula (and the audience) finally discover Gregory's innermost thoughts and secrets, which he had kept hidden beneath his charming exterior.

- *Arranged space* refers to the placement of objects within a fixed space (e.g., home, office). The arrangement of a room often serves as an indication of the social dynamics among the people who inhabit the space. For example, the primary television-viewing area in a home can furnish perspective into family dynamics. In America, the furniture in the TV room often revolves around the TV screen, even though this arrangement may make it awkward for people in the room to converse with one another. Where people sit in relation to each other as they watch is also an interesting microcosm of family dynamics. The person perceived as dominant often has the choice of the prime seat and is in charge of the remote control. In contrast, people from France, Italy, and Mexico position furniture to encourage interaction among. Conversation is important for them, and facing chairs toward a television screen stifles conversation.[31]

Tactile Communication

Tactile communication, or touch, can serve as a form of support, reassurance, intimacy, or sexual interest, or as an expression of emotions (e.g., anger, exhilaration). However as mentioned earlier, touching violations also can be an assertion of power and control by high-status individuals.

In media presentations, touching behaviors can reinforce verbal content or convey independent latent messages. For instance, politicians have mastered the art of holding a handshake for an instant longer than is normally expected, sending a message of personal regard, intimacy, and trust.

The specific meaning of touch is influenced by the following factors:

- *Culture.* As mentioned earlier, high-contact cultures include Arab countries, Latin America, and Southern Europe. Cultures less inclined to touch include Northern Europe and the United States.[32]
- *The nature of the relationship.* Lovers touch each other in different ways than mere acquaintances.
- *Region of the body that is touched.* A tap on the shoulder has a different meaning from a pat on the bottom.
- *Age.* Young and older people touch most frequently when communicating.
- *Context.* The place and occasion in which the touching behavior

Gaslight

Locations may serve as metaphors for aspects of characters' psyches. For instance, in the film *Gaslight* (1944), the attic represents the subconscious. In the film, Paula Alquist (Ingrid Bergman) marries the charming Gregory Anton (Charles Boyer), who knows a secret—Paula's aunt's jewels are hidden somewhere in the attic of the home that the couple has inherited. Gregory proceeds to "gaslight" Paula—convincing her that she is hearing things—so that he can dig around in the attic for the aunt's hidden jewels without attracting attention. The attic represents Paula's subconscious fears and buried memories of her aunt's death, adding to her compulsion to ignore the noises in the attic. (*Getty Images: Hulton Archive*)

occurs help determine its meaning. What might be suitable at a drive-in movie might not be acceptable at the office.

• *The type of touching behavior exhibited.* There are subtle yet discernible differences between pats, squeezes, brushes, and strokes.

Primary Colors (1998) is a film that provides an interesting commentary on the use of tactile communications in the political arena. In one scene, campaign manager Howard Ferguson (Paul Guilsoyle) and campaign aid Henry Burton (Adrian Lester) watch presidential candidate Jack Stanton (John Travolta) campaigning. Political consultant Richard Jemmons (Billy Bob Thornton) translates the meaning behind the touching behavior exhibited by Stanton in the scene:

> You know, I've seen him do it a million times now. . . . When [he puts] that left hand on your elbow or up on your bicep like he's doing now, very basic move, he's interested in you, he's honored to meet you. If he gets any higher, gets on your shoulder like that, it's not as intimate. It means he'll share a laugh with you or a secret, a light secret, not a real one, but very flattering. If he doesn't know you that well and wants to share something emotional with you, he'll lock you with a two-hander. Well, you'll see when he shakes hands with you, Henry.

Governor Stanton displays these five gestures throughout the course of the film. After the election, Stanton greets Henry with "the two-hander," which the audience understands as a sign of affection. However, had Henry not dropped out of the campaign at an earlier stage, he might have merited a "hug," the highest nonverbal expression of affection and respect.

As mentioned earlier, an image of people holding hands is a sign of affection, protection, and comfort. People holding hands often look relaxed and secure. Indeed, holding hands can actually have pronounced physiological impact. Professor James Coan declared, "We found that holding the hand of really anyone, it made your brain work a little less hard in coping."[33]

Physical Appearance

It is undeniable that physical appearance has an impact on ways in which people relate to one another. Attractive people are considered more socially desirable, credible, and persuasive than people considered

President Bush and Prince Abdullah holding hands

In Arab countries, holding hands is an act of respect and affection, such as when President George W. Bush held the hand of Crown Prince Abdullah of Saudi Arabia in Crawford, Texas, in 2005. (*Getty Images; photographer: Charles Ommanney*)

less attractive. In addition, good-looking people consistently receive preferential treatment.[34] Not only do we admire attractive people, but we identify with them and sympathize with their situations. Thus, even though film stars represent unapproachable ideals of beauty, audience members enjoy projecting themselves into their roles and situations.

In popular media programming characters often are defined by their appearance. Heroes and heroines are physically attractive, whereas villains often are physically displeasing in some way. Thus, ugliness is equated with evil. This practice can lead to falsely labeling an attractive person as "good" and an unattractive person as "bad."

The world of popular media programming operates according to a *hierarchy of appearance.* Physical beauty also is presented as emblematic of virtue. Thus, heroic characters are attractive because, on some level, they *deserve* it. Handsome heroes assume control of their lives and prevail over the villains—the inference being that these characters are "in the right" precisely *because* they are attractive. The heroes often are called upon to protect others—usually an attractive female. The implication is that only beautiful women are worth protecting.

Moreover, one way that we know that supporting characters are not as important as the stars is because they are not as attractive. In romantic comedies, attractive characters are engaged in a quest to find equally gorgeous partners. By extension, unattractive characters are suited only for each other. Comedy (or, worse, tragedy) occurs when people try to seek matches outside of their particular station. The cumulative media message is "know your place" when it comes to appearance.

For example, *When Harry Met Sally* (1989) is a romantic comedy that traces the relationship between Harry Burns (Billy Crystal) and Sally Albright (Meg Ryan). Harry and Sally maintain a platonic friendship. The dynamic of the film involves the two principal characters discovering what the audience can see: the two are "right" for each other (in large measure because they are both attractive).

Since they are only friends, Harry and Sally agree to fix each other up with blind dates: Harry with Marie (Carrie Fisher), and Sally with Jess (Bruno Kirby). They go on a double date, but it is clear that the two couples are physically mismatched. Jess has an obvious beer belly, the kind that hangs over his belt. And although actress Fisher is normally very pretty, her hairstyle, dress, and makeup are designed to make Marie look plain.

But while Harry and Sally struggle to find their romantic—and physical—counterparts, Jess and Marie get married. Unlike their attractive friends, Jess and Marie are content; their aims are not too lofty, and they happily settle for a partner whose appearance situates them within the same class in the hierarchy of appearance.

Eventually, Sally and Harry discover that they have been meant for each other all along. Order is restored to this universe, with the attractive and not-so-attractive couples finding their appropriate matches. Significantly, this hierarchy of appearance does not always apply to men—particularly when other cultural "virtues" are evident, such as wealth and power. Ironically, these measures of success become more pronounced as men grow older. Males in their fifties and sixties are at the peak of their salaries and influence.

In advertising, alluring models are typically the center of attention, as ordinary people stare enviously at them (ostensibly because of their appearance, but by implication, because of the product). These ads promote their products as a modern form of alchemy, in which base metals are transformed into gold. In this version, ordinary folks are transformed into the glamorous models—simply by using their products. However, a careful consideration of the ad can uncover this illogical premise. For example, in Pantene shampoo ads, a woman moves her head in slow motion, so that her lustrous hair sways gracefully and the light catches the nuances of her hair's texture and color. The latent message of the ad is that the shampoo is responsible for her lovely hair. After looking at the commercial, Leah Silverblatt, then nine years old, was asked whether the shampoo made the model's hair that pretty, or if the advertisers had selected a model who had beautiful hair in the first place. Leah immediately replied that the model probably had great hair to begin with.

This emphasis on appearance has become an essential factor in broadcast journalism as well. One classic illustration occurred in 1981, when Christine Craft was demoted from her position as a news anchor at a Kansas City television station at age thirty-six. Her boss, she said, explained that she came across on the tube as "too old, too ugly and not sufficiently deferential to men."[35] Now a Sacramento lawyer and Bay Area talk-show host, Craft sued the station.

Costumes

Costumes provide a wide range of information. For instance, clothing furnishes perspective into the worldview of subcultures and ethnic groups. Tom Zeller describes the underlying worldview of the costumes of "hipsters":

> Hipsters are always very conscious of what they are wearing and distinguish themselves by dressing creatively. . . . They possess an innate contempt for franchises, strip malls and the corporate world in general, . . . believe that irony has more resonance than reason . . . and enjoy declaring random things, like vodka martinis or exercise, passe.
>
> Underneath their apparent individualism, Hipsters conform just like everyone else.[36]

Moreover, costumes can represent *identity*. In the eighteenth century, the upper classes wore distinctive, expensive clothes that were beyond the means of the poor. Today, however, clothing choices transcend social class: lower-income people wear designer clothes (or knockoffs of designer clothes), while rich people walk around in tattered sweatpants.

Costumes also reveal *cultural preoccupations*. For instance, today's adults are dressing like kids as a reflection of their obsession with youth culture.

Media communicators use costumes as a dramatic device. For instance, costumes can reveal character in media presentations. Heroes wear bright-colored clothing, while villains wear disheveled, dark clothes. Costumes also function as an expression of a character's distinctive persona. For instance, wearing a trench coat in many of his films reinforced Humphrey Bogart's tough, ruthless image.

Costumes also dramatize thematic concerns associated with popular genres. In the gangster genre, the mob's flamboyant wardrobe is associated with violence, wealth, and power. Eugene Rosow comments, "The most reliably consistent trait of movie gangsters was their sartorial progression from dark and wrinkled nondescript clothing to flashy, double-breasted, custom tailored striped suits with silk ties and suitable jewelry."[37] The gangster's wardrobe epitomizes their paradoxical position in society; the characters appropriate the styles of high fashion to blend in and gain acceptance, but their clothing style is too extreme, and they are further ostracized by society. So they cultivate an "identified school of stylishness that, far from operating as camouflage, ultimately functioned like warrior dress"[38] In *Casino* (1995), director Martin Scorsese used costumes as a metaphor for the excesses in the lifestyle of the gangster. During the film, Ace (Robert De Niro) changes costumes fifty-two times; his wife, Ginger, (Sharon Stone) went through forty costume changes.

The choice of costumes can signal plot developments in a narrative. For instance, in the gangster genre, clothing often is emblematic of the mobster's rise from small-time crook to successful mobster, and his subsequent fall. Thus, in *Casino,* Ace's demise is documented by his choice of wardrobe. Toward the end of the film, Ace rises from his desk wearing a meticulously coordinated outfit (shirt, tie, socks, shoes, and boxer shorts)—minus his trousers. This signals a radical departure for a man who throughout the film has had a fixation with appearance. Clothes define a gangster's identity—both to himself and to the audience. Therefore, slipping into sartorial neglect signals the beginning of his fall.

In *Boyz n the Hood* (1991), director John Singleton uses costumes to chart the complex issues of racial identity and alienation facing a black youth moving into maturity in South Central Los Angeles. Concerned about her son Tre (Cuba Gooding Jr.), his mother, Reva (Angela Basset), sends him to live with his father, Furious (Larry Fishburne). Furious works as a mortgage broker in the neighborhood. Furious's clothes (chinos, striped shirts, knitted tops, and glasses) exhibit the conventional insignia of a black male socialized into a white middle-class culture. Conversely, the clothes of Tre's best friend, Doughboy (Ice Cube), are political statements against the established social order. The style of the youth conveys the message of aggression and defiance against the subordination of dominant white male hegemony. In addition, the clothes represent masculinity (as defined by the black community) and imply authority, control, toughness, and independence.

Thus, the costumes in *Boyz n the Hood* signify the fundamental choices facing the African American male in American culture. If Tre chooses the conventional, banal style of the white middle class, he merits acceptance into the dominant white culture but becomes alienated from his own sense of self, repressing his black, masculine identity. By donning the street uniform, Tre assumes 'hood affinity and masculine identity but suffers alienation from the mainstream American community and is relegated to the life of the streets.

In some cases, the costumes worn in media presentations become fashion trends, assuming a cultural significance. According to Professor Harriet Worobey, Joan Crawford's trademark dresses with shoulder pads were an expression of emerging cultural attitudes and preoccupations: "In the 1940s, Crawford was in her shopgirl/independent woman stage, starring in films such as *Mildred Pierce.* The shoulder pads indicated that she had power and was able to compete with her male co-stars. Women began to wear them because they wanted to emulate her. The clothes coincided with what was happening with women in the forties, who were having to join the workforce because of the war and were reluctant to give up this independence."[39]

Indeed, it can be argued that the costumes that appear in media presentations can *forecast* historical events. Reporter Stephanie Rosenbloom observes, "Just how much meaning should be read into fashion is a matter of debate. But few would disagree that clothes have always reflected the exuberance, the gloom, even the chaos of the moment." Barbara Bloemink, curatorial director of the Cooper-Hewitt National Design Museum, declares that fashion can "both sense and influence."[40]

For example, according to Anne Hollander, the author of *Seeing Through Clothes,* the class conflict leading to the French Revolution was heralded by the fashions of the time. Before 1789, women began wearing "simple, belted shifts," while men wore "plebeian garb" like "rough coats and unkempt neckwear."[41] Rosenbloom adds that the fashions of the sixties gave "shape and substance and color to the inarticulate impulses of the decade."[42]

Within this context, one of the striking trends at the 2005 Paris fashion show was the obscuring, by masks, hoods, hats, and swaths of fabric, of the faces of the models. According to Sarah Takesh, the founder of the Tarsian & Blinkley clothing company and a resident of Kabul, Afghanistan, a model's face was perhaps too beautiful to represent the moment. "There's such a dark blanket that has settled on the world right now," she said. Hollander agrees: The style, she said, was "muffled and hampered, taking off from the burka-clad idea; but it's essentially the same lack of female self-possession only in a different key."[43]

Costume has emerged as an important consideration in the persona of politicians. For instance, in April 2006, Democratic presidential hopeful Barack Obama's choice of "costume" for the *Late Show with David Letterman* made the pronouncement that he was, indeed, a serious candidate. "That is a tremendous suit you have on," Letterman told Obama. "That is a very electable suit."[44] Dori Molitor, the chief executive of WomanWise, explains, "Voters are looking for a new language and new thinking. Obama helps bring in that new language visually by breaking the dress code of blue suit, starched shirt and red tie."[45]

At the same time, wardrobe can be seen as a way to identify weaknesses in a politician, as when Richard Nixon wore lace-up shoes on the beach, looking decidedly like a geek. "You neither want to be seen as somebody who cares too much about appearance or too little," said Jay Fielden, the editor of *Men's Vogue.*[46]

Wardrobe also displays the double standard imposed on female politicians. "For women it's a totally separate game, a separate psychology," said lobbyist Juliana Glover, According to Glover, a female politician cannot afford to be too well turned out, or she risks being read as untrustworthy, a virago, or worse, a vixen.[47] For example, consider the following news story about Secretary of State Condoleezza Rice that appeared in the *Washington Post* in 2005:

> Secretary of State Condoleezza Rice arrived at the Wiesbaden Army Airfield . . . dressed all in black. She was wearing a black skirt that hit just above the knee, and it was topped with a black coat that fell to mid-calf. . . . As Rice walked out to greet the troops, the coat blew open in a rather swashbuckling way to reveal the top of a pair of knee-high boots. The boots had a high, slender heel that is not particularly practical. But it is a popular silhouette because it tends to elongate and flatter the leg. In short, the boots are sexy. . . .
>
> Rice's coat and boots speak of sex and power—such a volatile combination, and one that in political circles rarely leads to anything but scandal. When looking at the image of Rice in Wiesbaden, the mind searches for ways to put it all into context. It turns to fiction, to caricature. To shadowy daydreams. Dominatrix! It is as though sex and power can only co-exist in a fantasy. When a woman combines them in the real world, stubborn stereotypes have her power devolving into a form that is purely sexual.[48]

This article would be considered inappropriate if its subject was a male. For instance, it would be considerably more difficult to find stories commenting on George W. Bush's legs. Furthermore, this kind of article conveys the message that the basis for judging a female candidate is her appearance, which ultimately undermines confidence in her qualifications for public office. Indeed, by framing Rice's position of power in sexual terms, the article conveys the latent message that, in American culture, powerful women continue to intimidate males.

Accessories

Accessories are adornments that enhance personal appearance, such as makeup, hairstyle, eyeglasses, handbags, and cosmetic surgery. Accessories can send powerful nonverbal messages about an individual's credibility, power, likability, and competency. Through selection of attire,

President Bush in Pilot Costume

The selection of words and images can influence the ways in which people perceive events and people. To illustrate, in May 2003, President Bush, in pilot gear, landed a fighter jet on the USS *Abraham Lincoln* to announce "Mission Accomplished" in Iraq. The exterior of the plane was marked with "Navy 1" on the back and "George W. Bush Commander-in-Chief" just below the cockpit window. The media instantly picked up on this term, reframing the role and responsibilities of the president. (*Getty Images; photographer: Hector Mata*)

automobiles, and hairstyles, we can assemble a unique, distinguishable *identity*. Style has become a way to advertise ourselves within mass culture; our choices tell others who we are, what we stand for, and what others can expect from us.

In American political campaigns, candidates differentiate themselves through their choice of accessories. For example, during the 2004 presidential election, President George W. Bush wore French cuffs with gold cufflinks, which, according to Alex Williams, "reinforced an impression of executive acumen." In contrast, Democratic opponent John Kerry often wore a yellow wristband from the Lance Armstrong Foundation, an advocacy group for cancer survivors, "which may lend a dash of youthful athleticism."[49]

At times accessories actually *become* the message. Cherie Bank, medical reporter for WCAU-TV in Philadelphia, recalls reporting on a medical breakthrough involving the early detection of birth defects. "I anticipated calls from expectant mothers who wanted more information about the procedure. However, the first call I got was from a woman who wanted to know where I bought my earrings."[50]

Artifacts

The use of artifacts in media presentations can lend an air of authenticity to the presentation. For instance, in the film version of *The Portrait of a Lady* (1996), the filmmaker meticulously included trappings from the period, including clothing, furniture, and curios, which transported the viewer to nineteenth-century England and Italy. In addition, the sets are an integral part of many media genres, making the audience feel familiar in these surroundings. For instance, we expect saloons in old westerns to contain swinging doors, a player piano, a long bar, and spittoons on the floor.

In addition, media communicators use artifacts to comment on the attitudes, behaviors, and values of a historical period. For instance, in *Mad Men* (2007), a cable television drama set in the 1960s, the appearance of artifacts furnishes perspective into the growing materialism of the era. Matthew Weiner, who created and wrote the series, explains, "The story is told in the details, and those details have their own life. . . . The metal fixture that clasps like a clothespin onto the guest towel—my grandmother had it, my mother had it. It's actually written into the script."[51]

Vocalic Communication

Vocalic communication refers to the quality of the voice that conveys meaning, independent of the meaning of the words spoken. Vocalic communication includes the following elements:

- *Volume:* the relative loudness or softness in our voices. Loudness can signify dominance or conviction, while a low volume may suggest insecurity, submissiveness, or evasiveness.
- *Tone:* the characteristic quality or timber of the voice. A deep tone suggests authority, power, and confidence. Nasal voices are unattractive, lethargic, and foolish. Breathy voices are judged to be youthful and artistic for males, but artificial and high-strung for females.

- *Pitch:* the relative position of a tone in the musical scale; that is, whether the voice is high or low. Flat voices are seen as sluggish, cold, and withdrawn, while variety in pitch is dynamic and extroverted. A high-pitched voice may signal lying.[52] Ending a sentence with an elevated pitch ordinarily signals that the speaker is asking a question. However, this rise in pitch may also indicate that the speaker is uncertain about what he or she is saying. Conversely, lowering the pitch at the end of a sentence conveys certainty and authority.
- *Rate:* the pace or rhythm of delivery—how rapidly or slowly we speak. A person is generally regarded as speaking with greater intensity and earnestness as his or her speaking rate increases.[53] Media consultant Tripp Frohlichstein declares, "Too fast and listeners can't follow you. Too slow and you become ponderous and boring."[54]
- *Duration:* the length of time a communicator takes to emit a given sound or sounds. Drawing out a conversation is a dominance device, in which the speaker seeks to control the conversation.
- *Diction:* the clarity of pronunciation and articulation. Garbled diction can suggest confusion, ignorance, or deceit.
- *Silence:* the *absence* of sound. Because of the expense of producing a film or television program, time is a precious commodity. Consequently, *not* talking can be a dramatic—and effective—form of communication. Indeed, the power of actors such as James Dean or Clint Eastwood often comes not from what they say but from what they don't (or are unable to) express. In other contexts silence can be soothing and encouraging.
- *Laughter:* an involuntary emotional release that can express joy, approval, surprise, discomfort, anxiety, sympathy, or ridicule. The context of the laughter determines its exact meaning. For example, people who are nervous or feel that they are in a subservient position may laugh at inappropriate times. Various categories of laughter convey different meanings. In television programs, laugh tracks punctuate programs with chuckles, giggles, snickers, and guffaws, instructing the audience not only on what is funny, but on how funny the situation is.

Vocal cues such as dialect, tonal quality, inflection, speed of delivery, and accent transmit a wide range of information. According to psychologist Richard Wiseman, vocality can be a more accurate barometer of the communicator's intention than eye contact or gestures: "If you want to find out if a politician's lying . . . you're better turning away or shutting your eyes and just concentrating on the sound track."[55]

Dialect, tonal quality, inflection, speed of delivery, pitch, and pause inform the audience about the speaker's nationality, educational level, and social class. An accent, such as the postvocalic *R* that identifies a Bostonian or the Southern drawl, can pinpoint a person's birthplace. Accents can charm an audience; however, a heavy accent can interfere with the communication process.

A person with an accent may become the butt of jokes, undermining the seriousness of the message. For example, in the classic television series *I Love Lucy,* a running gag consisted of Lucy Ricardo poking fun at her husband's heavy Cuban accent (Lucy asks, "What do you mean, 'I've got a lot of 'splainin' to do?'"). Indeed, the history of American media is replete with exploitive films that minstralize, vaudevillize, and mimic black speech, diminishing the character of African Americans. However, according to film and cultural historian Clyde Taylor, authentic black dialect in indigenous films reveals not only black values, but the many "distinctive and richly expressive characteristics," such as semantic ambiguity, bold extravagant metaphor, and a prophetic mode of utterance.[56]

African American cultural expression can also be found in black music, which often moves black speech patterns into melody. According to jazz musician Phil Wilson, jazz was a form of dialogue among black musicians. While playing in all-white night clubs, black musicians used jazz to alert each other of coming trouble.[57]

Moreover, vocal cues can furnish insight into the *emotional context* of a speaker's remarks, including the type of emotion (e.g., anger, disappointment) and degree of emotional intensity. Vocal qualities also influence the impression that a speaker makes on the audience. A pleasing voice contributes to the credibility and attractiveness of the speaker. As a result, broadcast reporters train their voices to be low in pitch and resonant to give them an air of authority.

Nonverbal Indicators of Behavior

Nonverbal indicators provide a rich source of information about an individual's frame of mind and attitude. Terry Corpal, professor of criminal justice and a retired Secret Service agent, observes that nonverbal cues can furnish insight into human conduct: "By themselves, these behaviors may signify nothing. Collectively, they provide a tremendous amount of information about the person."[58]

These nonverbal cues can be applied to the analysis of media presentations as well. Actors adopt nonverbal mannerisms to express their characters' internal motivations and emotions. In addition, individuals covered by the media frequently lapse into unconscious nonverbal behavior patterns. Examining these unscripted verbal behaviors can serve as an indication of the media communicator's behavior and disposition.

Deception

Examining nonverbal behaviors can be an effective method of identifying instances of *deception.* Deception is a category of human behavior that includes doubt, lying, uncertainty, and exaggeration. Psychology professor Dr. Paul Ekman has developed a mechanism for reading subtle emotional cues from facial expressions. Using a facial action coding system (or FACS), Ekman is able identify *microexpressions*—immediate reactions that, while typically lasting less than a quarter of a second, display an individual's genuine emotions.

Ekman found that the forty-three muscles of the face work in observable, predictable ways when a person experiences a particular emotion— even when an emotion is so fleeting that the person experiencing it may not be conscious of it. Ekman explains, "While everybody can smile, most people can't move one crucial muscle around the eyes that must be moved to generate the physiology of happiness."[59]

In this way, the FACS can be used to detect liars. Ekman explains, "In a fake smile, only the zygomatic major muscle, which runs from the cheekbone to the corner of the lips, moves. In a real smile, the eyebrows and the skin between the upper eyelid and the eyebrow come down very slightly. The muscle involved is the orbicularis oculi, pars lateralis."[60]

Another way to detect deception is by looking for "evasive nonverbal behaviors." When questioning a suspect, Police Deputy Tom O'Connor begins by asking a series of routine questions in order to gauge the subject's normal nonverbal behavior pattern. O'Connor then asks more direct, probing questions and then notes any involuntary changes in nonverbal behavior: "The key from my perspective as a policeman is that we must put a person in a stressful situation (one in which they know that their responses have consequences, such as a loss of reputation or confinement). White lies often are undetectable because there are no huge consequences related to being caught. Nonverbal behavior cues are based specifically on what they do after they have heard and fully understand a critical question addressed to them."[61]

In this stressful situation, a person who is caught in a lie must concentrate on formulating a credible response. At that moment, the suspect is prone to let down his or her guard, displaying involuntary, unconscious nonverbal behaviors. O'Connor looks for downcast eyes (particularly before responding to a question), a low level of eye contact, shifty eye behaviors, lip biting, or noticeable changes in the pattern of breathing or frequency of swallowing. Other nonverbal signals of inner turmoil include hand rubbing or experiencing dry mouth.[62]

A suspect may also engage in a series of evasive nonverbal behaviors, such as dropping his or her head or clearing his or her throat, which O'Connor describes as "a delaying tactic—buying time to formulate an acceptable response."[63]

Another signal of deceit consists of hand-to-face gestures to cover up a lie. Pease observes that young children often cover their mouths with their hands "in an attempt to stop the deceitful words from coming out."[64] A variation of this hand-to-face gesture is the nose touch. Morris explains,

> Touching the nose unknowingly . . . during a verbal encounter often signals deceit. The person performing the action is unaware of it, which makes it a valuable clue as to their true feelings. Why unconscious nose-touching should be closely linked with telling lies is not clear, but it may be that, at the moment of deceit, the hand makes an involuntary move to cover the mouth—to hide the lie, as it were—and then moves on to the nose. The final shift from mouth to nose may be due to an unconscious sensation that mouth-covering is too obvious—something that every child does when telling untruths. Touching the nose, as if it is itching, may therefore be a disguised mouth-cover—a cover-up of the cover-up. However, some individuals report that they have felt a genuine sensation of nose ringing or itching at the very moment they have been forced to tell a lie, so that the action may be caused by some kind of small psychological change in the nasal tissue, as a result of the fleeting stress of the deceit.[65]

Another signal of deceit is when suspects fidget in their chairs. O'Connor observes that some suspects physically change their position when they are caught in a lie: "Their subconscious desire to leave the room is strong, so they move their bodies closer to the door."[66]

Indeed, sometimes a suspect actually will cross his or her legs, with one foot pointed toward the door—the place where they would like to be headed.

Sexual Attitudes

Nonverbal behaviors can furnish perspective into cultural attitudes. For instance, sexual attitudes often are communicated through nonverbal indicators. Men are permitted to be more sexually aggressive and therefore are more overt in their nonverbal cues, including winking and the dominant gaze. Another nonverbal sexual overture occurs when a man turns his body toward the object of his attention and points his foot at her. According to Pease, the gesture in which thumbs are tucked into the belt or the tops of the pockets also indicates sexual readiness: "The arms take the readiness position and the hands . . . highlight the genital region."[67]

Because females are more culturally constrained, they have had to be less direct in their expression of sexual interest. Consequently, women utilize a catalog of subtle nonverbal indicators of sexual interest. For example, a sideways glance, in which a female gazes sideways at the companion from a lowered head, signals secret approval. *Preening* behavior (e.g., smoothing his collar, smoothing his hair) is another sign of sexual interest. The head toss, in which the woman's hair sways over her shoulder or away from her face, is also considered a signal of preening. Licking the lips, slightly pouting the mouth, or applying cosmetics to moisten or redden the lips are all further indicators of a courtship invitation.[68]

Another nonverbal sexual cue is the body stroke, in which a female absentmindedly caresses her own leg. According to Morris, the latent meaning of the gesture is "I find you attractive": "When people find their companions attractive, they may unconsciously do to their own bodies what they would like their companions to do to them. . . . A casual stroking of the body while listening to a companion, or while talking to them, indicates a desire to be caressed by them, regardless of what statements are being made at the time. Leg stroking is the most common form of this reaction."[69]

Jan Hargrave observes that when a woman sits with one leg tucked under the other and points the folded leg toward the person who she wants to attract, the nonverbal message communicated is "I feel very comfortable with you. I'd like to get to know you better."[70] Another female sexual posture is the "leg twine," in which one leg is twined tightly around the other. Morris explains, "Because of the tight way in which the legs wrap around one another, it gives the impression of self-hugging, and this adds a mild sexual quality to the gesture."[71] Other indications of sexual interest include open legs while sitting or standing and rolling hips while walking.

However, as noted earlier, these nonverbal cues are not always reliable measures of sexual interest. At times, it is simply comfortable to position yourself in a particular way. Consequently, it is reasonable to regard these nonverbal cues as *indicative,* but certainly not a *guarantee* of sexual interest.

In the United States, the body language adopted by females is indicative of the cultural polarization between "good" and "bad" women in American culture. Images of virtuous women in photographs, television programs, and films display a modest, submissive demeanor, typified by soft smiles and a slightly tilted head. The virtuous woman refrains from looking directly at the object of her attention, instead looking with lowered eyes or with a sidelong glance. Her body language also displays her vulnerability; she often places an object (e.g., her hair, hands, or a male) between herself and the camera to shield herself. These virtuous women refrain from behavior or postures that might excite men. The model may sit sideways. If seated in frontal view, her legs are usually closed, or knees folded to the side. These women also typically keep their arms close to their bodies.

In contrast, the "bad" or immoral woman assumes a more direct pose. Her head is erect, and her eyes look straight into the camera. These women adopt open postures, moving their arms and legs away from their bodies, signifying sexual receptivity or aggressiveness. In entertainment programming, women who assume these nonverbal behaviors generally are villainesses or temptresses, whose transgressions are beyond redemption. For example, in a scene from the film *Basic Instinct* (1992), Catherine Tramell (Sharon Stone) positioned herself in a sexually provocative pose in front of a group of male interrogators to distract her questioners and control the interrogation.

In many media programs, these "bad" women are often killed off (as unfit to live) or exiled. In *High Noon* (1952), Helen Ramírez (Katy Jurado) was the former illicit lover of town marshal Will Kane (Gary Cooper). As the "bad" girl, Helen's dark hair and complexion and direct, defiant gaze and posture are juxtaposed with the pure blond innocence and demure demeanor of Amy (Grace Kelly), Kane's fiancée. Ironically, when an outlaw he put in prison returns with his gang to take revenge on Kane, it is the spurned Ramírez who defends Kane, while Amy chooses to leave him. Despite Helen's good heart, she must be punished for her moral transgressions, and she is forced to leave town. (Ironically, although Kane—the protagonist—was complicit in this moral transgression, he goes unpunished.)

Increasingly, however, these "immoral" nonverbal behaviors have become more widespread in mainstream media presentations. In fashion magazines such as *Vogue,* the models are routinely found in poses described earlier as belonging to "bad" girls: direct gazes, legs positioned in a provocative manner, and pelvis thrust forward, so that it is the closest body part to the camera. These models appear comfortable with their sexuality as a vital part of their total identity.

At the same time, this trend also can be regarded as a further exploitation of the bad-girl image: Webster University graduate student Samantha L. Harms observes, "In these ads, the company logos are placed prominently near the models' spread legs, in an effort to attract the attention of the readers. The ads definitely associate their products with sex."[72]

Nonverbal Communication Analysis: Smoking Behaviors in Film

Why do smoking behaviors appear so frequently in films?

Long before product placement emerged as a commercial incentive for the film industry, cigarettes were an integral part of the worldview of film. In 2000, women in Hollywood movies were twice as likely to smoke as women in real life (42 percent of female lead or supporting actors smoke on film, compared with 24 percent of U.S. women overall). Among males, 38 percent of actors smoke compared with 29 percent of men in everyday life.[73] In 2005, all five Oscar nominees for Best Actor played heavy smokers. Of the thirty finalists in the Academy Awards' six main categories, only *Pride and Prejudice* does not include smoking scenes. Among those with the more than fifty smoking scenes were *Brokeback Mountain, Capote, Good Night and Good Luck,* and *Walk the Line.*[74] Smoking behaviors are also prevalent in international films. For instance, Korean movies released in 2005 have an average of more than five and a half scenes that feature someone smoking.[75]

A nonverbal approach to media literacy can furnish perspective into smoking behaviors in films, as well as identifying cumulative messages about smoking that are conveyed in film. Because of its strong visual properties, smoking behavior can be a particularly effective form of nonverbal communication. Smoke creates a texture in the air as it catches the light, so that it can be used to create a mysterious, romantic, or surreal worldview.

Smoking behaviors can be an effective way to reveal character in films. For instance, Humphrey Bogart's image as a tough guy was exhibited by the way that he held and inhaled his cigarettes. In contrast, smoking gestures (e.g., lighting someone's cigarette, removing a cigarette from a cigarette case) can also be handled with savoir faire, reflecting an upper-class sophistication. For example, in *Now, Voyager* (1942), Charlotte Vale (Bette Davis) falls in love with debonair Jerry Durrance (Paul Henreid) on a South American cruise. In one scene, as the couple come to an understanding about their feelings for each other, Durrance proposes, "Shall we have a cigarette on it?" He suavely opens his cigarette case and extracts two cigarettes. Lighting both, he then gallantly hands one to Charlotte.

Because it is difficult to display internal states of consciousness in films, smoking behaviors can be used to signal what characters are thinking and feeling. Gestures such as twisting, flicking, or waving the cigarette are signals of emotional turmoil. In *The Man with the Golden Arm* (1955), Frankie Machine (Frank Sinatra) is an emotional wreck, on the verge of a nervous breakdown. In one scene, the camera focuses on Frankie's shaking hands as he tries to light a cigarette. Indeed, whenever Frankie becomes agitated, he lights up—the message being that smoking steadies the nerves.

An actor's smoking behaviors also indicate his or her character's level of self-esteem. Blowing smoke through the nostrils is a sign of a superior, confident individual. Allan Pease observes, "The faster the smoke is blown upwards, the more superior or confident the person feels; the faster it is blown down, the more negative he feels."[76]

Smoking behaviors in film can also project a character's attitude toward others. Blowing smoke straight ahead (in the direction of the other person) can be a statement of aggression, dislike, contempt, dominance, or indifference. According to Pease, extinguishing a cigarette also can be an expression of attitude toward others: "If the smoker lights a cigarette and suddenly extinguishes it earlier than he normally would, he has signaled his decision to terminate the conversation."[77]

Smoking is central to the worldview of many films and television programs, reinforcing the notion that cigarettes are integral to activities such as socializing at bars. Cigarettes also are a part of the wardrobe of glamorous professionals such as detectives, gangsters, show business personalities, and journalists.

In addition, filmmakers frequently use smoking behaviors as a *narrative device.* Film is a visual medium that emphasizes plot, or action—people doing things. Because movement is a key element in film, smoking behaviors draw the audience's attention during static scenes dominated by dialogue. In *Rebel Without a Cause* (1955), Jim Stark (James Dean) and gang leader Buzz (Corey Allen) pause for a smoke before dueling in a dangerous "Chickie Run." The cigarette break is a significant moment in the film. During this brief interlude, the two rivals reflect on the quest for meaning in a changing and impersonal world. Jim asks Buzz, "Why are we doing [the Chickie Run]?" Buzz replies, "You've got to do something." But as soon as they have finished their cigarettes, they again retreat behind the facade of cool detachment and resume their competition.

Smoking behaviors also can be a sign of intimacy between people. The communal aspects of smoking (e.g., offering someone a cigarette, lighting up together) often foreshadow later scenes in which the characters become closer. For instance, *Great Expectations* (1998) includes in a scene in which Estella (Gwyneth Paltrow) introduces Finnegan Bell (Ethan Hawke) to her friends, including her current lover, Walter Plane (Hank Azaria). Finnegan immediately pulls out a pack of cigarettes and, taking one, gives Estella his "last cigarette"—a measure of his devotion. Finnegan leans toward her to light her cigarette, so that the two characters are suddenly in very intimate proximity to each other. In this two-dimensional medium, the smoke forms a visual line, or *vector,* that connects characters physically and, by extension, emotionally as well. Having been excluded, Plane asks the waiter for a cigarette.

Further, smoking onscreen also has strong sexual implications. Critic Richard Klein observes that the phallic properties of cigarettes play a suggestive role in sexually volatile scenes: "In those aroused by the spectacle of masterly women giving themselves leisure (all nostril, mouth and fingers), smoking languorously and slow, the moment of lighting up seems to spark the most energetic erotic excitement."[78] Often when two characters meet and establish a sexual chemistry, one character (or both) pulls out a cigarette. Moreover, smoking after a lovemaking scene is a familiar cliché in film and television.

The use of cigarettes in media programs often is presented as a rite of passage to adulthood. For instance, in *Stand by Me* (1986), the young boys, out on their own for the first time, celebrate their independence by smoking cigarettes around a campfire.

Trainspotting (1996) offers a nihilistic worldview, in which characters are on their own, with nothing (not even parents) to rebel against. The characters are locked in the present, and smoking cigarettes (and shooting heroin) represents a rebellion against themselves—against their futures.

Actors also use smoking behaviors as a performance prop. George Burns and Groucho Marx used cigars for dramatic pause and emphasis. For instance, they controlled the timing of their lines by lighting the cigars. They also waved the cigars around for emphasis and (in Groucho's case) wagged the cigar in a suggestive way after a sexually suggestive quip.

Conclusion

Even though the appearance of smoking in films initially was noncommercial, films served as a very powerful indirect advertisement for tobacco products. Clearly, smoking remains a very attractive activity in films. Smoking is central to the worldview of many films, reinforcing the notion that cigarettes are an integral part of the culture. Smoking accompanies particular activities, such as socializing at bars and sexual encounters. Moreover, smoking is used as a symbol of rebellion, a rite of passage to adulthood, or a communal activity that promotes a sense of membership in a group.

Cigarettes also are used as a dramatic device to advance the plot. Lighting a cigarette establishes a pause in the action for new disclosures and fresh insight into character and relationships. Cigarette smoking often functions as a bonding ritual between characters in the narrative; the communal aspects of smoking (e.g., offering someone a cigarette, lighting up together) offer opportunities for characters to pause in the action and honestly share their thoughts and feelings.

The nonverbal approach to media literacy identifies the cumulative messages about smoking in film. This approach furnishes perspective into the continued popularity of smoking, despite efforts to educate the public about its dangers.

Summary: Nonverbal Analysis of Media Content

I. Nonverbal communications analysis can help the audience member to decipher media messages, by the following four lines of inquiry:

A. Do the nonverbal communication behaviors reinforce verbal messages? Explain.

B. Do the nonverbal communication cues provide subtextual information about the speaker? Explain.

C. Are there "unscripted" nonverbal behaviors that are at variance with the verbal message? Explain.

D. Do the media communicators manipulate nonverbal behaviors to create a particular image or impression?

E. How does the study of nonverbal communication furnish perspective into cultural attitudes, values, behaviors, preoccupations, and myths that define a culture?

F. What role do nonverbal cues provide in the depiction of media stereotypes?

II. Nonverbal communication behaviors

Facial expressions   Eye behaviors
Posture   Gestures
Proxemic communication   Tactile communication
Vocalic communication   Physical appearance
Accessories

See the grid above to identify the nonverbal communication behaviors that apply to the following questions:

A. What types of nonverbal communication behaviors does the
   subject display?
B. What functions are fulfilled by these nonverbal communication behaviors?
   1. Do these nonverbal communication behaviors classify
      information? Explain.
   2. Are these nonverbal communication behaviors intended
      to persuade? Are they successful?
   3. Are these nonverbal communication behaviors used to
      regulate the communication process? Explain.
   4. Are these nonverbal communication behaviors intended
      to establish or maintain the communication relationship?
      Are they successful?
   5. How do you interpret the nonverbal communication be-
      haviors?
   6. What emotions are conveyed through nonverbal com-
      munication behaviors?
   7. Do the nonverbal communication behaviors support or
      conflict with the verbal communication?
C. What do these nonverbal communication behaviors reveal
   about the subject's character, state of mind, or attitude?
D. What do these nonverbal communication behaviors suggest
   about the subject's status or credibility?
E. What messages are conveyed by the communicator's nonverbal communication behaviors?
   1. Do the nonverbal communication behaviors reinforce
      verbal messages?
   2. Do the nonverbal communication behaviors reveal "un-

scripted" nonverbal behaviors that are at variance with the verbal message?

3. Do the nonverbal communication behaviors reveal "scripted" nonverbal impression-management behaviors? What are the intended messages?

III. Additional questions to analyze specific nonverbal communication behaviors

   A. Posture

      1. What are the characters' postural styles (rigid, relaxed, nervous, calm, friendly, contentious, attentive)?

      2. What messages do these postures convey?

   B. Proxemic communication: What kinds of proxemic communications are taking place?

      1. Personal space: What is the physical distance between the characters?

      2. Group formation

      3. Fixed space

         a. What does the architecture tell you about the characters' lifestyle?

         b. What is your emotional response to the environment (warm, formal, private, familiar, distant, confining?

   C. Tactile communication

      1. Which characters touch each other? Who initiates the touching?

      2. What does the touching signify?

   D. Vocalic communication

      1. What tone of voice is used?

      2. Is there an accent or dialect?

      3. How fast does the character speak?

      4. Are there long silences or pauses, and what does this mean?

   E. Physical appearance

      1. What is the shape of the body (obese, thin, muscular)?

      2. What does the body type tell you about the character?

      3. What are the comparative heights of the characters?

      4. Does this signify anything as to dominant-subordinate relationships?

   F. Accessories

      1. How are the characters dressed, and what does this tell

you about the character (social class, education, ethnic origin)?

2. What artifacts does the character wear?
3. What types of clothing are the main characters wearing?
4. What other material accessories (e.g., home, technology) do the characters have?

4

Mythic Analysis

Introduction

Why is it that we watch reruns and formulaic stories over and over again? What is it that draws us it to these media presentations? One reason might be that these stories are telling (or retelling) myths.

In contemporary culture, with its emphasis on rational, scientific explanation, there is a tendency to discount or deny the value of myth. However, writing in 1873, Max Mueller argued that mythology exists in the modern age, whether or not we are willing to acknowledge it: "Depend upon it. There is mythology now as there was in the time of Homer, only we do not perceive it, because we ourselves live in the very shadow of it, and because we all shrink from the full meridian light of truth."[1]

Today, the oral tradition—the primary source for passing myths from generation to generation—has nearly disappeared. In this vacuum, the media have emerged as primary channels for the transmission of myth. Mircea Eliade contends that although times have changed, people continue to seek solutions to life crises, albeit unconsciously, through the channels of mass communications: "A whole volume could be written on the myths of modern man, on mythologies camouflaged in the plays that he enjoys, in the books that he reads. The cinema, that 'dream factory,' takes over and employs countless mythical motifs— the fight between hero and monster, initiatory combats and ordeals, paradigmatic figures and images."[2]

A mythic approach can help make media content accessible in the following ways.

- To identify the *mythic functions* of media programming

- To provide perspective on media content as a *retelling* of traditional myths
- To identify *mythic elements* in media programs (and the meanings behind these elements) as a way to approach critical analysis of the narrative
- To identify *cultural myths* in media programs that furnish perspective into that culture

Note: Several points of clarification need to be made in considering the mythic approach to media. First, a distinction must be drawn between form and content. Not all media content qualifies as myth. The media (e.g., film, Internet) are simply channels of information. Thus, while a medium is not in itself mythic, it may serve as a modern conveyer of myth. Consequently, a first step in a mythic analysis involves identifying mythic elements in media presentations.

The question of *intention* also must be considered: Are media communicators consciously drawing upon myth for inspiration? Are they committed to conveying mythic tales? Perhaps. Ultimately, though, the question of artistic intention is irrelevant. At times, media communicators simply are trying to entertain—or make a profit. However, in the process of telling stories about themselves and their world, media communicators tap into a wellspring of universal mythic concerns. Moreover, in the absence of traditional sources of myth telling, people desperately strive to discover meaning in other areas. Psychologist Rollo May observes, "In such directionless states as we find ourselves near the end of the twentieth century, it is not surprising that frantic people flock to the new cults, or resurrect the old ones, seeking answers to their anxiety and longing for relief from their guilt or depression to their anxiety and longing for something to fill the vacuum of their lives."[3]

One final note: There is some possibility that readers might regard this discussion of mythology as an attack on their personal belief systems. While it is easy to remain detached in a discussion of ancient Babylonian mythology, an analysis of your religion (e.g., Christianity or Buddhism) as myth may be another matter entirely. In the definition of myth, the authors note that a myth may or may not be true, and we recognize that it is beyond our capability to make this determination. The scope of this approach is merely to examine common mythic functions, mythic elements, and narrative components of myth as a way of furnishing perspective into media presentations.

Overview of Myth

A myth is any real or fictitious story, recurring theme, or character type that gives expression to deep, commonly felt emotions. In the most general sense, myths may be distinguished from simple narratives, in that they appeal to the consciousness of a people by putting human beings in touch with elemental feelings associated with the experience of being human. Joseph Campbell explains, "What human beings have in common is revealed in myths. Myths are stories of our search through the ages for truth, for meaning, for significance. We all need to tell our story and to understand our story. We all need to understand death and to cope with death, and we all need help in our passages from birth to life and then to death. We need for life to signify, to touch the eternal, to understand the mysterious, to find out who we are."[4] Myths can be multilayered, so that they may operate on several of these levels simultaneously.

Myths may be grouped into three general areas: *nature myths, historical myths,* and *metaphysical myths.* In the prescientific age, *nature myths* provided explanations for natural events, including meteorological, astronomical, terrestrial, chemical, and biological phenomena. Nature myths describe the origin of things, like the formation of rivers, or of some momentous past occurrence, such as the great deluge.

Historical myths chronicle significant events and rulers of previous civilizations. These tales serve as prehistories of ancient civilizations that often kept no written records. Historical myths may also provide information on the genealogy of gods, kings, and peoples, as well as the naming of particular places and people.

Metaphysical myths furnish insight into the mysteries of being human and an inhabitant of this world. Metaphysical myths explore the elemental part of the human experience: creation, birth, death, divine presence, good and evil, and the afterlife. Mythic scholar Gilbert Highnet explains, "[Myths] deal with the greatest of all problems, the problems which do not change because men and women do not change. They deal with love; with war; with sin; with tyranny; with courage; with fate; and all in some way or other deal with the relation of man to those divine powers which are sometimes to be cruel, and sometimes, alas, to be just."[5]

Psychoanalysts Sigmund Freud and Carl Jung maintain that myths originate in the subconscious, the repository for all universal human experience. Individuals come into contact with this shared experience through their dreams. Myths, then, represent an *externalization* of the elemental experiences and aspects of self that each person encounters as part of being human. By projecting these universal impulses, experiences, and conflicts, human beings are able to put their experiences into perspective. Henry A. Murray explains, "Though the imagery is necessarily derived from the external world, the reference is internal. In no other way, as Plato insisted, can certain profound truths be genuinely conveyed to others. Mythic stories and symbols that depict the 'night journey' of the introverted soul, the encounter with the monster in every person's 'depths,' liberation from imprisoning modes of feeling and of thought, reconciliation, spiritual rebirth, the beatific state of grace and redemption—experiences of this nature—are expressed in language that must be taken figuratively, symbolically, and imaginatively."[6]

Thus, human beings do not *invent* myths; they *discover* them as part of our universal unconscious. For example, Rayshawn Campbell, a fifth-grade student at Flynn Park School, University City, Missouri, composed an original story that, unbeknownst to him, is a variation of the Greek myth of Cronus and Zeus:

> Once there was a mean giant named Jim. He couldn't stand kids. He always would try to eat them. One day the kids were playing outside past their curfew. So Jim followed them home. When they got in, he waited for a while. Jim knocked and knocked again. They didn't open the door.
>
> Jim shouted, "Let me in." The kids said, "We know it's you, Jim. So back off. Leave us alone." So he slipped behind their house and waited until their mom got home. She said, "Let me in," sweetly. They let her in.
>
> Then Jim went to the bakery and bought some sugar. When their mom left again, Jim ate the sugar to make his voice sweeter. He went back to their house and knocked on the door. He said sweetly, "Let me in." Then they opened the door.
>
> Jim chopped their heads off and ate their bodies. He put their heads on the post. When their mom got home she saw their heads on the post. She said, "Ooooo, Jim got my babies." She heard a "Zzzz" sound and saw Jim. Immediately, she cut open his stomach took her kids' bodies out and sewed their heads back on. Then she put two big stones in Jim's stomach. When Jim woke up, he was thirsty. He went to the lake. And when he bent down, he fell into the lake, sank to the bottom, and turned into stone.[7]

The ancient version of the Cronus-and-Zeus myth is as follows:

> Cronus was now the lord of the universe. He sat on the highest mountain and ruled over heavens and earth with a firm hand. The other gods

obeyed his will and early man worshiped him. This was man's Golden Age. Men lived happily and in peace with the gods and each other. They did not kill and they had no locks on their doors, for theft had not yet been invented.

But Cronus did not set his monstrous brothers free, and Mother Earth was angry with him and plotted his downfall. She had to wait, for no god yet born was strong enough to oppose him. But she knew that one of his sons would be stronger than he, just as Cronus had been stronger than his father. Cronus knew it too, so every time his Titaness-wife Rhea gave birth, he took the newborn god and swallowed it. With all of his offspring securely inside him, he had nothing to fear.

But Rhea mourned. Her five sisters, who had married the five other Titans, were surrounded by their Titan children, while she was all alone. When Rhea expected her sixth, she asked Mother Earth to help her save the child from his father. That was just what Mother Earth had been waiting for. She gave her daughter whispered advice, and Rhea went away smiling.

As soon as Rhea had borne her child, the god Zeus, she hid him. Then she wrapped a stone in baby clothes and gave it to her husband to swallow instead of her son. Cronus was fooled and swallowed the stone, and the little god Zeus was spirited away to a secret cave on the island of Crete. Old Cronus never heard the cries of his young son, for Mother Earth let noisy earth sprites outside the cave. They made such a clatter, beating their shields with their swords, that other sounds were drowned out.[8]

Later, Zeus successfully deposed Cronus and, setting his brothers and sisters free, established the rein of the gods on Mount Olympus.

Rayshawn's story contains some remarkable similarities to this Greek myth. Both versions focus on male authority figures who are threatened by members of the younger generation. The children are protected by the mother, so that they can fulfill their destinies. Interestingly, both tales used the same motifs—the adult males planning to swallow the children and the mother substituting stones for her offspring.

Thus, myths often focus on the *deep truth* of human experience. That is, regardless of whether myths are factually accurate accounts of historical events, mythic tales speak to an inner truth in a way that science cannot. Psychologist Rollo May declares, "It does not matter in the slightest whether a man named Adam and a woman named Eve ever actually existed or not; the truth about them in Genesis still presents a picture of the birth and development of human consciousness which is applicable to all people of all ages and religions."[9]

In many myths, gods are portrayed as having human shape, feelings, and motives, though on a grander scale than their mortal counterparts. This personification makes the mysteries of the universe more intelligible to human beings. At the same time, these stories of the gods also can be regarded as allegorical tales about human beings, which put the experiences of men and women into meaningful perspective.

Functions of Myths

Myths fulfill a range of *functions,* or purposes, many of which now are also served by media programming. One of the disarming features of myth is that its functions appear to be so *natural;* that is, its functions are obvious and assumed by the audience. Critic Roland Barthes explains, "[Myth] transforms history into nature. We now understand why, in the eyes of the myth-consumer, the intention . . . of the concept can remain manifest without however appearing to have an interest in the matter: what causes mythical speech to be uttered is perfectly explicit, but it is immediately frozen into something natural; it is read not as a motive, but as a reason."[10]

This principle also applies to myths conveyed through the channels of mass communication. Although media programs often serve a variety of mythic functions, the audience tends to accept these programs as natural, without question. Consequently, a useful approach in mythic analysis is to consider media programming in terms of the following traditional functions of myth.

To Inspire Awe

Myth has the ability to move people out of everyday experience, into the realm of the extraordinary. Joseph Campbell explains, "The first function of mythology is to waken and maintain in the individual a sense of wonder and participation in the mystery of this finally inscrutable universe."[11]

Because preternatural events and heroic exploits are not part of everyday existence, we seek myth to affirm that the extraordinary is possible, that witches, ghosts, and supermen exist, and that mortals are capable of grand and transcendent acts.

In like fashion, media programming has the ability to transport its audience to a different realm of experience. Film, television, and recorded music operate on an *affective* (or emotional) level, so that audience members do not merely understand the story on a cognitive basis but are moved beyond their own immediate experience. Indeed, one of the primary functions of special-effects films such as *Star Wars, Spider-Man,* and *The Matrix* is to immerse people in an alternative experience.

Myth and media share another awe-inspiring capability as well. Both myths and media presentations contain elements of horror, destruction, and tragedy that evoke fear and dread among members of the audience. Both Oedipus and news reports of the 9/11 attacks remind people of the horrific possibilities of life.

To Facilitate Self-Actualization

Psychologist Rollo May observes that by putting human beings in touch with their own submerged feelings, myths can have a cathartic, or healing effect: "In reading the mythic tale, we feel cleansed as if by a great religious experience. . . . The world and life have a deeper quality that reaches down into a person's soul. . . . Love and joy and death confront one another in these depths of emotion."[12]

One of the attractions of media programming—even popular, formulaic programs—stems from this self-actualization function. Dramatic programs focus on elemental conflicts between good and evil, life and death, and questions of living honorably in an unjust world. Sitcoms are morality plays, in which characters must contend with the consequences of their transgressions, such as deceit or betrayal of their community. Disney cartoons such as *Hercules* and *The Little Mermaid* focus on issues of identity. Thus, even if programs appear repetitive, simplistic, and unchallenging on the surface, they satisfy an innate hunger to see these primal conflicts acted out on-screen.

Moreover, human beings seek myth as a way to break through their personal isolation, enabling them to move into full membership in the community of human beings. Joseph Campbell declares,

> In his life-form the individual is necessarily only a fraction and distortion of the total image of man. He is limited either as male or as female; at any given period of his life he is again limited as child, youth, mature adult, or ancient; furthermore, in his life role he is necessarily specialized as craftsman, tradesman, servant, or thief, priest, leader, wife, nun, or harlot; he cannot be all. Hence the totality—the fullness of man—is not in the separate member, but in the body of the society as a whole; the individual can only be an organ.[13]

Media programming also offers individuals an opportunity to share experiences with others, whether they are rooting for their favorite team on *Monday Night Football* or reveling in a feel-good movie.

To Exalt

Myths provide a means for people to honor significant events and people. In like fashion, the media elevate people and events to mythic status. Media attention can transform *ordinary* events into *extraordinary* occasions. For example, the Super Bowl has been transformed into an occasion— Super Sunday. Conversely, the media magnify achievements merely by focusing on them; if it appears on television, it *must* be important.

The media have assumed a *mythologizing* function in contemporary society. The pervasiveness of media coverage gives the media figure an air of omniscience. For example, information on basketball star Kobe Bryant and his family is everywhere—on television, in print, in films, and in cyberspace. Advertisers frequently present their spokespersons performing mythic deeds to boost their products' appeal. The close-up shots of Bryant making acrobatic shots make him appear omnipotent. While certainly Bryant's skills on the basketball court are superb, media coverage endows him with an air of invincibility. ESPN SportsCenter highlights his spectacular plays, while editing out his missed shots and errant passes. In fact, the media have truly merged reality and myth. Slow-motion replays accentuate his graceful moves and keep him suspended in midair indefinitely.

Entertainment programming also has begun to merge reality and myth. In *Space Jam* (1997), basketball superstar Michael Jordan operates in a magical world, in which he talks with animals and, thanks to special effects, defies gravity and other mortal constraints.

At the same time, the media *demythologizes* mythic figures and events. Unlike the Greek polytheistic culture, which recognizes many qualities in its mythic heroes, American culture tends to simplify its characters into absolutes of good and evil. The intense scrutiny of the media magnifies the flaws of people in the public eye. Editor Tony Frost of the tabloid paper the *Globe* asserts that his paper is responding to a basic desire to tear down our mythic heroes: "We have inherent morality. We believe in the lowest common denominator. Very few stars behave the way they should in private. That's what makes them interesting. We put them up on the pedestal, and they fall down and it's their own doing. . . . Bam, we've got a story."[14]

For example, in January 2007 Senator Barack Obama's announcement of his intention to run for president was received with the excitement generally accorded a rock star. Newton Minow, a Chicago lawyer who served in the Kennedy administration, declared, "This is the sort of thing you get once in a generation. This is a connection between what the voters need and what the voters want. This is the first time I've felt it since Jack Kennedy."[15] As columnist Jeff Zeleny reported, "The next phase of his political development will inevitably draw intense and less flattering scrutiny."[16] This phase began in March 2007, when 125 newspapers throughout the country ran the story that in January, Obama had accumulated $375 in fines for outstanding parking tickets seventeen years before as a student at Harvard Law School in the late 1980s. (He paid the fine in January 2007.) This media scrutiny magnifies the human flaws of Obama, while undermining public confidence in politicians in general.

In this climate of intense media scrutiny, it is increasingly difficult for human beings to maintain an exalted status. For instance, in 2007, Michael Richards's racial tirade at a nightclub was brought to public attention after being picked up by YouTube. While intriguing to audiences, this phenomenon contributes to a cynicism among the public, as people are stripped of their belief in mythic heroes.

To Provide Meaning

Myths also establish and reinforce beliefs. People choose to believe in myth, even though many of the stories involve extraordinary beings and events that challenge logical explanation. Could the infant Hercules strangle snakes placed in his crib? Did God create the world in six days? Belief in these myths involves an act of faith that transcends logic. Even if people are dubious about the literal truth of a myth, they often believe in its metaphorical aspects. For instance, the biblical time frame for creation can be interpreted as relative—God's conception of a day may translate into eons. And even if a myth is untrue, over time it may assume a *mythic reality;* that is, a myth is repeated with such frequency that people believe it to be true.

To Instruct

When myths are accepted as truth, they represent the accumulated knowledge and wisdom of a society and therefore serve as a primary source of information dealing with history, natural phenomena, and religious and ethical principles. In like fashion, individuals model their behaviors and define their expectations based on the behaviors of media figures. Some programs instruct through positive examples. However, other media presentations instruct by glorifying negative, self-destructive, self-indulgent, or violent actions.

To Provide Order

Myths furnish explanations in the face of what appears to be an overwhelming and chaotic world. In that sense, myths provide reassurance, as well as a sense of direction: where we have been, where we are, and where we are going. In the same way, a media presentation presents an ordered worldview that offers the comfort of structure to people's lives. This might explain why much media consumption is habit driven. For instance, people tend to read the newspaper in the same order and in the same location or routinely tune in to the news before retiring for the night.

As Ritual

A ritual is a ceremonial act that is an extension of the belief system of an organization, religion, or myth. Rollo May explains the relationship between ritual and myth: "[Rituals are] physical expressions of the myths. . . . The myth is the narration, and the ritual—such as giving presents or being baptized—expresses the myth in bodily action."[17] Thus, rituals reaffirm faith in the essential validity or authenticity of the myth. Henry A. Murray observes that the ritualistic retelling of myths, such as the story of the birth of Christ at Christmastime, serves "to propagate and periodically revive and reestablish veneration for the entities and processes it represents."[18]

Media presentations often function as rituals that act out and resolve myths. Looking at the media as ritual can help explain the popularity of some programs that we watch—either as reruns or simply as variations of the same formula—again and again. Consequently, watching a rerun or a formulaic program may have value as ritual, reaffirming mythic themes and values that are critical to our belief system. For example, Professor Joseph Schuster was astonished to discover how many times students in his script-analysis class at Webster University had seen

Star Wars: "I had eleven students in my class. Each student had seen *Star Wars* at least twice. One student reported that he had seen the film seventy-eight times. On average, the students in the class had seen the film approximately 18.3 times."[19] These students do not return to *Star Wars* to find out how the story *ends;* after seventy-eight viewings, this should be rather obvious. Rather, their gratification comes from watching the narrative *unfold,* to reencounter the elemental conflict between good and evil and to experience the satisfying resolution of the narrative.

To Promote Social Conformity

Myths often present a worldview that supports and validates the prevailing social order. In that sense, myths can be seen as *reactionary,* promoting conformity to the belief system of those in control of society. Murray explains, "The forces that are aligned with the group's welfare, with its hopes for the future, being beneficent in direction, are exalted as the good powers. The opposing and hence maleficent forces are portrayed as evil."[20]

In that regard, cultural myths play a fundamental role in an individual's socialization by telling stories that reinforce the prevailing societal standards of success and failure. In many cultural myths, the triumph of good over evil is dependent on the characters' adherence to the values and goals of dominant culture. (For further discussion, see Chapter 1, Ideological Analysis.)

Media and the Transmission of Myth

Many contemporary media programs can be regarded as modifications, variations, or extensions of traditional myths. For instance, in 2000, the Coen brothers produced *O Brother, Where Art Thou,* a film adaptation of the Homeric myth the *Odyssey.* In 2004, another film adaptation of a Homeric myth was released: *Troy,* starring Brad Pitt. Indeed, it can be argued that one of the reasons that we watch the same formulaic media programs over and over is because these stories are transmitting myths that tell us about ourselves.

Comparing and contrasting traditional myths as they have been adapted by various societies can be a useful avenue for discovering the differences between cultures. For instance, creation myths are common to nearly all cultures. However, in the Judeo-Christian version, God is preeminent and supreme, existing before the universe. The book of Genesis declares that he created the heaven and earth in six days, and then he rested. In contrast, Babylonian myth reflects a different conception of divinity, in that the universe preceded the existence of the gods. According to the Babylonian myth, the merging of sweet water (Apsu) with salt water (Tiamat) gave birth to the gods. Considering Babylon's arid climate, it is not surprising that everything originated with water.

Norse mythology takes yet another perspective on creation. The Norse creation myth establishes a human-driven world, very dark in orientation, in which the end of the world has already been foretold. According to Norse myth, the fusion of two contrasting elements, fire and ice, created Ymir, the Frost Giant, who had a human form. The giants then produced a new race of gods. The gods then conspired to murder their progenitor and used his body to make the earth and the seas. Significantly, this myth does not acknowledge an omnipotent power; instead, the gods are created by mortal beings (giants), rather than the other way around. And unlike in the two other versions of the creation myth, the Norse gods were not immortal; the prophesy declares that the gods would die when the giants and demons rose against them.

Indeed, the alterations in a classic myth can provide insight into a culture. For example, Foster R. McCurley observes that the myth of Adam has been reconfigured into an American cultural myth: "The Adamic myth portrays the American as the innocent primal human, possessing virtually unlimited potential and set at the beginning of history. This view of Adam, of course, is based on the Biblical story of Genesis 2, and does not include the story of rebellion and limitation which follows on its heels in Genesis."[21]

Myths are to be found in all media; for instance, the myth of Hercules appears in print, television, and film. However, the characteristics of interactive media provide a platform that is particularly conducive to mythic storytelling. Digital media represent the combination of all established media: print, photography, graphics, audio, and video. As a result, these media can present stories that are mythic in their ability to defy the laws of nature: Characters are capable of heroic feats, and events appear supernatural.

For instance, *The Darkness,* a game that premiered in 2007, tells an epic story of good versus evil, filled with magic and mythic heroes, villains, and minions. The premise of the story involves a young thug, Jackie Estacado, who is being pursued by gangsters who are trying to kill him at the behest of his old mobster boss, Paulie. However, as Charles Herold explains, the story soon moves into the mythic realm:

> Jackie's next surprise consists of two demonic heads that suddenly sprout from his shoulders. These are manifestations of the evil entity that has chosen Jackie to be its host. Jackie also acquires several powers that help him in his one-man war against the mob. He can open a small black hole that sucks in enemies, or send one of the heads through vents and along ceilings to take out unsuspecting victims. Jackie can also summon savage child-size creatures called Darklings to serve as his minions." [22] While the game itself is quite bleak, concerned with its unsubtle symbolism of as Charles Herold explains, "a criminal subsumed by his inner darkness."[23]

Within this context, a worthwhile question to consider is: Why does a traditional myth appear in this particular culture at this particular time? For example, in 2005, NBC presented a six-part miniseries about Satanists and the end of the world, based on the biblical book of Revelations. According to writer–executive producer David Seltzer, the current state of the world may be feeding interest in the show's subject matter. Seltzer cited thirty-five current wars worldwide, any one of which could be a flash point leading to an apocalypse: "People are very nervous about where they're heading for the sake of their children and their children's children, and I think it's time [for people] to explore their relationship to the hereafter and the now and determine whether or not there's a part mankind can play to forestall the nuclear bubble breaking and the world coming to an end. . . . With all the geological, social, political world events lining up with what the Book of Revelation says are the end of days, it is time to start taking it seriously."[24]

A related line of inquiry explores ways in which modern adaptations depart from the original. Bruce Weber notes that the popular 2004 Sunday evening programming schedule for HBO included shows that were derivative of traditional myths:

> What is "Six Feet Under" if not a contemporary study of funerary ritual—an exhumation of the issue that consumed the Greeks, Romans and Egyptians, the passage between life and afterlife. And "Sex and the City"? Surely, the decadence in dress and behavior recall Rome under Caligula. Granted, "Curb Your Enthusiasm" has no classical antecedent. But "The Sopranos" is rooted in "The Oresteia," the progenitor of all family tragedies. Uncle Junior is Nestor-like, the very embodiment of

wisdom, no? The two Tonys have that Agamemnon and Menelaus thing going, sibling loyalty and love tempered by rivalry and frustration. In Paulie Walnuts, the dumb brute warrior, we have a clear descendant of Ajax. And Carmela, betrayed to the breaking point, is Clytemnestra.[25]

In addition, media programming may feature traditional mythic characters who are reconfigured in the media. The warriors of professional wrestling capture the attention and adulation of the public because, in many respects, they represent a modern adaptation of mythic heroes like Hercules. For instance, although the Greek myth of Troy focused on the complex relationship between the gods and their mortal counterparts, the contemporary version focuses exclusively on the warriors—Achilles, Hector, and Agamemnon. In a film review of *Troy* (2004), Phillip Mc-Carthy notes, "Inevitably it all comes down to Brad Pitt's body. It's been seriously pumped, buffed and preened in his new movie, *Troy,* and those signature golden locks of his haven't looked quite as wild, untamed and, yes, shampoo-commercial gorgeous since *Legends of the Fall* 10 years ago."[26]

Mythic Elements in Media Presentations

Mythic elements such as mythic plots, themes, characters, motifs, and images frequently appear in media presentations. These mythic elements serve as a code for the reader, which furnishes a wealth of meaning to the text. Murray maintains that "[Mythic elements are] very commonly sufficient to bring the complete mythic event to the consciousness of those who are familiar with it."[27] Thus, recognizing these mythic elements in media presentations can be a useful way to uncover meaning in a media presentation.

Mythic Plots

A plot is a planned series of events in a narrative, progressing through a struggle of opposing forces to a climax and a conclusion. According to Ronald B. Tobias, there are a finite number of mythic plots, which have been retold countless times, from antiquity to contemporary films, comics, and video games: "We use the same plots today that were used in the world's oldest literature. . . . If you found a plot that had never been used before, you're into an area that is outside the realm of shared human behavior. Originality doesn't apply to the plots themselves but to how we present those plots."[28] Thus, one way to account for the appeal of many media programs—no matter how redundant they may seem—is that they are incarnations of mythic plots.

One common mythic plot is the *quest,* in which characters embark on a journey at the beginning of the narrative. Examples include Sir Galahad's quest for the Holy Grail and *Indiana Jones and the Temple of Doom* (1984). Joseph Campbell explains, "These deeply significant motifs of the perils, obstacles and good fortunes of the way, we shall find inflected through the following pages in a hundred forms. The crossing first of the open sewer, then of the perfectly clear river flowing over grass, the appearance of the willing helper at the critical moment, and the high, firm ground beyond the final stream (the Earthly Paradise, the Land over Jordan): these are the everlastingly recurrent themes of the wonderful song of the soul's high adventure."[29]

Throughout the ages, the quest has been a vehicle for mythic themes dealing with the search for identity and truth (see discussion, "Mythic Themes"). By the conclusion of the quest, the hero and heroine have changed in some manner. The questions are (1) What have these characters learned as a result of their quest? (2) How have these lessons enabled the hero and heroine to triumph over adversity at the end of the story? The audience also participates in this quest, making discoveries with the characters during the course of the journey. Linda Seger explains, "As we watch the story unfold, we may think of our own heroic journeys. . . . The journey of the story may also remind us of our own inner journeys, as we seek value and meaning in our lives."[30]

The quest frequently appears in stories focusing on the adolescent search for identity. (See discussion, "Mythic Themes.") Often what emerges as consequential is the quest itself; that is, the relationships, growth, and movement toward the goal ultimately are more meaningful than the actual attainment of the goal. An example from classic myth is Odysseus's quest to return home after the Trojan War. According to the myth, an impulsive lack of respect for the gods (surely an adolescent act) provoked the gods into orchestrating events so that it took nearly ten years before he saw his home. Thematically, Odysseus was not yet ready to assume the mantle of adulthood. In the course of his quest, Odysseus faced a series of trials that tested his resolve and fortitude. Odysseus was forced to contend with the issue of identity, assuming a series of disguises in order to make his way from place to place. Ten years later, he arrived home as an adult, ready to assume his role as king of Ithaca and husband to Penelope. He finally cast off his disguise and vanquished his enemy, who had usurped his throne and threatened his wife.

The quest motif has also become incorporated into American culture, as expressed in countless media presentations. Reporter Holland Cotter traces the appearance of the quest motif in media presentations:

> The books: Thoreau's "Walden," Dickinson's poems, Whitman's "Specimen Days" and Jack Kerouac's "On the Road." It was the Kerouac novel, first published 50 years ago, that inspired the trip. Americans have, or at least once had, a thing for quest-journeys. You find evidence in 19th-century paintings of wilderness to the horizon. In literature John Bunyan's "Pilgrim's Progress" was a national best seller before the Civil War, second only to the Bible. Its redemptivist impulse powers Thoreau's perambulations. [In the novel *On the Road*], Jack Kerouac, a confessed religionist, used Bunyan's dream trip from the City of Destruction to the Gates of Heaven as his literary model.
>
> In the 1950s a cult of the frontier enjoyed a popular revival. Davy Crockett and the space race provided safe, secular options to two kids, two cars and 9 to 5. The stage-savvy Beats, with their motorbike saints, were part of the getaway package. Then in the early '60s the poetics of travel turned political, with civil rights marches, Freedom Rides and songs about all the roads a man must walk down before you call him a man.[31]

The *death and resurrection* plot occurs when the hero suffers apparent death, only to return later in the story (e.g., the story of Christ). This storyline reflects the cycle of nature: life, death, and resurrection. In some media presentations, regeneration may take the form of a wedding, birth, or triumph over the villains. Many media presentations feature comebacks by a character who initially has been defeated, à la *Rocky* or *Cinderella Man*. These comebacks are the result of an internal, spiritual renewal, linked to the character's commitment to the values that ultimately make him or her triumph. A variation of this plot occurs when the hero's reputation is tarnished. He is branded as either a coward (e.g., *High Noon*) or a fraud (e.g., *The Natural*). In either case, the hero suffers a death-in-life, only to reemerge triumphant at the denouement of the film.

A related plot can be termed the *harrowing of hell,* in which the hero willingly confronts death for the public good. This motif illustrates the courage and strength of character of the hero as he or she voluntarily encounters death. At the same time, this motif puts the audience in touch with their own deepest sense of dread and terror as they watch the hero's descent into hell.

In an interview with Bill Moyers, Joseph Campbell discusses the harrowing of hell in *Star Wars* (1977),

> M: My favorite scene was when [the heroes] were in the garbage compactor, and the walls were closing in, and I thought, That's like the belly of the whale that swallowed Jonah. . . . Why must the hero do that?
>
> C: It's a descent into the dark. Psychologically, the whale represents the power of life locked in the unconscious. Metaphorically, water is the unconscious, and the creature in the water is the life or energy of the unconscious, which has overwhelmed the conscious personality and must be disempowered, overcome and controlled.
>
> In the first stage of this kind of adventure, the hero leaves the realm of the familiar, over which he has some measure of control, and comes to a threshold, let us say the edge of a lake or sea, where a monster of the abyss comes to meet him. . . . In a story of the Jonah type, the hero is swallowed and taken into the abyss to be later resurrected—a variant of the death-and resurrection theme. The conscious personality here has come in touch with a charge of unconscious energy which it is unable to handle and now must suffer all the trials and revelations of a terrifying night-sea journey, while learning how to come to terms with this power of the dark and emerge, at last, to a new way of life. . . .
>
> You see, consciousness thinks it's running the shop. But it's a secondary organ of a total human being, and it must not put itself in control. It must submit and serve the humanity of the body. When it does put itself in control, you get a man like Darth Vader in *Star Wars,* the man who goes over to the consciously intentional side.[32]

Circe plots focus on the implications of change. One version of this mythic plot involves a person's physical transformation, as in Odysseus, when the sorceress Circe turned Odysseus's crew into pigs. Another variation involves a person undergoing significant change in wealth or social status.

In the *imminent annihilation* plot, the characters (and audience) become aware of an impending catastrophe. For instance, in Homer's *Iliad* (the story of the fall of Troy), the emphasis immediately shifts to individuals' personal responses to the news of the approach of the Greek army. In *Independence Day* (1996), the beginning of the film establishes the impending invasion by the aliens. The remainder of the film examines the personal impact of this catastrophe on the individual characters, the United States, and world at large.

Adam and Eve plots feature stories of temptation and corruption. These stories examine how the average person can be tempted by sex, power, or money to commit immoral or antisocial acts. Tobias explains, "The story of temptation is the story of the frailty of human nature. If to sin is human, it is human to give in to temptation. But our codes of behavior have established a price for yielding to temptation. The penalties range from one's own personal guilt to a lifetime without parole in the state penitentiary. . . . The battle rages: yes and no, pro and con, why and why not. This is conflict, and the tension between opposites creates the tension. Knowing what to do and actually doing it are sometimes oceans apart."[33]

Paradise plots are an extension of the Adam and Eve plot. In the paradise plots, the characters have been in harmony with nature (as well as with their own natures). However, something has upset this harmonious condition, and the characters are cast out of paradise. The paradise plots focus on the characters' efforts to return to an earthly paradise. Paradise myths also symbolize the characters' efforts to regain the original states of innocence and harmony they have lost.

Other mythic plots that appear in media presentations include the following:

- *King Midas.* In myth, Midas was a king who worshiped wealth above all other things and got his wish that everything he touched would turn to gold. But the "golden touch" proved fatal when his food, his clothes, even his loved ones, became dead gold under his hand. King Midas, like many legends, points out the moral that spiritual, not materialistic goals are, in the end, the most satisfying.
- *Faust.* In the Faust story, a man makes a pact with the devil, exchanging his ultimate salvation for the earthly pleasures of youth, wealth, and love. There are at least two conventional endings to the Faust plot: one in which Satan cashes in on his contract with the damned, and the other in which the central character is saved by the love or self-sacrifice of a virtuous woman, whose purity defeats the powers of darkness.
- *Frankenstein.* The tale about the coming of the machine gave us this plot theme of "the creator destroyed by his creation." That man should not play God is a powerful dramatic premise.

- *The fatal flaw.* "In each man are the possible seeds of his own destruction," which is another way of saying that mankind, being human and mortal, is capable of evil as well as good. This plot was perhaps first told describing a physical flaw, such as the myth of Achilles' heel. The Greek hero's mother, attempting to make her son invulnerable, dips him as a child in a magic stream, holding him by his heel. But she neglects to bathe that part of his body and so provides his enemies with a way of destroying him. Told in a more sophisticated version, it can unfold as the story of how alcoholism, dope addiction, or any overpowering obsession can bring about a person's downfall.
- *The fatal choice.* This plot applies to almost any story in which a wrong or right turning or decision can affect a long chain of events and circumstances.
- *Rivalry.* The original murder plot was that of Cain and Abel in the Bible. Murder can be told as a suspense or detective story, or it can be the basis of absorbing human drama in which the question of an individual's responsibility for the welfare of other men and women is questioned: "Am I my brother's keeper?"
- *The pact with God.* This plot generally unfolds in one of two ways: A person faced with impending disaster or death vows that if he is saved he will "turn over a new leaf" and be a good man or woman for the rest of his life. The conflict arises when his prayer is answered but he is confronted with a number of temptations that try his character severely. The other usual variation is the dedicated man or woman of God confronted with a strong motivation or desire to get out of holy vows and return to the wider world.
- *Beauty and the beast.* Like his mother, Venus, Cupid represented physical love in folklore, and Psyche, a Greek girl, was the symbol of the soul or spiritual love. When they married, it was on condition that Psyche never look upon him, to prevent recognition of the fact that he was a god. Psyche's sisters spread the rumor that he must be a monster and so piqued her curiosity that she broke her promise and destroyed her marriage and her chance for happiness. In another beauty-and-the-beast story, by taking pity on a frightful beast, a beautiful girl is able to transform him into a handsome prince. The moral here is that the eyes of love can make all things beautiful. This plot is exemplified by *Knocked Up* (2007), a film by Judd Apatow, in which Alison Scott (Katherine Heigl), a beautiful

woman, spends one night with Ben Stone (Seth Rogen), a slacker, and becomes pregnant. In his efforts to do the right thing by Alison, Ben grows up, so that by the end of the movie he has emerged as a fit partner and father.

- *Damon and Pythiasny.* This is a classic friendship story, illustrated by Damon and Pythias, in which a friend may, or at least offers to, give up his life and fortune for his beloved companion; complications arising therefrom. It may be a war story of two servicemen, or it may be the story of another kind of severe testing of a close relationship between two men or even two women.
- *David and Goliath.* This is the story of the little guy, who, small in stature (or position) but great of heart, wit, and courage, defeats brute strength in a giant bully, and points out a heartening moral. The power of brains verses brawn, in the overcoming of brutality or unreasoning strength by ingenuity and valor, is part of humanity's history as well as its folk literature. The overthrow of a tyrant by a seemingly helpless people is another application of this tale.
- *The triangle.* This is perhaps the oldest and most reliable of all plots, dating back to the story of Adam and Eve and the serpent (who in some versions is a woman named Lilith).
- *The savior (or mysterious stranger).* The story of Jesus is unique, yet it has been retold in other terms and other circumstances. Mr. X in soap operas, or the mysterious stranger who comes out of nowhere, solves problems, and disappears into nowhere, embody an absorbing concept.[34]
- *Revenge.* Revenge plots focus on "retaliation by the protagonist against the antagonist, for real or imagined injury."[35] This plot deals with issues of civil verses "higher" justice, individual culpability, and the self-destructive aspects of revenge.

Mythic Themes

A theme is the central idea expressed in a narrative, either implied or explicitly stated. Mythic themes raise issues pertaining to the human condition, as well as human beings' unique relationship to the universe. There is a close relationship between plot and theme. A theme is an abstract idea that is given expression or representation through a character or plot. Thus, in the *Odyssey,* the structured sequence of action revolves around the hero's quest to return home. The theme of this myth involves the hero's search for identity; it is only when he fully discovers who he is that he is ready to return home.[36]

Mythic themes correspond to what Rollo May has identified as a series of *existential crises* that accompany the stages of human development. Media programs often contain mythic themes that articulate these existential crises.

Birth

Many mythic tales attempt to explain the miracle and mystery of creation: both how and why the world was created. These stories reflect human beings' efforts to assign meaning to this seemingly random act of nature. A cosmic variation of this existential stage consists of myths featuring a hero whose birth has extraordinary significance (e.g., Hercules, Moses). Birth myths also account for the origin and nature of gods.

For example, *Contact* (1997) is a film in which astronomer Eleanor Arroway (Jodie Foster) discovers the presence of life on another planet. Much of the narrative focuses on the young woman's efforts to convince her male supervisor to take her (and her work) seriously. Underlying the story is the reason that she is so passionate about her work. Through her discovery, she (and the audience) are taken back to essential questions about creation and the order of the universe.

Infancy

This stage originates in young children between the ages of five and six, when they first become aware that human beings are born of union between man and woman. One theme related to this stage of awakening is the *Oedipal longing,* named after the famous Greek myth. Sigmund Freud first interpreted this myth from a sexual perspective—the son's desire to eliminate his rival (father) and possess his mother. Later, however, Carl Jung applied a spiritual interpretation to the Oedipus myth, focusing on the symbolism of the mother as the source of life. Within this context, the Oedipus myth responds to humans' growing awareness about their inevitable separation from the protected womb of the mother. Although this separation is a part of life, this step is, at the same time, a form of death, as the individual can never again recapture the same sense of safety and connectedness to the source of life. This stage of separation is found in the Peter Pan myth, which has

E.T.

Mythic themes correspond to what Rollo May has identified as a series of *existential crises* that accompany the stages of human development. To illustrate, in the classic sci-fi film *E.T.* (1982), the emotional moment of the extraterrestrial's final separation from Elliott, his earth buddy, touches the audience because it corresponds with the stage of *infancy* when children first become aware of the inevitable separation from the protected womb of the mother. (*courtesy of Universal Studios Licensing LLP*)

been retold countless times in media presentations—most recently in *Finding Neverland* (2004).

This existential crisis is also reflected in stories in which characters must let go of loved ones as they pass away. For instance, in Disney's *Bambi* (1942), the young deer and his mother are trapped by hunters and are forced to flee. In her efforts to save her son, Bambi's mother is killed. Once he has reached safety, Bambi (and the audience) become aware of the tragedy and mourn their mutual loss.

A derivative story line involves characters who must bid farewell forever, which is a form of death-in-life. In *E.T.: The Extra-Terrestrial* (1982), the extraterrestrial's return home meant that he would be separated forever from Elliott, his new earth buddy. The emotional moment of E.T.'s departure signaled a form of death—as defined by a final separation. A third variation of this theme involves tales of abandonment, in which a character is deserted and must cope with feelings of rejection and isolation. A comedic example of this theme is the *Home Alone* films.

According to Murray, additional thematic concerns are associated with this stage of awakening:

- A statement of need and helplessness in a perilous, unnourishing, or hostile environment and the wish for an omnipotent, omniscient, and benevolent protector, provider, and director
- Narcissism and the wish to be omnipotent and superior to others (psychic source of countless self-glorification and heroical myths)
- Curiosity and the wish to obtain an appealing *graphic* explanation of how babies are created
- Dread of temptation and punishment (psychic source of numerous images of demonic [satanic] tempters, threatening indignant deities, and myths of crime and punishment [e.g., Sodom, Gomorrah, and the Deluge])
- Collective motivations, such as fear of starvation and a consequent decline of social and regal vigor in a barren, dry environment leading to ardent wishes for the revival of fertility and of vigor (psychic source of the important death-and-resurrection myth)[37]

Adolescence

This category of mythic themes originates in adolescents' need to assert their independence as part of the process of establishing their own identities. Fundamental to this stage is the drive to test taboos, or limits that have been imposed on individuals, by either nature or society. The desire to break away from one's earthly existence is expressed in the Icarus myth, in which young Icarus and his father Daedalus fly, having constructed wings made of feathers glued with wax. But despite his father's warning, Icarus becomes intoxicated with his new powers of flight and soars too close to the sun; in the process, the heat melts the wax, and Icarus plunges into the sea and drowns.

This existential crisis is expressed in stories of revolt or rebellion against the established order (parents, society, and the gods). For instance, in Herman Melville's classic American novel *Moby Dick,* Captain Ahab, the dark hero, is faced with his own mortality, as symbolized by the white whale. Ahab thunders, "I would strike the sun if it insulted me." Though egotistical, this assertion of independence is essential in the development of the self. Many popular films of the 1950s such as *Rebel Without a Cause,* starring James Dean, and *The Wild One,* starring Marlon Brando, focused on this adolescent existential crisis. By defying authority figures such as their parents and the police, these actors became cultural mythic icons, epitomizing teenage angst and rebellion. At one point in *The Wild One,* a girl asks Brando, "What are you rebelling against?" Brando coolly replies, "What have you got?"

A common adolescent thematic issue is the role of fate verses that of free will. Classic myths like the *Odyssey* raise questions about whether human beings are independent entities who control their own destinies, or merely players who act out a script that has been written for them. In many media programs, the protagonists carve out their own destinies in the face of a culture that has already prescribed their futures. This empowerment theme underlies many advertisements as well. These ads suggest that their products enable us to overcome our human limitations. Nike tells us to "Just do it" and declares, "Gravity, you are no friend of mine."

Another theme connected to the crisis of adolescence is *love and romance.* Many classic myths, including those of Aphrodite, Cupid, and Psyche, deal with the beauty and transcendent power of love, as well as its many complications—jealousy, loss of trust, and rejection. In like manner, film and popular music place a heavy emphasis on the travails of love and romance—responding to the strong adolescent market, as well as the adolescent sensibilities in adults.

A related theme connected to the crisis of adolescence involves people who are unwilling (or unable) to confront their "adult" responsibilities. For instance, the television series *I Hate My 30s* (2007), presented on VH1, a music video channel targeting young adults, deals with the travails of reaching this age and adolescence as a stage of preparation for adulthood.

In the film *The 40-Year-Old Virgin* (2005), Andy Stitzer (Steve Carell) is stuck in an adolescent purgatory. Despite being an adult, he remains a virgin, defined by the kinds of frustrations and repressed fantasies that are typical of kids in junior high school. In this world of diminished expectations, he cannot find work commensurate with his education—he is a stock "boy" in a technology discount store.

The world of this film is populated by males who find it difficult to make the transition to adulthood. Both Andy and his buddies are terrified

The Wild One

The Wild One, starring Marlon Brando, is a prime example of a popular 1950s film focused on the adolescent existential crisis. Brando became a cultural mythic icon, epitomizing teenage angst and rebellion. (*Getty Images; Columbia TriStar*)

about emotional commitment as well, so only Jay (Romany Malco) has anything remotely approaching a lasting relationship in the movie. The romantic subtheme of the film focuses on Andy's prepubescent, "secret" crush on Trish (Catherine Keener), which operates at an adolescent level of sophistication and maturity.

Steve's buddies provide advice and support throughout the film. However, the latent message is that the most this world can offer is the comfort and support of friends—not as resolution to one's problems, but as temporary solace and respite from one's condition. Ironically, this is precisely what the program is also offering its audience—a cheap laugh and commiseration with film friends who appear to understand their plight.

Adulthood

The crisis of adulthood focuses on the ultimate acceptance of human limitations (or taboos). The Greek myth of Prometheus offers a classic example of this theme. As the gods distributed the gifts of life to the creatures of earth, humans were left out. As a result, human beings lacked the strength, swiftness, and protection (fur or feathers) of other animals. Prometheus, a Titan, took pity on these creatures and stole fire from the gods to give to humans. In doing so, Prometheus brought civilization to humans; however, Zeus then punished Prometheus, chaining him to a rock:

> An eagle red with blood
> Shall come, a guest unbidden to your banquet.
> All day long he will tear to rags your body,
> Feasting in fury on the blackened liver.[38]

In this mythic tale, Prometheus was a tragic hero, doomed to suffer like the humans he befriended; for although he could see beyond his chains, he was confined forever. In like manner, human beings must come to terms with their own mortality.

In this stage, human beings are both terrified and fascinated by death. Freud explains, "Freud postulates that the organism has an innate tendency to revert to its initial state. This instinct, which would lead to self-destruction, has to be diverted outward by the developing organism. . . . The death instinct represents one of the two major classes or drives and motives, which—for psychoanalysts—comprise all motivational processes."[39]

Rollo May observes that accepting one's finitude is vital to love and compassion: "We are able to love passionately because we die." But significantly, media presentations rarely address this theme, for several reasons. First, the "target audience" for films and television programs are generally people between sixteen and twenty-four years of age—too young to seriously address this issue. Also, media presentations in which the characters experience a loss of control hardly fit into the feel-good mode of commercially successful media presentations. Thus, although films like *The Notebook* (2004) and *Away from Her* (2006) actually do resonate with a sizable audience, the scarcity of presentations with adult mythic themes reflects our general unwillingness to confront this stage or grieve—for loved ones and, ultimately, for ourselves.

Genre and Myth

One of the appeals of genres is they lend themselves to particular mythic themes. For example, the sports genre lends itself to the tales of heroes whose physical prowess becomes legendary. Further, these stories dramatize how these heroes overcome adversity, which enables them to beat the odds and win, thanks to heart and determination. For example, *Cinderella Man* is a dramatization of boxer James J. Braddock (Russell Crowe). Braddock, who earned the heavyweight championship of the world during the Great Depression, became a symbol of hope. Felled by injuries, Braddock had been forced to support his family by going on public assistance. Braddock's comeback in the ring touches on the theme of the underdog whose road to the heavyweight championship is fueled by determination and the support of his family.

Mythic Figures

Mythic figures appear throughout media presentations. The more we understand about the mythic antecedents and mythic aspect of these characters, the more we can appreciate the context and impact of their counterparts in media presentations.

Sometimes mythic figures are transplanted directly from classical myth. For example, a television ad for BMW depicts a winged figure racing an automobile. Although the ad makes no effort to identify

Cinderella Man

One way to account for the appeal of many media programs is that they are incarnations of mythic plots. To illustrate, the *death and resurrection* plot occurs when the hero suffers apparent death, only to return later in the story. This storyline reflects the cycle of nature: life, death, and resurrection. A variation of this plot is the comeback tale in films like *Cinderella Man* (2005), in which boxer James Braddock (Russell Crowe), who was initially defeated, comes back and wins the heavyweight championship. (*courtesy of Universal Studios Licensing LLP*)

the character, the wings on his hat are a clear reference to the Roman god Mercury, who, as Jupiter's messenger, is associated with swiftness. Added to the mythic context of the ad, the race takes place in an ancient, Roman-looking coliseum. This allusion reinforces the ad's message about the speed and agility of the BMW, which easily wins the race against Mercury. Beyond this obvious allusion to speed, the selection of Mercury in the commercial has other implications as well. Mercury also was the god of commerce and the market, protector of traders such as BMW.

For the uninitiated in the audience, the inclusion of these direct mythic referents in media programming introduces people to mythic figures. The audience learns to associate the winged figure with swiftness without formally knowing anything about Greek mythology.

Mythic Archetypes

Characters appearing in media presentations often reflect *mythic archetypes*. According to psychologist Carl Jung, an archetype is a projection of humans' collective or universal unconscious. In its simplest terms, an archetype corresponds to the various sides of Self in human beings, representing different aspects of the psyche. All archetypes, taken together, make up the Self. The balance, or relationship between the archetypes, determines the personality of an individual. The goal of Jungian psychology is to work toward the proper "constellation" of all of the archetypes to achieve a balanced personality.[40]

These archetypes recur throughout human history and exist as a projection of humans' universal experience. Over the ages, these archetypes, or aspects of Self, have been externalized in the form of mythic characters. In the same way, archetypes are found in media presentations as projections of Jung's universal Self. These archetypes may assume many forms, or *archetypal images,* which are determined by the culture and the individual storyteller. Thus, Odysseus and Rocky are both images of the hero archetype.

Mythic archetypes often appear in media presentations in the form of *stereotypes.* One reason that media stereotypes are so readily recognizable is because they resonate within us; that is, the stereotypes reflect basic sides of Self. This mechanism enables people to scapegoat others and, in the process, distance themselves from their own impulses.

The *Hero archetype* epitomizes the best in human character and achievement. The hero archetype offers an opportunity for the audience to get in touch with their own heroic attributes.

Joseph Campbell has identified several types of archetypal hero:

- *Hero as warrior.* Myths often extol the hero's strength, athleticism and power. However, in some myths (e.g., David and Goliath), the hero is overmatched physically but prevails due to heroic intangibles: courage, quick-wittedness, or faith. The adventures of the warrior symbolize the inner conflicts confronting all humans. For example, Campbell interprets myths in which medieval knights slay dragons as "[s]laying the dragon in me: slaying monsters is slaying the dark things."[41]
- *Hero as lover.* The hero and heroine also may distinguish themselves as paragons of love. Examples of young tragic love include the Greek myth of Pyramus and Thisbe and Shakespeare's Romeo and Juliet.

- *Hero as world redeemer.* This mythic hero is a crusader who resists injustice and oppression. These heroes inspire others through their idealism and selfless commitment to a cause—even at the cost of their own lives. An example of world redeemer found in media programming includes the character of William Wallace (Mel Gibson) in the film *Braveheart* (1995).
- *Reluctant hero.* At times, the hero is a reluctant agent who requires the assistance of a mentor to act. For example, in *The Matrix* trilogy of films (1999–2003), Morpheus acts as a mentor for Neo. He chooses and guides the young man, who at first doubts that he is "the one," as Morpheus insists. (See discussion of the mentor later in this discussion of Mythic Characters.)

The *villain* is the embodiment of the corruption and sterility of society, and of life itself. As such, villains are associated with winter, darkness, confusion, sterility, moribund life, and old age.[42] In both mythic tales and media presentations, evil is generally externalized, appearing in the form of objects, animals, people, and metaphysical beings, such as devils and witches. In this sense, the villain is a projection of the audience member's own evil, impure, or weak impulses. For instance, some myths vilify the snake as the embodiment of evil, an example being the Adam and Eve story. This externalization of evil enables people to distance themselves from these very complex and disturbing impulses within themselves. Villains fall into the following general categories:

- *Usurpers* seize the power, position, or rights of another, by force and without legal right or authority.
- *Criminals* intentionally break the law or regulations for personal gain.
- *Violators* disregard the wishes or preferences of an individual to violate another individual. This can involve either physical violence (e.g., assault or rape) or emotional violence.
- *Betrayers* breach a confidence, are disloyal, or deceive another.
- *Corrupters* are guilty of spiritual villainy. They are immoral, dishonest, and depraved and can contaminate others by seducing them to betray their own principles.

The mentor archetype represents those aspects of Self that are in supreme authority. This superior master and teacher is an ideal figure, the embodiment of order and rationality. Christopher Vogler points out that in the course of the hero's journey, the mentor provides support, motivation, inspiration, and guidance: "The relationship between hero and Mentor is one of the most common themes in mythology, and one of the richest in its symbolic value. It stands for the bond between parent and child, teacher and student, doctor and patient, god and man. The Mentor may appear as a wise old wizard (*Star Wars*), a tough drill sergeant (*Officer and a Gentleman*), or a grizzled old boxing coach (*Rocky*)."[43]

Archetypes often fulfill specific functions within a narrative. For instance, the Mentor is often the voice that expresses the central theme or insight of the narrative. At a pivotal moment in the narrative, the mentor expresses a revelation, prophesy, or counsel that the hero (and audience) should heed. The hero's success is determined by his or her ability to absorb and apply the counsel of the mentor during the course of the narrative.

Threshold guardians are characters who attempt to block the path of the heroes and test their powers. Threshold guardians often assume the form of henchmen, bodyguards, gunslingers, mercenaries, guards, doormen, or lieutenants of the chief antagonist. Threshold guardians also may be well-intentioned supporters who are opposed to the hero making changes. In this case, the threshold guardian represents our own uncertainties as we contend with change. Christopher Vogler explains, "These Guardians may represent the ordinary obstacles we all face in the world around us: bad weather, bad luck, prejudice, oppression, or hostile people. But on a deeper psychological level they stand for our internal demons: the neuroses, emotional scars, vices, dependencies, and self-limitations that hold back our growth and progress."[44]

Threshold guardians appear at crucial points of a story, when the main characters are faced with critical choices. For example, in *Robin Hood,* the hero faces a series of threshold guardians (Will Scarlett, Friar Tuck, and Little John) before he is prepared to lead a revolt against Prince John, who has assumed the English throne in the absence of his brother, King Richard. In the 1939 film version, Robin (Errol Flynn) is literally blocked from crossing a stream by Little John (Alan Hale). Robin decides to test Little John's mettle by fighting him with cross staffs. Robin is actually beaten by Little John but learns the lesson that it is not his physical prowess that is most important in his effort but, rather, his leadership and sense of purpose.

The *herald* brings a challenge to the hero and announces the coming of significant changes. In Greek mythology, Hermes was the messenger god, who was charged with dispatching messages from Zeus. Vogler explains, "Typically, in the opening phase of a story, heroes have 'gotten by' somehow. They have handled an imbalanced life through a series of defenses or coping mechanisms. Then all at once some new energy enters the story that makes it impossible for the hero to simply get by any longer. A new person, condition, or information shifts the hero's balance, and nothing will ever be the same. A decision must be made, action taken, the conflict faced."[45] Heralds may be manifested as dreams, visions, oracles, or foreshadowing devices. The herald also may signal the *need* for change. Vogler notes, "Something deep inside us knows when we are ready to change and sends us a messenger."[46]

The victim is a weak or vulnerable character who succumbs to the forces of the world, the will of others, or his or her own self-destructive tendencies. This figure is a projection of the weaknesses of human beings. The victim is deficient, morally, physically, or emotionally, and frequently is in need of protection by an outside agent—either a hero or divine intervention. A variation of this archetype is the character who has been victimized by forces outside of his or her control, such as fate or injustice. Female characters frequently are cast in the role of victim in media programs, reflecting cultural attitudes with respect to the female gender.

The divine child (puer aeternus) corresponds to the infantile side of Self. Numerous myths feature a child as hero, including Hercules, Moses, and Chandragupta (from the fourth-century B.C.E.), the founder of the Hindu Maurya dynasty. This archetype is marked as special at birth, epitomizing the nobility and divinity within all human beings. Stephen Walker observes that the divine child reflects both immaturity and spiritual purity: "For Jung, what is 'infantile, childish, too youthful in ourselves' is also what carries the promise of future development: 'the Puer Aeternus means really your most devoted attempt to get at your own truth, your most devoted enterprise in the creation of your future; your greatest moral effort.'"[47]

The divine child appears prominently in contemporary media presentations, reinforcing the American cultural myth of youth culture (see discussion, American cultural myth). Contemporary media programming suggests that the American culture prizes this side of Self. In the horror and science fiction genres, it is the children who are able to see the supernatural forces that are beyond the comprehension of adults.

Occasionally the function of a character changes during the course of a narrative. Vogler refers to these characters as *shape-shifters:* "Shape-shifters change appearance or mood, and are difficult for the hero and audience to pin down. They may mislead the hero or keep him/her guessing, and their loyalty or sincerity is often in question."[48] In myths, wizards, witches, and ogres are often shape-shifters; they have the ability to alter their appearance through disguises or physical transformation. For instance, Margaret Finan points out that in the Harry Potter books and films, Lupin's friends, Sirius, Peter, and James, learn how to become a particular kind of shape-shifter called Animagi, in order to provide companionship to Lupin while he is transformed into a werewolf. The following passage from *Harry Potter and the Prisoner of Azkaban* explains this transformation:

> "Yes, indeed," said Lupin, "it took them the best part of three years to work out how to do it. Your father and Sirius here were the cleverest students in the school, and lucky they were, because the Animagus transformation can go horribly wrong—one reason the Ministry keeps a close watch on those attempting to do it. Peter needed all the help he could get from James and Sirius. Finally, in our fifth year, they managed it. They could each turn into a different animal at will."
>
> "But how did that help you?" said Hermione, sounding puzzled.
>
> "They couldn't keep me company as humans, so they kept me company as animals," said Lupin. "A werewolf is only a danger to people. They sneaked out of the castle every month under James's Invisibility Cloak. They transformed. . . . Peter, the smallest, could slip beneath the Willow's attacking branches and touch the knot that freezes it. They would then slip down the tunnel and join me. Under their influence, I became less dangerous. My body was still wolfish, but my mind seemed to become less so while I was with them." . . .
>
> "Well, highly exciting possibilities were open to us now we could all transform. Soon we were leaving the Shrieking Shack and roaming the school grounds and the village by night. Sirius and James transformed into such large animals, they were able to keep a werewolf in check. I doubt whether any Hogwarts students ever found out more about the Hogwarts grounds and Hogsmeade than we did. . . . And that's how we came to write the Marauder's Map, and sign it with our nicknames. Sirius is Padfoot. Peter is Wormtail. James was Prongs."[49]

Characters may also assume *emotional masks* by hiding their true natures or motives. For example, *A History of Violence* (2005) is a film that begins with a slow four-minute single take (camera shot) that eases the audience into the tranquil midwestern town of Millbrook, Indiana, inhabited by normal families and model citizens, where nothing out of the ordinary seems to happen. The story centers on Tom Stall (Viggo Mortensen), a devoted, caring father, and loving, attentive husband. The audience is lulled into this idyllic existence until Carl Fogarty (Ed Harris) a Philadelphia gangster, shows up at Tom's diner and announces that Tom is really a different person, "Joey, you're trying so hard to be this other guy, It's really painful to watch." The town and audience are temporarily fooled into thinking that Fogarty has mistaken Tom for someone else. But as the story unfolds, the audience detects slight shifts in Tom's facial expression that discloses Joey's real identity. Tom's startled wife, Edie (Maria Bello), observes one of these transformations after Tom and Fogarty have a deadly confrontation in front of the Stall home. "It's not what I heard. It's what I saw. I saw Joey. I saw you turn to into Joey right before my eyes. I saw a killer, the one Fogarty warned me about."

As Tom drives to Philadelphia for a contentious encounter with his brother Ritchie (William Hurt), Tom's body language begins to take on a more rigid, tough stance. When Ritchie's driver, Rubin (Ian Mathews), meets him in a bar and asks him, "Are you Joey?" Tom/Joey replies in an Italian American dialect, "Yeah, I'm Joey," making the transition back to Joey complete. The previously mild-tempered Tom reverts back and remains murderous Joey until business with his brother, a symbolic Cain and Able confrontation, is completed. Afterward, Joey performs a symbolic cleansing ritual in the lake in front of his brother's house to wash away all traces of homicidal Joey before he shifts back to gentle Tom and returns to Millbrook with the hope that he will be welcomed back into the family fold as Tom.

Villains may also serve as heralds, who either issue a direct challenge to the hero or dupe the hero into becoming involved. This ambiguity has a dramatic function, introducing doubt and suspense into the story. Vogler declares, "In some stories, it's the task of the hero to figure out which side, positive or negative, he is dealing with."[50]

Shape-Shifting in Virtual Worlds

Second Life is a virtual reality system that provides an opportunity for individuals to dissociate from their culturally authored identity and shape-shift to a virtual self (i.e., an avatar character that represents him or her). Without the constraints of social sanctions, users can shape a self much different from their "real selves." For example, if a male user switches gender, his female avatar may experience sexual harassment, or a shy in-hibited person may wish to create an avatar that is outgoing and assertive in order to present a self he or she would like to be in real life. Many alter their physical appearance to an idealized self or reverse the aging process by shaping a younger more animated version of their real-life self.

With a few clicks of the mouse, "residents" can change appearances and alter personalities as they teleport across the cyberterrain to develop relationships in any of the numerous virtual environments, from coffee shops, bike trails, and nightclubs to housing communities. Some long-term "residents" even reshape their persona by engaging in virtual careers totally different from their real jobs such as architects, interior designer, mayors, and cruise directors. In virtual worlds such as Second Life, you are who you shape-shift to be.

Mythic Motifs

A motif is a recurrent thematic element, such as an idea, symbol, or incident, employed in mythic narratives. Understanding the significance and context of these mythic motifs can enrich one's understanding and appreciation of media presentations.

In the *personification* motif, objects, plants, animals, and gods are endowed with human features, emotions, personalities, and speech. For instance, cartoon figures such as Mickey Mouse or Barney assume human characteristics. Even in cases in which they cannot speak, animals such as Flipper and Lassie seemingly possess human intelligence and emotions.

For example, *Arctic Tale* (2007) is a coming-of-age tale, in which Adam Ravetch and Sarah Robertson, a husband and wife who have spent the better part of two decades filming in the Arctic for television nature shows, sifted through more than 800 hours of their footage of wildlife to assemble a narrative in which the animals adopt human characteristics. Andrew C. Revkin explains the project:

> The film tells the story of Nanu, a young bear, and Seela, a walrus. Their stories are related, fable style, by Queen Latifah, and include scenes ranging from the wrenching, when a bear cub falters and fades in a relentless blizzard, to the comic, when a heap of basking walruses erupt into a flatulent chorus after bingeing on clams. (An adult can eat 4,000 a day.)
>
> [The story is] complete with humanlike villains and heroes, including a walrus "Auntie" who gives her life in defense of Seela.[51]

By making nonhumans act in human ways, the filmmakers allow audiences to better understand the motives and sensibilities of the world at large. In addition, this motif creates an environment that enables myths to comment on human issues and concerns. For instance, in *Arctic Tale,* the animals are forced to contend with the effects of global warming—an ecological danger that affects humans as well.

Science fiction films have extended the personification motif to aliens; for instance, despite their cosmetic differences, creatures in *Star Trek* operate on a human level. In some science fiction programs, technology has been personified as well. In the *Star Wars* films, the druids R2-D2 and C-3PO maintain an all-too-human relationship, bickering and worrying about each other.

The mythic motif of *magic* admits the audience into an extraordinary world of possibilities that transcend natural laws, logic, and human limitation. As Sir James George Frazer notes, magic is a form of wish fulfillment: "A dramatic representation of the natural processes which [human beings] wish to facilitate; for it is a familiar tenet of magic that you can produce any desired effect by merely imitating it."[52]

Magicians such as Merlin are *shaman*—mystics who use their magical powers to see into the future and influence events to promote the welfare of the human community. However, magic also has a darker, more dangerous side. Villains may employ magic to achieve their own self-serving ends or to wreak havoc on the heroes. For instance, Odysseus's adventures led him to the Island of Dawn, which was inhabited by the sorceress Circe. She turned his crew into swine, and it required all of Odysseus's cunning to convince her to restore his crew to human form.

Occasionally, humans attempt to use magic and, in the process, threaten the natural order; being human, they are ill equipped to control this power. Examples include Pandora and young Harry Potter from the books and films.

Magic is a common motif in media programming as well. One reason that magic is prevalent in media presentations is simply because film and television *can* produce the illusion of magic. Indeed, futuristic technology often assumes the visage of magic wands. For example, in *Star Trek* people "magically" disappear as they are beamed from one locale to another.

The entertainment sensibility of media admits to the possibility of magic through the willing suspension of disbelief. In the world of media, horses talk, dandruff shampoos make you popular, and the cavalry always arrives on time. Even the technology of the media is "magical"; at the end of a scene, the people and surroundings disappear, replaced by new images.

Significantly, in numerous films such as the Harry Potter series, it is the young people who are able to recognize the use of magic, since they have yet to become so cynical that they would close their minds to the paranormal possibilities of life (for further discussion, see "Cultural Myths" in this chapter).

Prophesy is a mythic motif in which predictions foreshadow the events of the story. In many classic myths, prophesies take place through an oracle—a shrine at which prophecies are made known. These oracles are divine in origin and therefore are regarded as reliable sources of information. However, these prophecies are often enigmatic statements or allegories; the exact meaning behind the prophecy becomes clear only as the story unfolds. In media presentations, an oracle may assume more pedestrian forms, such as a letter or mysterious stranger who provides a clue about upcoming events in the story.

In the introduction of entertainment media programs such as print or broadcast news, a "foreshadowing" of what will be covered is provided, as is the order in which the news is presented. In newspapers, the lead paragraph provides a summary of what the article will substantiate, in more detail. The introduction often also serves as a microcosm of the story, establishing the premise, as well as specifying the setting, characters, and situation. The body of the narrative, then, is the fulfillment of the "prophecy" presented at the beginning.

Production elements may also provide clues about future events. For instance, in *Jaws* (1975), the distinctive theme music recurs throughout the film, signifying that danger is lurking under the surface.

Mythic Symbols

Mythic symbols operate as a language that provides clues and cues for the audience. According to psychoanalytic theory, mythic symbols originate within the human imagination, as a manifestation of collective unconscious, and thus have a shared meaning for the audience.

In myth (and media), the *primal elements of nature*—fire, water, and air—have a fundamental connection and significance. The exact connotation of these elements may be determined by context. For instance, fire may represent evil, as illustrated in the fires of hell. However, fire also can symbolize knowledge, power, and enlightenment. In the Greek myth of Prometheus, fire was the element that distinguished humans from other animals. Fire also can be used as a defense against forces of evil (witches) or predators (animals).

As a primal element, water is associated with birth (the water in the womb), and the origin of species (the primordial swamp). In addition, water is a sacred element representing purification. Examples from myth include Catholic holy water and the biblical story of Noah and the flood. Water also symbolizes death and rebirth. Baptism is a ritual in which a person undergoes spiritual regeneration by being immersed in water.

Ancient myths divide the universe into three *cosmic spheres:* hell, earth, and heaven. Similarly, in media presentations, locations on earth often possess a symbolic significance derived from their proximity to these cosmic zones. Places located at great heights situate human beings close to heaven. Consequently, scenes in which the characters experience a revelation or epiphany often occur on rooftops, balconies, ladders, staircases, towers, or mountaintops. These elevated areas often provide the setting in which the climax and denouement of the plot take place.

Conversely, the lower recesses of the earth are closest to hell; as a result, it is often in these settings that the most sordid aspects of the human mind and spirit manifest. For example, in Quentin Tarantino's film *Pulp Fiction* (1994), Butch (Bruce Willis) is a professional boxer who has been ordered to throw a boxing match; instead, he double-crosses his boss, Marsellus, pockets the money he has bet on himself, and prepares to skip town. But as luck would have it, Butch literally runs into Marsellus as the underworld leader is crossing the street.

Marsellus chases Butch into a pawnshop, where the clerk stops the altercation. Then, in a shocking turn of events, the clerk takes them prisoner, forcing them downstairs to the recesses of the cellar. There they are bound and gagged, and Marsellus is sodomized. This scene is disturbing to the characters (and to the audience as well); just as we think that Tarantino's characters couldn't be more evil, we are introduced to new depths of depravity.

The *circle* has a mystical quality, representing the endless, cyclical conception of time (e.g., the zodiac and clock faces). This shape has direction and is complete; as a result, it is associated with endlessness and wholeness. In many cultures, the circle is a symbol of the sun and, as a result, signifies warmth and life.

However, while the circle joins people and things together, it also *separates,* setting objects apart (e.g., a social circle). In some ancient civilizations, the circle was a symbol of protection. Stonehenge and Avebury are examples of ancient use of the circle to mark the boundary of a sacred area. Similarly, a Babylonian rite involved laying a circle of flour around a person's sickbed to keep demons away.

The circle was also used by magicians in medieval Europe as a way to delineate sacred space: "[T]he circle is not only intended to keep something out but also to keep something in—the magical energy which the magicians will summon up from within themselves in the course of the ceremony. . . . If it were not for the circle the energy would flow off in all directions and be dissipated. The circle keeps it inside a small area and so concentrates it. The same motive lies behind the circle of people who link their hands at a seance."[53]

According to Eva C. Hangen, the universal significance of the circle is embodied in the following cultural artifacts:

- Circle of fire: monastic chastity, magic, inviolability
- Wedding ring: continuing devotion and love
- Four circles linked to a fifth, larger one: the words of wisdom
- In Mexico, two serpents entwined into a ring: time without end
- In China, a circle separating two serpents: the two Principles claiming the universe[54]

(For more discussion, see Chapter 5, "Analysis of Production Elements.")

A *reflected surface* such as a mirror often reveals an individual's unexplored self or inner secrets, furnishing knowledge not yet known or revealed. An example of this symbol is the evil queen's looking glass in *Sleeping Beauty,* which discloses the truth about the queen's ugly nature—a truth that the queen cannot admit to herself. In other myths, people look in the mirror and see a reflection of their deepest dreams and desires. For example, *Harry Potter and the Sorcerer's Stone,* written by J.K. Rowling, includes a chapter titled "The Mirror of Erised." Harry gets up in the middle of the night and looks in the mirror: "It was a magnificent mirror, as high as the ceiling, with an ornate gold frame, standing on two clawed feet. There was an inscription carved around the top: 'Erised stra ehru oyt ube cafru oyt on wohsi.'"[55]

Webster University student Lee Ann Tapscott reversed this inscription and found the following message: "I show not your face but your heart's desire." She explains, "A mirror reflects what we want it to reflect. . . . Not only do we do that with our own personal selves (our personal mirrors) but we do that with other people, with our personal lenses. Other people can be a source of reflection for us like the mirror . . . we get lost in our perceptions of ourselves through others, and of other sources."[56]

Mirrors frequently appear in the Film Noir genre, suggesting deception. In many films, a character's reflection serves as a symbol of degeneration. Foster Hirsch explains, "Reflections in mirrors . . . suggest doubleness, self-division, and thereby underline recurrent themes of loss or confusion of identity; multiple images of a character within the same shot give visual emphasis to the dual and unstable personalities that are rampant in the genre."[57]

Cultural Myths

A country's media presentations often reflect its own set of *cultural myths*. Cultural myths are a series of beliefs that are tied to self-concept—how a people or group sees itself. Consequently, examining cultural myths can provide insight into the attitudes and preoccupations that define a society.

In addition to the universal myths discussed above, each culture develops its own set of myths that express its predominant concerns and preoccupations. Today, the media has assumed a vital role in the transmission of cultural myths. For instance, through countless hours of watching westerns on film and television, American audiences have become acquainted with the California gold rush, the stand at the Alamo, the Battle of the Little Big Horn, and the gunfight at the OK Corral. Even if these stories are not factually accurate, they contribute to the myth about the settling of the American West.

A 2007 Subaru ad used Japanese cultural mythology to sell its product to an American audience. Stuart Elliott explains,

> Subaru will promote the 2008 Impreza WRX by invoking the history, heritage and popular culture of its home country, Japan. . . . [The ad] tells a tale of a man from a futuristic city "in a land of forbidden secrets" . . . who is fated to become the master of a powerful jungle creature, i.e., the WRX. "Somewhere in the jungle, the legend is reborn," asserts the headline of a print advertisement that depicts a dragon perched atop a mountain. The text begins, "From the East it comes, conceived in thunder, born in lightning." . . . "Prepare to meet your destiny," the ads proclaim.[58]

Cultural myths also can reveal *shifts* in societal attitudes, behaviors, values, and preoccupations. For example, the 1950s were characterized by a longing for stability—a return to normalcy following the disruption of World War II. The 1950s culture valued convention and conformity. Consequently, situation comedies of the 1950s such as *Leave it to Beaver* and *Ozzie and Harriet* presented an ideal worldview, in which the nuclear family was the center—both in terms of activity and as the locus of identity. By the 1970s, however, programs such as *Married with Children, The Simpsons,* and *The Family Guy* featured dysfunctional families, in which the parents' shortcomings impede the children's efforts to grow into well-adjusted human beings. It should be noted that the humor of these programs is based on the audience's familiarity with the cultural myth of the ideal family, acknowledging that the world has changed since the 1950s.

American Cultural Myths

American culture has a rich tradition of cultural myths, reinforced and perpetuated through the media.

The *New World myth* stems from the "discovery" of America by Europeans in the fifteenth century. The New World became a symbol of innocence and hope, in contrast to the tired civilization of Western Europe. The downside of this cultural myth is that for many Americans, the world began with the discovery of the New World. Consequently, Americans display a shocking ignorance and contempt for history.

Manifest Destiny is an extension of the cultural myth of the New World. As the new "chosen people," Americans regard themselves as the standard-bearers of a new civilization. The cultural myth of manifest destiny was the philosophical foundation of the Monroe Doctrine, a political policy originating in the nineteenth century, which held that the United States was the guardian of the Western hemisphere and had both the right and the duty to expand throughout the North American continent. Today, the American news media reinforces this myth of manifest destiny. The amount of international coverage in newspapers and television is minuscule, and the majority of international coverage focuses on allies of the United States or international news items that directly affect America.

The mythic frontier is also an extension of the New World myth. As settlers spread west in the nineteenth century, America offered the prospect of a fresh beginning. According to Frederick Jackson Turner, the mythic frontier is characterized by "restless energy, individualism, self-reliance, the bounteousness and exuberance which comes with freedom."[59] Having shed the vestiges of civilization, man was free of corruption. This populist myth is rooted in the democratic ideal; instead of status being determined by social class, success was based on an individual's innate qualities—courage, imagination, determination, honesty, and integrity. The myth of the frontier also was associated with abundance and opportunity. America was blessed with seemingly boundless resources. Farmers would use up a patch of land, burn it, and then move on.

Over time, the mythic frontier evolved into the *myth of the Old West*. As depicted in countless novels, films, and radio and television programs, the mythic Old West generally was set between 1865 (the end of the American Civil War) and 1890. In the face of the significant changes in American culture, the myth of the frontier has remained constant. The western myth has been incorporated into other genres, such as science fiction (the *Starship Enterprise* exploring "the last frontier"), and police programs. However, heroes now drive trucks or ride motorcycles rather than horses.

The *myth of progress* is predicated on the belief that life will get better. In the New World, change (as opposed to tradition) was accepted as a way of life. Immigrants worked diligently so that their children could go to college and succeed. According to David Nye, technologies such as the axe, water-powered mills and factories, canals and railroads, and irrigation acquired social meaning as symbols of progress in the construction of the New World. By employing these implements of technology Americans felt that they had the power to transform nature and produce a "new creation, a new civilization."[60]

Representations of dominance over nature propagated throughout the culture and, subsequently, changed social practices that continue to fuel America's mythic enterprise of transformation in both private and public ventures. For years, technological innovations continued to improve Americans' comfort level. Scientific discoveries extended the life span of the average citizen. Advertisers have responded by linking their products to this cultural myth. These ads promote the products as "new and improved" and send the message that we should purchase a new product because it will be better than the old one. However, Rollo May sees some dangers in what he refers to as "the seduction of the new": "But this addiction to change can lead to superficiality and psychological emptiness. . . . This compulsion toward change can be an effort to escape responsibility, Self, the anxiety of the human paradox and the anxiety of death. . . . The price for this evasion is a deep loneliness and a sense of isolation."[61]

Significantly, for the first time, Americans have begun to express doubts about this myth of progress. According to *New York Times* reporter David Leonhardt, "In one typical poll from 2007, only 34 percent of people said they expected today's children to be better off than people are now, down from 55 percent when a similar question was asked in 1999."[62] Statistics would appear to back this loss of faith in the myth of progress. Americans have every reason to be concerned. A 2007 study reveals that men who are now in their thirties earn less than their fathers' generation did at the same age. In 1974, the median income for men in their thirties, in today's inflation-adjusted dollars, was $40,210. In 2004, the annual earnings for this group had dropped to $35,010.[63]

Idiocracy (2006), a futuristic film by Mike Judge, reflects this loss of faith in societal progress, depicting a world in which civilization has taken a giant leap backward. Private Joe Bauers (Luke Wilson), the definition of an "average American," is selected by the Pentagon to be the guinea pig for a top secret hibernation program and awakens 500 years in the future. He discovers a society that has so regressed that he is now the "smartest guy in the world." Reading has become an activity strictly for "fags," and the public responds only to messages dealing with sex and violence. Further, the "tools" of society are mostly broken, with no one capable of fixing them.

The *Horatio Alger myth* has become emblematic of the American Dream. Horatio Alger was an author of juvenile fiction about young boys who achieved success through hard work and perseverance. Greeley explains, "[The Horatio Alger myth] is essentially a breaking with the finite conditions of earthly [really working-class] life so that one can transcend oneself and scale the heights. . . . [It] symbolizes the desire of all men to be able to rise out of their finite existence. Is the 'rags to riches' myth so very different from the magic flight of the god king or the seven steps of Buddha?"[64]

The Horatio Alger myth contains a very optimistic message about achieving success by following the American Dream. The Horatio Alger myth celebrates the fundamental democratic principle of America—not that everyone will be successful, but that everyone has a *chance* to make it in America (no matter how great the odds). However, the Horatio Alger myth can have negative ramifications as well.

A related myth, adjusted for gender, is the *Cinderella myth,* which has also been retold countless times in the media. Recent films such as *Maid in Manhattan* (2002) tell the tale of Marisa Ventura (Jennifer Lopez), a member of the lower class whose charms enable her to find her Prince Charming. In this Cinderella tale, which is directed at an adolescent audience, this backward notion of easy upward mobility—which defies recent socioeconomic studies—is so tenacious that it exists even in films directed at an adult audience, such as *Pretty Woman* (1990).

These myths minimize the amount of effort required for minorities to overcome various cultural hurdles and are presented as a rationale to preserve the status quo. Individual members of subcultures who manage to succeed are offered as proof that the system works for all. Caryn James explains,

> What these movies reveal is not just film's addiction to fantasy, which audiences expect and embrace, but also to the Big Lie that class is meaningless in American life. [They all have] a similar message: not that America is a classless society, but that class is as fluid as water and upward mobility a cinch.
>
> The idea, of course, goes back to the Founding Fathers' egalitarian goals, and quickly became so ingrained in the national mythos that what Tocqueville wrote in 1840 could stand as the motto for the J. Lo movie as well as its ancestors like *Sabrina* and *Working Girl*: "At any moment a servant may become a master." The amalgam of American idealism and rags-to-riches dreams is irresistible.[65]

In reality, according to Kevin Phillips, the increasing gap between the median American family income and the richest 1 percent has been "a point of national discussion for over a decade." By the turn of the twenty-first century, "Aristocracy was a cultural and economic fact" in the United States.[66] (For further discussion, see Chapter 1, "Ideological Analysis.")

The cultural myth of the *all-sufficiency of love* holds that romantic love is a mystical force that is essential to a person's survival. Love is vital to a person's self-esteem, identity, and existence. Conversely, loss of love is equated with loss of self, so that maintaining a relationship—any relationship—is critical to a person's well-being. Popular song titles provide insight into the American myth of the all-sufficiency of love, including the following:

- "There's No Living Without Your Loving"
- "You Are My Everything"
- "You Are My Sunshine"
- "All You Need Is Love"
- "One Hand, One Heart"
- "Can't Help Falling in Love"
- "(Everything I Do) I Do It for You"
- "The Only One"
- "You Got It All"
- "I Was Born to Love You?"

The Creation of New Cultural Myths

As societies evolve, new cultural myths emerge, which then are reinforced and disseminated through the media. For instance, a number of contemporary songs point to a shift in the cultural myth of romantic love discussed above. Columnist David Brooks cites the following examples of songs that are a far cry from earlier hits like "Can't Smile Without You" and "Ain't No Sunshine When She's Gone":

- "Before He Cheats," by Carrie Underwood. This is a song about a woman who catches her boyfriend in a bar fooling around with someone else—but she's not wounded or insecure. She's got nothing but contempt for the slobbering, cologne-wearing jerk. She's disgusted by the bleached blond girly-girl who's leading him on and who doesn't even know how to drink whiskey. As she rages, she's out there in the parking lot rendering a little frontier justice—slashing his tires, taking a baseball bat to his headlights, carving her name into his leather seats.
- "U + Ur Hand," by Pink. This second song is about a woman out for a night on the town, very decidedly without men. She's at the bar doing shots with her girlfriends and she's not in a Cole Porter frame of mind. She snarls at the pathetic guys who come up offering to buy her a drink, telling them, "Keep your drink, just give me the money. It's just you and your hand tonight."
- "Girlfriend" by Avril Lavigne. The third song is performed in the manner of an angry cheerleader chant, a sort of drill-sergeant version of the eighties Toni Basil hit, "Mickey." It's about a woman who tells a guy to make his loser girlfriend disappear so she can show

him what good sex is really like. Or as she sneers, "In a second, you'll be wrapped around my finger, cause I can . . . do it better! She so stupid! What the hell were you thinking?"[67]

Brooks continues,

> If you put the songs together, you see they're about the same sort of character: . . . hard-boiled, foul-mouthed, fed up, emotionally self-sufficient, and unforgiving. She's like one of those battle-hardened combat vets, who's had the sentimentality beaten out of her and who no longer has time for romance or etiquette. She's disgusted by male idiots and contemptuous of the feminine flirts who cater to them. . . . These iPhone Lone Rangers are completely inner- directed; they don't care what you think. They know exactly what they want; they don't need anybody else. She's also, at least in some of the songs, about 16.
>
> This character is obviously a product of the cold-eyed age of divorce and hookups. It's also a product of the free-floating anger that's part of the climate this decade. But as a fantasy ideal, it's also descended from the hard-boiled Clint Eastwood characters who tamed the Wild West and the hard-boiled Humphrey Bogart and Charles Bronson characters who tamed the naked city.
>
> When Americans face something that's psychologically traumatic, they invent an autonomous Lone Ranger fantasy hero who can deal with it. The closing of the frontier brought us the hard-drinking cowboy loner. Urbanization brought us the hard-drinking detective loner.
>
> Now young people face a social frontier of their own. They hit puberty around 13 and many don't get married until they're past 30. That's two decades of coupling, uncoupling, hooking up, relationships, and shopping around. This period isn't a transition anymore. It's a sprawling life stage, and nobody knows the rules.[68]

Brooks points out that the shift in the social landscape has caused young females to "romanticize independence," much as they had previously idealized the notion of equating love with identity and self-actualization:

> The heroines of these songs handle this wide-open social frontier just as confidently and cynically as Bogart handled the urban frontier. Of course it's all a fantasy, as much as "The Big Sleep" or "High Plains Drifter." Young people still need intimacy and belonging more than anything else. But the pose is the product of something real—a response to this new stage of formless premarital life, and the anxieties it produces.
>
> In America we have a little problem with self and society. We imag-

ine we can overcome the anxieties of society by posing romantic lone wolves. The angry young women on the radio these days are not the first pop stars to romanticize independence for audiences desperate for companionship.[69]

Vladimir Propp's morphology can be a useful methodology for identifying a unifying structure in cultural myths. Propp dissected the fairy tale, divesting it of its individual embellishments in order to identify its skeletal formula. He then traced the sequence of elements in a story to discover the basic structure common to this genre of tales. Propp found that the number of structural elements, or *functions*, known to the fairy tale is limited and complete. Each function may contain a number of alternatives, which provides variety within the stories. For example, Function IV is entitled, "The Villain Attempts to Deceive His Victim in Order to Take Possession of Him or of His Belongings." However, three general plot alternatives are available under this general function: (1) "The Villain Proceeds to Act by the Direct Application of Magical Means"; (2) "The Villain Uses Persuasion"; and (3) "The Villain Employs Other Means of Deception or Coercion."

In addition, the basic structure of the narrative is subject to some degree of variation:

- Some functions may be omitted from a tale, while the order of the other functions remains the same.
- At times, the sequence of a tale is rearranged.
- Interpolated episodes occasionally are inserted in the middle of a tale, complicating the plot.[70]

For example, over the last fifty years, the UFO tale has emerged as a cultural myth. Numerous stories have circulated about the existence of unidentified flying objects, most notably the alleged crash of an alien spacecraft in Roswell, New Mexico, in 1947. This preoccupation continues today, with the popularity of UFO tales on television and film.

Vladimir Propp's morphology can be used to identify the unifying structure in the UFO myth. Despite the distinctive embellishments of individual UFO stories, the essential structure of the UFO myth is uniform, reflecting a constant set of questions, issues, and concerns. The essential structure of the UFO myth is as follows:

    I. Introduction
        A. Background
        B. Establishing the truthfulness or veracity of the account
   II. Circumstances leading to the sighting
        A. Temporal-spatial determination (time, day, location)
        B. Weather conditions
        C. Status of protagonist
            1. Personal background
            2. Accompaniment (alone or in a group)
            3. Activity preceding sighting
  III. Initial sighting
        A. Reaction(s) of protagonist
            1. Astonishment
            2. Disbelief
            3. Disregard
            4. Puzzlement
            5. Fear
            6. Curiosity
            7. Helplessness
        B. Rational or physical explanation immediately offered
        C. Affirmation of sighting
        D. Alerts members of "immediate circle"
        E. Hero in physical contact with UFO
        F. General impression of phenomenon
  IV. Description
        A. UFO
        B. Aliens
    V. Protagonist seeks personal verification
        A. Explanation
        B. Exploration
  VI. Confrontation with UFO
        A. More detailed, closer description of UFO
        B. More detailed, closer description of aliens
        C. Indirect contact with UFO—aliens alter environment
 VII. Protagonist seeks outside verification
        A. Family, friends, lovers, or other objective witnesses
            1. Response(s)
               a. Disbelief
               b. Belief

        c. Investigation
   B. Authorities (police, military, and government)
      1. Response(s)
        a. Disbelief
        b. Belief
        c. Investigation
        d. Cover-up
   C. Decides not to seek verification
VIII. Direct contact with UFO
   A. Communication with UFO
   B. Physical contact with UFO
      1. Aliens are friendly
      2. Aliens are hostile
        a. Protagonist taken prisoner
        b. Aliens hostile to people or the environment
      3. Protagonist interaction with aliens
  IX. Departure of UFO
   A. Leaves alone
   B. Takes someone or something from earth
   C. Alien(s) are vanquished
   D. Leaves undiscovered by authorities
   E. Leaves discovered by authorities

    This morphology furnishes a complete framework for the UFO tale, while at the same time providing for considerable variation within each story. Each general function contains a number of alternatives; for instance, the wide possibility of responses to the initial sighting ranges from a denial of the phenomenon to coming into physical contact with extraterrestrials. This basic structure also provides opportunities for individual embellishments, so that in different tales, aliens may assume a variety of shapes and dispositions.

    Beyond the differences in specific detail (appearance of the aliens, location, etc.), a slight manipulation of the formula drastically alters the narrative. As in Propp's morphology of fairy tales, reversing the order in which functions appear creates wide plot variations. For instance, if the protagonist confronts the UFO (Function VIII) *before* he or she seeks personal verification (Function V), the emphasis of the story shifts from the hero as an active participant in the adventure to the hero as a victim of the phenomenon.

When seen as a whole, the UFO myth provides insight into concerns, preoccupations, and circumstances that are characteristic of this culture. First, UFO tales are distinctly local in setting, as the stories focus on the intrusion of the foreign into very familiar territory. This cultural myth is also linked to cultural and historical events. According to Amy Harmon, the origin of the UFO myth is rooted in the political and technological climate of post–World War II society: "The nation's interest in UFO's began at the dawn of the atomic age, when fears over the Cold War and anxieties about new doomsday technologies coincided with thousands of reported sightings in the years that followed the Roswell incident."[71]

At the same time, this new cultural myth operates on many of the levels of the traditional myths discussed earlier. The UFO myths provide insight into phenomena of the past, ranging from unusual formations in the terrain to unexplainable influences on ancient civilizations that would enable people to interpret, for instance, the Sphinx, or Stonehenge. The UFO myth also answers other phenomenal questions concerning the universe, including the form and substance of other planets.

The UFO myth also addresses metaphysical questions concerning the distant stars and planets that people long have observed with wonder. Chris Carter, creator of the popular TV series *The X-Files,* observes that the emergence of this myth is a response to the narrow and literal confines of our materialistic culture: "We need mysteries, we need stories, we need something beyond the temporal."[72] Human beings no longer are the center of the universe but are part of a larger community. The revelation of a populated universe also raises questions about creation—how, when, and why earthlings were created as part of this larger universe.

In addition, the UFO myth furnishes a new type of mythic character—the extraterrestrial. If not superhuman like mythic gods and heroes, these extraterrestrials are technologically superior to humans. The aliens serve as a foil for their human counterparts, furnishing perspective into human foibles, aspirations, and concerns. According to Benson Saler and Charles Ziegler, "The UFO myth serves as an expression of anti-Government sentiment and the age-old yearning to believe we are not alone in the universe . . . the popular belief in superior technological beings . . . For some, aliens replace or augment conventional religious beliefs."[73]

American cultural myths may be exploited for political purposes. According to author Susan Faludi, in 2002, the Bush administration used the cultural myth of *women captives* to make the case for the war in Afghanistan. The woman captive myth refers to stories in which a female is abducted and held captive. Ultimately, she is rescued from captivity by male protectors. In this cultural myth, the captors are members of a racial or ethnic subgroup that has been demonized. Faludi traces captivity narratives to Puritan times, when Mary Rowlandson described how she was taken captive by Native Americans during a raid on her village of Lancaster, Massachusetts. Faludi says, "One of its hallmarks was the idea that . . . women's weakness was required to shore up male strength, and the most sort of dramatic form of female vulnerability is sexual defilement, so these images of rape were all over popular culture in the second half of the nineteenth century." During the Civil War era, captivity narratives focused on women who were abducted by "savage freed black men who were alleged, completely wrongly, to have perpetrated an epidemic of rape."[74]

According to Faludi, the Bush administration concocted a story surrounding the capture of Private Jessica Lynch to marshal support for the war in Afghanistan in 2003. Lynch was a member of an army maintenance company that was ambushed during the initial march to Baghdad in March of 2003. She was injured when the Humvee she was in crashed into a Mack truck, and it jackknifed. Lynch was taken to an Iraqi hospital. Faludi maintains that the official account of her rescue was revised to fit the parameters of the captive myth:

> The story we heard originally was that these, you know, Special Ops teams of brave men, armed with a night vision video camera so they could film themselves, came battling into this Iraqi hospital, which was supposedly overrun with Fedayeen death squads, and they rescued Lynch. The military hustled out a video of this drama only three hours later and woke up all the reporters in the middle of the night so they could see it.
>
> Well, as it turns out, there was no battle. I mean, it took them six minutes, and there wasn't one casualty. And there were no Fedayeen death squads, as the military actually knew, because they had been alerted by an Iraqi translator. It was just, you know, a bunch of doctors and nurses trying to take care of Lynch and actually trying to return her to the US military.[75]

In her testimony before Congress on April 24, 2007, Jessica Lynch elaborated: "At my parents' home in Wirt County, West Virginia, it was under siege by media, all repeating the story of the little girl Rambo from the hills of West Virginia who went down fighting. It was not true. I have repeatedly said, when asked, that if the stories about me helped inspire our troops and rally a nation, then perhaps there was some good. However, I am still confused as to why they chose to lie and tried to make me a legend, when the real heroics of my fellow soldiers that day were legendary."[76]

Thus, this account of Lynch's rescue was used as a rationale of what's going on in Afghanistan with regard to the protection of Afghani women. Faludi explains, "Two weeks after the invasion in Afghanistan, the White House officials were saying . . . we're going to show ourselves to be dominant and invincible by taking care of these helpless women."[77]

In some cases, American cultural myths are invented for commercial purposes. For example, one of the most innovative attractions at Disney's MGM Theme Park in Orlando, Florida, is the Tower of Terror. (Another Tower of Terror opened at Disney-France in late December, 2007.) As passengers ride up an elevator in an old "haunted" hotel, they are told a tale about a group of passengers who never made it to the top floor, but as the elevator plunged to the basement, these people disappeared, never to be found. At this moment, the elevator drops, leaving the passengers breathless and exhilarated. One way to enhance the impact of the ride is for the audience to became fully acquainted with the legend before entering the attraction. Consequently, in October 1997, Disney produced a television program, *Tower of Terror,* in which the protagonists investigate the legend and "meet" the ghosts. The program appeared on *The Wonderful World of Disney,* on ABC, which is also owned by Disney. Consequently, the myth, which has a distinct corporate ring to it, has become part of the public consciousness.

Heroes of Cultural Myths

Cultural heroes are often physical embodiments of cultural myths. The heroes of cultural myths embody the highest aims and ideals of a society. In that regard, these figures can be seen as cultural archetypes. Taken collectively, these heroes make up the cultural ideal. For example, the male Hollywood movie stars of the 1930s and 1940s embodied aspects of this ideal self. Examples include:

- Rugged individualism: John Wayne
- Sophistication, charm: Cary Grant
- Boyish innocence, purity: Jimmy Stewart
- Urban toughness: Humphrey Bogart
- Dangerous insolence: Robert Mitchum

These Hollywood stars were not *actors,* per say, but *personas;* that is, while actors strive to become subordinate to the roles they play, the popularity of these stars was based on a constant mythic identity that they brought to each role. Thus, John Wayne remained the same essential figure in each film, whether he was appearing in a western or a military drama. Collectively, these film stars form a composite of the ideal male in American culture during this period.

When a culture is constant, so are its cultural heroes. Consequently, while the individual performers change, the essential *types* remain the same. For example, John Wayne, Arnold Schwarzenegger, and The Rock are generational representatives of the rugged individualist archetype. The rugged individualist epitomizes the virility, self-sufficiency, and independence of the American male, demonstrating that people can determine their own fate through the exercise of individual choice.

The rugged individualist is affiliated with the American cultural myth of the frontier discussed above. As Rollo May notes, this cultural hero is distinctly American and would not have appeared in the myths of other cultures: "[Individualism] was unknown in the Middle Ages . . . and would have been considered psychotic in classical Greece."[78] (See earlier discussion on American cultural myth.) According to Gary Wills, John Wayne's popularity stems from his association with this cultural myth—an association that grew only more fervent as the cultural myth of the frontier became more fragile in the face of cultural change: "Wayne's innate qualities are not enough to explain so large a social impact. He had to fill some need in his audience. . . . When he was called the American, it was a statement of what his fans wanted America to be. . . . [H]e stood for an America people felt was disappearing or had disappeared, for a time 'when men were men.'"[79]

At the same time, cultural mythic heroes may also embody some of the shortcomings within a culture. For instance, the rugged individualist is a narcissistic figure whose self-absorption undermines the spirit of community within a society.

Heroes such as Clint Eastwood's *Dirty Harry* character are mavericks who regard the system as an obstacle to their heroic quest. According to Rollo May, the rugged individualist is a lonely individual who "has few if any deep relationships and lacks the capacity for satisfaction or pleasure in the contacts he does have."[80] The rugged individualist accepts his isolation, giving him a melancholy, if not tragic air. May maintains that this alienation is a manifestation of America's "cultural rootlessness."[81] America is a country without any common, indigenous myths; immigrants came to America bringing a variety of mythic traditions from their own countries, and mainstream America has not accepted Native American myths as part of its cultural tradition. May concludes that this state of isolation produces an anxiety that is expressed in our being a violent people.[82]

As the culture changes, different mythic figures assume positions of prominence within the society. Andrew Greeley contends that cultural heroes emerge to fit the times, citing the elections of Dwight Eisenhower in 1952 and 1956, and John Kennedy in 1960. "In the early 1950s the American people needed a father god to reassure them. They were provided with one. In the early 1960s . . . the people needed a young warrior god who would lead them to victories in the face of new challenges."[83]

However, when one archetype dominates the cultural myths of a society, it can signal imbalances within the society. As discussed earlier, contemporary American media programs and advertisements promote youth culture, featuring versions of the divine child (*puer aeternus*). Adult actors now are taking second billing to child stars. In many popular films it is the children who demonstrate the ability to adapt to the complexities of modern society. In contrast, the inept, inflexible adult characters are seemingly incapable of exercising the authority that is typically found in traditional cultures. Indeed, adults often are absent altogether, as in the *Home Alone* films. Another category of popular films features adults who act like children (e.g., *Knocked Up* and *Step Brothers*).

However, psychologist Carl Jung warns that in order for an individual (or a culture) to achieve psychic balance, the divine child archetype needs the salutary wisdom of the mentor. An improper constellation can result in "dangerous flights from fancy."[84] Further, people with this psychic imbalance may disintegrate when confronted with reality.

Advertisers have long exploited the deep-rooted appeal of mythic heroes. Marlboro, which was originally marketed as a women's cigarette in 1929 (and used the slogan "Mild as May), dwindled to one-quarter of 1 percent of the U.S. market by 1950. In 1954, the Burnett advertising agency changed the target market to men and introduced the cowboy— the archetypal image of the rugged individualist—as the face of the product; sales jumped 107 percent by 1956. By 1997, Marlboro generated sales of $10 billion. David Dangoor of Philip Morris said the campaign worked because the cowboy "lived by his own principles. It's believable that a man would only smoke a cigarette he likes."[85]

Michael Gill of the J. Walter Thompson Advertising Agency observes, "In advertising, as in most fiction, you need to tap into the subconscious of your audience. The Marlboro Man seemed to have done that. . . . With the Marlboro Man, of course, this man is the symbol of the West—the cowboy. There's a feeling of confidence—that he's in charge. He's always either alone or, sometimes, with other men. But he's never with women— that's not part of the myth. . . . When people smoke or drink they're not doing it casually, they're doing it to be associated with something that improves their feeling about themselves."[86]

Moreover, some politicians assume the personas of cultural heroes in an effort to exploit public attitudes. For instance, the Bush administration cultivated the image of President George W. Bush as a cowboy on the eve of the war in Iraq. Reporter Susan Faludi notes,

> On the eve of the Iraqi invasion, the president's advisers were working hard to embed George W. Bush inside the script of the American Western. Rejecting the widespread European frustration with Mr. Bush's Lone Ranger act, Vice President Dick Cheney used his "Meet the Press" appearance to make clear that the president is "a cowboy" who "cuts to the chase." Mr. Bush's blunt talk, the vice president told Tim Russert, is "exactly what the circumstances require."
>
> The president has done his part. For some time now, Mr. Bush has been obliging, dutifully working his way through the Western cliche checklist: "smoke 'em out of their holes"; "hunt 'em down"; "go it alone"; "wanted: dead or alive."[87]

Cultural Symbols

Cultural symbols are representations of otherwise intangible aspects of the cultural life of a society. These symbols are subtly incorporated into media presentations, without particular fanfare. Recognizing these symbols can enrich the audience's understanding of media messages embedded in the text.

- One cultural symbol is *small town America,* a place that is characterized by "family values" such as honesty, loyalty, and volunteerism. A classic example of this cultural symbol is Bedford Falls, the small town in Frank Capra's *It's a Wonderful Life* (1946). This mythical town is equated with the simple life, defined by order and permanence in contrast with the complexity and chaos characteristic of urban life. In small-town America, the nuclear family is the source of the strength and identity of its citizens.

In some respects, the *suburb* is an extension of the cultural symbol of small-town America discussed above. According to Hal Himmelstein, suburbia embodies the harmony between humans and nature: "[The suburb is] a place where sanity prevails, a place of full employment; conventional white, white-collar corporate families; clean streets, well-kept weedless lawns, neatly trimmed hedges, and, in the older suburbs, an occasional freshly painted white picket fence."[88] Even the names of many of the suburban developments have a mythic flavor. Examples found in the suburbs of St. Louis, Missouri, include Olympia Gardens, Arcadia Estates, Clarendon Hills and Plantation Estates, a name that recalls the American cultural myth of the antebellum South.

The suburb emerged as a cultural symbol in post–World War II America. People retreated to the suburbs as a refuge from the effects of urbanization. Suburbia also was a psychic retreat, reflecting individuals' unwillingness to confront social problems.

As presented in the media, suburbia epitomizes success and control. For example, in the 1950s sitcom *Leave It to Beaver,* the ultimate enemy is *change.* Indeed, the brick homes that make up the set are seemingly impervious to the forces of nature. Within the worldview of the series, problems are reduced to funny, trivial irritants, which are easily resolved within a thirty-minute time frame: Wally discovers girls, Beaver loses his library book.

- *Guns* symbolize power, masculinity, and control. Consequently, the person who wields this weapon is dangerous, violent, and attractive. On the surface, the National Rifle Association's campaign over gun rights is founded on constitutional issues. However, at heart, the primal concern of the NRA is over the gun as cultural mythic symbol of the American character.
- In twentieth-century America, the *automobile* has emerged as a mythic symbol of mobility, control, prestige, and sexual prowess. Greeley observes, "It is clear that modern America's devotion to the automobile is not just ironically similar of primitive man to sacred objects. It is a manifestation of the same human tendency at work— the inclination man has to worship an object that is particularly dear

to him or in which he is especially dependent, and to elevate it from the order of the profane to the order of the sacred."[89]

Mythic Analysis: Into the Wild

Into the Wild (2007) is a mythic tale of a boy's coming of age in the Alaskan wilderness. Many mythic elements frame Christopher Mc-Candless's (Emile Hirsch) story as an epic tale. *Into the Wild* is an initiation story, in which McCandless embarks on a quest that leads him to the Alaskan wilderness. The film is divided into "chapters" that mirror Rollo May's existential crises: infancy, adolescence, adulthood, and the final stage.

The mythic hero's journey is initially a flight from his parents, whose dysfunctional relationship shook Chris's faith in people. Maintaining that people put too much stock in human contacts, Chris rejects his connections to human beings, instead preferring the solace and beauty of the wild, traveling to Alaska.

During his journey, the mythic hero meets a series of threshold guardians: Wayne Westerberg (Vince Vaughn); a hippie couple, Rainey (Brian Dierker) and Jan Burres (Catherine Keener); Tracy, a young girl (Kristin Stewart); and finally Ron Franz (Hal Holbrook), an old man. All of these characters offer similar advice to the young man. The old man imparts wisdom, telling Chris that "Forgiving his parents will unlock the love in his heart.

At the conclusion, Chris is trapped by the surging river, a metaphor for how he is trapped by his unwillingness to forgive his parents. As Chris lies starving, he reflects on the lessons of these threshold guardians and finally admits that "happiness is only real when shared." His death is, then, a release: he is no longer trapped; his spirit moves into nature.

We (Don't) Need Another Hero
Myth and Our "Heroes"
Ouida Gordon Jones

In mythology and legend, a hero is regarded as a person noted for feats of courage or nobility of purpose. Although Western societies believe that there is no longer a need for stories of myth, today the exploits of mythic heroes are passed from generation to generation through media presentations.

According to Art Silverblatt, myth is "any real or fictitious story, recurring theme, or character type that gives expression to deep, commonly felt emotion."[90] According to Silverblatt, "the audience tends to accept these mythic programs as natural, without question."[91]

Silverblatt maintains that one of the *functions* of myth is "To Inspire Awe . . . myth has the ability to move people out of everyday experience, into the realm of extraordinary. Because preternatural events and heroic exploits are not part of everyday existence, we seek myth to affirm that the extraordinary is possible."[92] Through the mythic process the characters become fantastic. Within this context, the NBC television show *Heroes* tells stories of ordinary people who are able to affect change in our impersonal, mass culture.

As the viewer is introduced to each of the characters in *Heroes,* the excitement builds because the characters are ordinary people from all walks of life.

In *The Power of Myth,* Campbell observes that in mythic tales, the hero is initially a flawed character: "The only way you can describe a human being truly is by describing his imperfections. The perfect human being is uninteresting. . . . It is the imperfections of life that are lovable . . . the humanity, the thing that makes you human and not supernatural and immortal—-that what's lovable."[93]

Thus, various episodes of *Heroes* feature an Internet stripper with multiple personalities, a man with a criminal past who uses his power to get out of jail, a man who will struggle with his choice of evil over good, and a cheerleader with the power to regenerate who somehow will tie all the characters together. In the course of the narrative, each character discovers the goodness (and/or evil) within them, enabling them to achieve feats of heroism.

According to Campbell's *Hero with a Thousand Faces,* the hero's adventure always consists of three stages:

- *Departure* deals with the hero's call to adventure or hailed to go on a quest
- *Initiation* refers to the trials the hero will face or "road of trials"
- *Return* refers to the hero's decision to return home (or not) with the skills and/or knowledge the hero acquires on the journey[94]

Heroes shows the characters in various stages of their journey. Some characters accept their call to adventure more readily than others. For example, Hiro Nakamura (from Tokyo, Japan) has developed the ability to teleport and bends the space-time continuum.

In Chapter 1, "Genesis," Hiro's character is naive and unsure of himself. He can be described as an idealistic, inept, high-pitched-voiced nerd who wears glasses. However, in Chapter 4, "Collision," and Chapter

5, "Hiros," he comes back from the future to warn Peter Petrelli of the importance of saving the cheerleader, Claire Bennet. It is at once clear to the viewer that the Hiro who has come to warn Peter Petrelli is not the same person the audience has grown affection toward. This Hiro is confident in his mannerisms, posture, and vocal tone. His trademark glasses are also noticeably absent, and he carries a sword. Based on these factors, the viewer is aware that (future) Hiro has shown a level of achievement in his journey. In other words, the viewer gets a glimpse of how the *initiation* segment of the journey has matured Hiro, even though the viewer is not yet aware of his specific trials. At the same time, by warning Peter, Hiro initiates his *return* even though it is in the context of his future self. It is also apparent that for Hiro his journey is not complete. It must be noted that the show *Heroes* is told in a nonlinear fashion. As a result, because of his ability to time travel, Hiro has gone through all three stages but vacillates between them as well.

The mythic elements found in *Heroes* are actually centuries old. Mythologist Joseph Campbell theorized that there is a fundamental pattern found in myths around the world. He referred to this as the *monomyth*. In his book *The Hero with a Thousand Faces,* Campbell explains, "Throughout the inhabited world, in all times and under every circumstance, the myths of man have flourished; and they have been the living inspiration of whatever else may have appeared out of the activities of the human body and mind. It would not be too much to say that myth is the secret opening. . . . [T]he symbols of mythology are not manufactured; they cannot be ordered, invented, or permanently suppressed."[95]

Within the first minute and thirty seconds, it is evident that *Heroes:* "Chapter 1—Genesis" uses mythic elements to tell the story of these mythic heroes. The first scenes are filled with mythic symbolism. In the opening of the show, viewers are presented with a black screen with white letters that read:

> In recent days, a seemingly random group of individuals has emerged with what can only be described as "special" abilities.
> Although unaware of it now, these individuals will not only save the world, but change it forever. This transformation from ordinary to extraordinary will not occur overnight. Every story has a beginning. Volume one of their epic tales begins here.[96]

The camera cuts away, revealing a picture of a slowly turning earth; the sun is shining behind it, and then it becomes an eclipse (a symbol that is also used within the series title). The voice of the narrator is then heard: "Where does it come from? This quest, this need to solve life's mysteries, when the simplest of questions can never be answered? Why are we here? What is the soul? Why do we dream? Perhaps we'd be better off not looking at all. Not delving, not yearning. That's not human nature. Not the human heart. That is not why we are here."[97]

Eclipses "appear often in the mythology and literature of different cultures and different ages, most often as symbols of obliteration, fear, and the overthrow of the natural order of things. The word *eclipse* comes from a Greek word meaning 'abandonment.' Quite literally, an eclipse was seen as the sun abandoning the earth." The underlying message to the viewers is that there are going to be problems on a global scale that threaten all of humanity. Will the heroes abandon the earth?

The eclipse has its place in mythology and has produced stories around the world. Indian mythology tells the story of Rahu deceiving the gods, and as a result Rahu is beheaded for his treacherous ways. As a result, it is believed that Rahu "eats" the sun every few years. The ancient Chinese believed that dragons swallowing the sun caused eclipses. The Chinese word for solar eclipse is *resh* or *Sun-eat.* African mythology tells of a snake emerging from the ocean that grew so large that it moved upward into the sky and swallowed the sun.[98]

Looking at the variety of mythic stories about the eclipse strengthens Campbell's monomyth theory. The stories clearly show a common theme despite coming from diverse parts of the world.

Keeping in mind that *Heroes* is told in a nonlinear fashion, the characters from *Heroes* are from different parts of the world, that is, Japan, India, and the United States. With each episode the viewer and the characters become aware that humanity is at risk. The achievement of the characters will be for them to come together as a cohesive unit to save the world.

Further, throughout the show, many of the characters experience altered states through dreams. The opening sequence takes the viewer through Peter Petrelli's "dream" flight. Simultaneously through the narration the viewer sees that Chapter 1 is titled "Genesis" and Peter is on the roof of a building. Peter steps off the roof as if he is going to fly. Although viewers never actually see Peter fly, the camera simulates the motion of flight. For a moment the viewer goes along for the ride. The flight ends in the shining sun. The viewer is then brought back to reality and is made aware that Peter has awakened from a dream.

The use of dreams in *Heroes* is prevalent and is significant in myth. In his book *Jung on Mythology* Robert Segal maintained that Jung believed there are differences between dreams and myths, but they are also parallel. In essence dreams are an important part of the telling of myth: "In many dreams and in certain psychoses we frequently come across archetypal material, i.e., ideas and associations whose exact equivalents can be found in mythology. From these parallels I have drawn the conclusion that there is a layer of the unconscious which functions in exactly the same way as the archaic psyche that produced the myths.

... Myths carry fantasy thinking beyond dreams to the external world. Mythic thinking is thinking about the world, which is transformed into a dream-like fantasy."[99]

Thus, the popularity of *Heroes* can, in part, be attributed to its mythic elements. Indeed, *Heroes* has become so popular that it has inspired the CNN show *Anderson Cooper 360* to include a nightly segment called *Heroes*. The segment became so popular that an award show was created to honor these people. The description for the award show read: "CNN Heroes: An All Star Tribute. Ordinary people receive honors for extraordinary acts."[100] H*eroes* has managed to bring people together despite race, socioeconomic background, age, and gender. The popularity of the show can be linked to the need to know why we as human beings are here and our purpose. It is clear that this need transcends all races and cultures. We must realize that the need for myth and its heroes does not exist independently of each other but rather interdependently. We need myth and its heroes to tell the tales of our struggles and triumphs. In many ways the existence of myth rejuvenates our spirit, validates our existence, and gives us purpose as humans in this world. In centuries past and in centuries to come, one thing remains the same. Myth and its heroes will always give us hope to find our own hero . . . the hero within ourselves.

Summary

I. A mythic approach can help make media content accessible in the following ways:
   A. To identify the *mythic functions* of media programming
   B To provide perspective on media content as a *retelling* of traditional myths
   C. To discover *mythic elements* in media programs (and the universal meanings behind these elements), which provide insight into the narrative
   D. To examine media programs as modern *cultural myths,* which furnish insight into contemporary life
II. A useful methodological framework for mythic analysis is as follows:
   A. Does the media presentation fulfill any of the functions of myth? What does this reveal about media content?
   B. What is the role of the media in the mythologizing process?
      1. In what ways do the media mythologize people and events?

      2. In what ways do the media demythologize people and events?

C. Does the media presentation retell classic myths?

      1. Why does a traditional myth appear in this particular culture at this particular time?

      2. In what ways has this adaptation been altered from the original?

      3. What do these adaptations signify with regard to cultural attitudes, beliefs, values, and preoccupations?

      4. Is the media presentation a reconfiguration of traditional myth? Explain.

D. Does the media presentation contain any mythic themes? What insights does an understanding of these mythic elements provide into the text?

E. Does the media presentation feature any mythic figures? What insights does an understanding of these mythic figures provide into the text?

F. Does the media presentation contain any of the following? What insights does an understanding of these mythic elements provide into the text?

      1. Mythic plots

      2. Mythic motifs

      3. Mythic symbols

G. Does the media presentation reflect cultural myths?

      1. What do these cultural myths reveal about the predominant values, concerns, and preoccupations within the culture?

      2. What do the cultural myths reveal about shifts within the culture?

      3. Are new cultural myths being created and conveyed through the media? Explain.

      4. Does the media presentation contain any of the following?

         a) Cultural mythic themes

         b) Cultural mythic figures

         c) Cultural mythic symbols

5

Analysis of Production Elements

Overview

Production elements refer to the *style* and aesthetic quality of a media presentation. An awareness of stylistic elements such *editing, composition, point of view, angle, connotation, graphics, color, lighting, shape, movement, scale, sound,* and *special effects* contributes to our appreciation of media content and provides insight into media messages. Production values are roughly analogous to grammar in print, in that these elements influence the following features:

- The way in which the audience receives the information
- The emphasis or interpretation placed on the information by the media communicator
- The reaction of the audience to the information

Production elements often touch the audience on an emotional level, creating a mood that reinforces manifest messages or themes. Through production elements, the media communicator creates an environment that enables the audience to experience (as opposed to merely understand) the messages. For example, horror films generate feelings of fear in audience members, which enables them to identify with the experiences of the characters on-screen.

Media communicators strive to create seamless, self-contained productions that conceal the process of designing and assembling the presentation. Because many of these constructed meanings slip past conscious awareness, they predispose viewers to think about the presentation from the point of view of the media communicator. During the production process, the media communicator actively selects, manipulates, and coordinates various technical elements that support media messages. For instance, when producing horror films, media communicators manipulate lighting, music and screen space to arouse intense feelings of terror in the audience. Stylistic elements may also convey independent messages, such as the glamour associated with screen violence.

The analysis of media production elements has several objectives: (1) This approach enables individuals to understand how production elements are utilized to construct meaning in media presentations. (2) Examining production elements offers an excellent way to identify both manifest and latent messages as well as themes within a media text. (3) This approach can increase an individual's awareness of the ways in which production elements affect him or her personally, as well as the wider audience.

Editing

Editing refers to the selection and arrangement of information. Editing is a process in which many elements are pieced together to give meaning to a presentation. Editing decisions can send a wide range of messages regarding media content.

Inclusion and Omission

Given time and space limitations, critical editing decisions involve both what to *include* and what to *omit* from a media presentation. These decisions have been reached before the presentation reaches the public; as a result, the audience is not in a position to make a critical judgment about the selection process. For example, printed in the upper right-hand corner of the *New York Times* is the motto "All the News That's Fit to Print." This statement conveys that editing decisions have been made prior to publication, and what is "fit to print" has been determined by the editors.

The advent of blogs significantly influences what mainstream media such as the *New York Times* deem fit to print. A case in point: At Republican senator Strom Thurmond's one hundredth birthday party, Republican senate majority leader Trent Lott stated proudly that his state, Mississippi, aligned itself with Thurmond during his 1948 presidential campaign. Thurmond's presidential platform defended racial segregation, issuing campaign statements such as, "All the bayonets of the Army cannot force the negro into our homes, our schools, our churches,"[1] Lot continued lamenting that "if the rest of the country had followed our [Mississippi's] lead, we wouldn't have had all these problems over all these years, either."[2]

The *New York Times* and other mainstream media such as CNN chose to ignore these remarks until political blogs, namely, Josh Marshalls's http://www.talkingpointsmemo.com and Andrew Sullivan's http://andrewsullivan.theatlantic.com brought these comments into focus and fueled the fires with demands for Lott's resignation. The *New York Times* and other major news networks were forced into covering this racist indiscretion, making Lot's position untenable and forcing his resignation. Paul Krugman's Op-Ed piece in The *New York Times* credited blogs as a pivotal force in bringing the Lott issue into public view: "Talkingpointsmemo.com is must reading for the politically curious, and . . . more than anyone else, [Marshall] is responsible for making Trent Lott's offensive remarks the issue they deserve to be."[3]

Rahul Kumar, deputy editor of *OneWorld South Asia,* observes that the combination of technology, blogs, and the Iraq war has "spawned an era of embedded journalism," whereby "freelance journalists, soldiers and Iraqi youth brought, in large measure, images of war that would never have made the public domain."[4] These weblogs are akin to the mouse that roared in that they are reconfiguring the media infrastructure. According to Kumar, weblogs force mainstream media to cover stories they would otherwise ignore. Blogs, he says, have fueled content and ideas that are being incorporated into books, films, the recording industry, and even online exhibitions of war photographs.[5]

In film and television, the issue of inclusion and omission is critical. The shooting ratio in a Hollywood feature film production is approximately 10 to 1. That is, ten feet of film has been shot for each foot of film included in the final print. The same principle applies to television. In the news, a reporter may collect thirty minutes of interviews and background information for a story. However, he or she must compress this information to fit within a news slot of (at best) three minutes.

One way to analyze the editing process is to examine a variety of newspapers or television programs appearing on the same day. The same topic may be expanded or addressed from different points of view—or omitted altogether. Therefore, questions to consider include:

(1) What important stories have been ignored or downplayed? (2) What important details are left out and why? (3) How much information can be covered in these brief TV segments? (4) Who orders the segments and to whom are they important? (5) What is the primary purpose of most lead segments?

For example, on NBC's *Dateline,* Ann Curry featured the pioneering surgeries of the Aguirre twins, whose brains were joined at birth. *Dateline* continued their coverage of the twins over the next two years, providing updates as to the twins' progress and rehabilitation.[6] These experimental procedures and personal tragedies, however, usually affect only one or two people and their respective families. Regrettably, long-term processes, such as poverty and lack of health care, which affect more than 47 million people, 8.5 million of whom are children, rarely are considered newsworthy. Also, coverage for the 1,800 unnecessary deaths that occur due to lack of access to health care amounts to a blip on the radar screen.[7]

In another poignant example, the *Project for Excellence in Journalism* reported that cable and radio talk shows dedicated 37 percent of their programming to tabloid celebrity Anna Nicole Smith the week flowing her death, while more important issues, such as the debate over the Iraq war, received only 14 percent coverage, and coverage about political candidates vying for the White House amounted to 10 percent.[8]

Arrangement

The order in which news segments are presented provides a subtle way of telling the audience what is important. Because this process is far from being an exact science, newsroom editors and staff exercise *news judgments* about what is newsworthy based on their personal experiences, worldviews, backgrounds, and political pressure. As a result, the placement of news may vary dramatically from news outlet to news outlet (e.g., newspapers and television stations). An example is the Bush administration's effort to build a case for war against Iraq and the subsequent coverage dealing with the controversial issue as to whether Iraq possessed weapons of mass destruction.

For about a year and a half beginning in September 2002, former chief UN weapons inspector Scott Ritter and four respected journalists compiled compelling evidence that Iraqi facilities did not contain weapons of mass destruction. This information challenged the Bush administration's justification for preemptive attack that claimed the Iraqi regime had been busy stockpiling chemical, nuclear, and biological agents.

Unfortunately, these stories refuting weapons of mass destruction were relegated to the back pages of the *Washington Post* and the *New York Times,* connotatively lessening their significance and, consequently, giving them little traction.[9] In contrast, journalist Judith Miller's influential 3,500-word article supporting the war with its captive headline, "U.S. Says Hussein Intensifies Quest for A-Bomb Parts," received prominent front page status.[10] Television stations such as CNN and CBS echoed the clarion call for war, but by January 2004, the *New York Times* had issued an apology for the Miller article supporting the rationale for war; however, the mea culpa was too little too late.[11]

In regard to all media coverage pertaining to weapons of mass destruction, both before the war and after, the University of Maryland's Center for International and Security Studies concluded that, on the whole, the articles and segments were weighted in favor of the administration's arguments and failed to air dissenting views.[12]

Issues of arrangement also exist in film and television. Walter Cronkite, whose television career spanned more than thirty years, became a cultural icon and one of the most trusted men in America. During his nineteen years as *CBS Evening News* anchor, Cronkite's signature sign-off, "And that's the way it is," not only promised to present all the news; with it, Cronkite also pledged to give us the news in its order of importance. Most television stations across the country proffer the same assurance with slogans like "Where the News Comes First" (KSDK-TV), "Coverage You Can Count On" (WKRG-TV), and "News Edge" (KXAN-Fox 7). These slogans imply that quality news in order of importance will follow, but oftentimes this is not the case.

Frequently, news segments are either superficial or tabloid in nature. For example, on June 8, 2007, Defense Secretary General Robert Gates made an important announcement that he was dismissing Peter Pace as joint chiefs of staff and military adviser for the Iraq war. MSNBC, however, joined the announcement late due to its coverage of international playgirl Paris Hilton's appearance in court. In the midst of an interview with military analyst Rick Francona regarding the significance of the Pace dismissal, a scrolling banner rolled across the screen alerting viewers to "breaking news." Anchorwoman Contessa Brewer abruptly cut off the interview with Francona saying, "Here's Paris Hilton now," as the camera surveyed the drama outside Hilton's home and her ride back to court.[13]

That evening NBC nightly news "in depth," along with other stations, rearranged its news rundown to cover the aborted interview, once again arranging the news to focus on Paris Hilton. The Hilton tabloid saga occurred in an issue-laden week. Among the major events were two major presidential debates, immigration legislation, and rising U.S. tension with Russia over the missile defense system in Europe.[14]

Although news coverage on TV newscasts seems substantial, it is most often a fast-moving hodgepodge of sound bites and images lacking in-depth information from which the viewer can make an informed decision. The nightly news is akin to catching history on the run. To further demonstrate the quality and depth of information presented, professor Gary Schwitzer analyzed 840 health news stories on four television stations in Minneapolis–St. Paul, Minnesota, for a four-month period. One of the most troublesome findings was that health segments were thirty seconds or less single-source stories, with many touting sensational claims and coupled with hyperbole and elements of commercialism.[15]

Theme sequencing is an editing device whereby linkages are established between seemingly disparate stories. For instance, weather reports (featuring stories of stormy, inclement conditions, or high pollen counts) are often sponsored by cold medicines, thus sending a cumulative corporate message. The weather report triggers memories of cold or allergy symptoms, while the commercials show the viewer how to get relief. The visuals establish a chain of associations between wintry weather, cold symptoms, and relief with use of the advertised product.

In addition, examining the relationships among the articles, segments, and commercials is a way to uncover hidden messages. For example, three top government officials were conducting a "town meeting" at Ohio State University in hopes of gathering support for the government's decision to bomb Iraq. During the broadcast, CNN injected several commercials for the new video release of *Air Force One* (1997). The film is about President James Marshall's (Harrison Ford) victory over terrorists.

Editing for Contrast

Visual media such as photographs, television, and film employ editing techniques to highlight differences among settings, locations, or characters. In the film version of Henry James's novel *The Wings of the Dove* (1997), director Iain Softley utilizes editing to dramatize the differences between classes. In one sequence, Kate (Helena Bonham Carter) and her rich guardian, Aunt Maude (Charlotte Rampling), attend a wedding reception. The camera moves around the vast reception hall while the sedate, wealthy guests discuss trivial topics. The scene then dissolves to an overcrowded dimly lit pub where Kate's lover, a journalist, stands in the midst of a loud, disheveled group arguing political and social issues. This juxtaposition of scenes visually establishes Kate's conflict— securing her position of wealth, versus marrying Merton (Linus Roache), a working-class man with limited prospects.

Alternatively, director Alfonso Cuarón contrasted class and social difference without editing. His *Y tu mamá también* (2002) delivers a road story about two clueless, self-centered Mexican teenagers in the foreground, while a vivid, kaleidoscopic view of Mexico's twisted social, political milieu, and class difference runs parallel in the background throughout the film.

Editing for Rhythm

Editing can be fast or slow, depending on the duration of each shot in the edited sequence. The variable combinations of edited shots can be characterized as "music of the image." In music, a sequence of eighth notes is much faster than a cluster of whole notes. Likewise, in editing for film and television, a sequence of short shots is much faster than a grouping of shots long in duration. Individual shots can be as short as one-twenty-fourth of a second or as long as ten minutes. The rhythm has an impact on the rate at which the audience absorbs the information, and this, in turn, determines how much attention an audience can give to a particular aspect of the narrative.

The rhythm of editing also can influence the mood of a piece (e.g., frenetic versus tranquil). Rapidly edited shots build tension, indicate urgency, and create a rushed atmosphere. Long takes use up more time; however, when they are edited in sequence, they can create suspense. Long takes with minimal changes in camera position and lighting for a specific shot (setups) can also deliver the desired lyrical flow to romantic narratives and impart a feeling of stability. For example, the long wedding sequence at the opening of *Soul Food* (1997) gives the audience time to meet the characters and observe the social interaction within the context of a community ritual. The subsequent long sequences at "Big Mama's" (Irma P. Hall) weekly Sunday dinners dramatize the importance this forty-year tradition plays in keeping this African American family together.

Media communicators often employ rhythmic editing techniques for purposes of emphasis. In his gangster film *Goodfellas* (1990), director Martin Scorsese edited in freeze frames to emphasize the significance of particular events. During the opening sequence, young Henry's (Christopher Serrone) father is beating him. Suddenly, the action is frozen—and then the father's beating resumes. As the audience watches the film, they gain insight into how this moment has shaped Henry's outlook on life. This editing technique also furnishes perspective into the adult Henry's (Ray Liotta) behavior toward other characters later in the film.

In a subsequent sequence, we see Henry igniting explosives and again the frame freezes while Henry stands and watches. Scorsese comments, "[A] point was being made in his life. There is an explosion and the freeze frame, Henry frozen against it—it's hellish, a person in flames in hell. . . . It is important where the freeze frames are in that opening sequence. Certain things are embedded in the skull when you're a kid. Extract a moment in time."[16]

In contrast, *The Bourne Ultimatum* (2007) emphasizes the relationship between the main character and time. Editing Jason Bourne's (Matt Damon) actions before they are completed not only speeds the action but creates a "sense of uneasiness" surrounding Bourne and his actions. It underscores Bourne's being at odds with his environment and forces the audience, along with the character, to understand his identity piece by piece.[17] To evoke this sense of Bourne's "incomplete character and fragmented state of mind," editor Christopher Rouse made thirty-seven cuts in the first minute of the film.[18]

Spatial Editing

Spatial editing establishes connections between different characters or locations. For example, in the film *A Mighty Heart* (2007), journalist Daniel Pearl (Dan Futterman) and his wife Mariane (Angelina Jolie) leave their home together but jump into different cabs and head their separate ways. Danny navigates the crowded streets of Karachi, searching for an elusive contact that will lead him to an interview with Sheikh Gilani, a cleric and head of a militant Islamic group. Simultaneously, Mariane travels about the city, the supermarket, and then home to prepare the dinner they will share with friends on their last night in Karachi. As they communicate by phone throughout the day, the film intercuts between the two, establishing a link between their parallel actions. The frequent phone conversations to check on each other's whereabouts within the chaos and noise of Karachi and the visual editing back and forth between the two hints at the potential dangers each faces as they move within and around the city.

Temporal Editing

Alternating images of an individual with flashbacks, memory shots, dream images or flash-forwards offers an opportunity for the media communicator to comment on the subjective nature of time. In *The Notebook* (2004), director Nick Cassavetes used flashbacks to dramatize the courtship, separation, and reunion of two young adolescents, Noah (Ryan Gosling) and Allie (Rachel McAdams), who fall in love while Allie and her family spend their summer on Seabrook Island, South Carolina. The story opens six decades later in a posh nursing facility where Noah, now called Duke (James Garner), takes up residence to be with Allie (Gena Rowlands), who now suffers with Alzheimer's. As Duke reads from the tattered pages of the notebook, flashbacks depict their love story, written years earlier by Allie, and Duke harbors hope that his repeated readings will help her recover her memory and restore their marital bliss.

Composition

Composition, or where a character or object appears on the screen (or page), directs the viewer's eye to the part of the page or scene intended by the media communicator. Media communicators must work within the predetermined size of the page or screen. Where the character or object is placed within the screen area determines not only the amount of attention it receives, but its relative importance as well. The most stable and prominent viewing area is the center of the screen.

When the elements (characters or objects) within the picture's frame are balanced (equally distributed around the center), there is a sense of stability, thus minimizing tension in the viewer's mind. If the interrelationships linking the event, character, and/or object within the frame are unbalanced (images are off center or weighted heavily on one side), then this creates instability and heightens the sense of tension for the viewer.

The media communicator may strategically place objects and figures in one of the major sections of the frame to evoke an emotional response and convey messages. For example, when focal interest is drawn to the top of the screen, it suggests ideas dealing with power, authority, and aspiration. Generally, characters or objects positioned at the top of the screen command a greater sense of importance than other figures in the frame.

Conversely, objects or characters at the bottom of the screen represent subordination, vulnerability, and weakness. When figures of equal size are used, a dominant-submissive relationship between two figures can be displayed by placing the dominant figure at the top of the screen and the subordinate member at the bottom. Media communicators also can transmit feelings of isolation or insignificance by positioning a character to the right or left side of the frame. These feelings are intensified if the rest of the page or screen is relatively barren.

When part of the object on the screen is missing and not in our field of vision, we mentally complete the image. This perceptual response to the phenomena is called *gestalt,* or *predisposition to order.* Our minds want to fill in the spaces that we cannot actually see. This allows us to perceive the whole even though we actually see only a portion of it. For example, in a close-up shot where the top of the forehead is out of the frame, the viewer will mentally extend the figure to complete the image so that it is automatically implied that off-screen space contains the person's unseen or cutoff portion. The completion of the image is called *psychological closure.*

Using both the off-screen and on-screen space connects these spaces. The powerful illusion of reality inside the frame encourages the perception that a larger scene continues outside the frame. Thus, the imagined space outside the screen extends the visible space. Fundamentally, "the off-screen may be defined as the collection of elements (character settings, etc.) that, while not being included in the [screened] image itself, are nonetheless connected to that visible space in imaginary fashion for the spectator."[19]

Figures placed on the edge of the frame looking at or approaching the unknown outside the frame suggest that the most important visual element resides outside the frame. This can arouse a sense of mystery, suspense, or fear in the viewer. Fear of what we cannot see is synonymous with fear of the unknown. For example, in the television series the *X-Files,* characters were often seen looking up toward space, looking for the unknown outside the visual frame.

Another important element of composition is the amount of white space that separates pictures, graphics, and headlines. Research has found that white space in printing takes on the significance of a pause, a visual silence. Cultural historian Walter Ong declares that white space loosens the visual authority, appears more accessible, and invites dialogue. It serves as a guide to action, akin to turn taking in verbal conversation. When newspaper contents are tightly arranged, however, they assume a stance of completeness and the voice of final authority. The visuals of a tightly filled newspaper present a sense of closure, which discourages argument or dispute.[20]

The composition or layout of a production establishes a visual pattern that directs the audience's or reader's attention. For example, on December 24, 2007, the front page of the *Albany Times Union* carried the headline "Credit bills piling higher," printed in bold Franklin Gothic condensed type; it should have commanded attention, but the heavy type and seriousness of the issue were diminished or even negated by the commanding four-column color visual of happy shoppers placed next to it. The overhead color photo of people walking in the mall captured and directed readers' eyes down to the Jansen light serif headline "Shop till you drop . . . a bundle." A smaller, second photo beneath the larger one showed two smiling women "taking a break" from their shopping spree. The composition (layout, typeface) imparted more significance and importance to spending than to the alarming rise in credit card debt.[21]

Advertisers who must work within the constraints of the printed page also depend on both composition and placement to guide the reader's eye to the message. A recent advertisement for Clinique's anti-aging cream illustrates this point. Pictured on the left-hand side of the page is a large pocket watch. A cluster of weathered, aged wood shards accumulates between the eight and four on the clock face (representing the weathering agent of time). One shard is broken off and placed pointing at the bewitching hour of twelve. The tilted watch is prevented from falling by a jar of Clinique's "advanced stop signs eye" cream, which is placed to its right. The bright shiny lid of the jar appears to brighten the top rim of the watch where the two meet, as opposed to the bottom of the watch, which is dull, connoting the positive effect of the cream. Metaphorically, the contents of this fertile, green jar is a "cluster-buster"[22] that eliminates wrinkles and "stops" the clock on the aging process.

Format

Format refers to organization and layout. In an effort to increase circulation and attract new readers, many major newspapers have reformatted their papers. In May of 2002, the *San Francisco Examiner* changed from broadside to tabloid format and integrated extensive use of color throughout the paper. Robert Gower, design director at the *Examiner,* reasoned that in addition to differentiating the *Examiner* from the competition, "We [also] felt the niche existed in San Francisco for an urban tabloid and that our voice was already one of a tabloid."[23] The *Wall Street Journal* launched its new format in January 2005. Among the many changes, the *Wall Street Journal*'s designer, Mario Garcia, says he incorporated a "restrained and subtle use of color" to attract new readers and more advertisers. To keep abreast with the new industry standards, he shrank the width of the paper from sixty inches to forty-eight inches and expanded the "What's News" column on the front page. Garcia also inserted little boxes that summarize longer articles and identify the article's Web presence. The sum total of changes would mean "better navigation, enhancement of the content, and the use of more color to enhance the visual appeal."[24]

Gordon Crovitz informed readers that the "new content features, new ways to navigate the newspaper and innovations in aligning the print *Journal* and the *Wall Street Journal* online" would make it easier for the journal to be an essential source of information throughout the day.[25]

Point of View

Point of view refers to the source of information—who tells the story. Point of view has an impact on:

- How a story is told
- What information is conveyed
- The audience's orientation and sympathies

Point of View in Print

News stories often present information from the point of view (POV) of the reporter. As mentioned earlier, before a story appears in print, the reporter must research the topic. After gathering this information, the reporter chooses what information to include, what to exclude, what is emphasized, and what is omitted. Consequently, the story is not recorded but filtered through the perspective of the reporter.

Charlotte Ryan illustrates how a story can be written to fit a preconceived point of view:

Version 1: Rats Bite Infant
An infant left sleeping in his crib was bitten repeatedly by rats while his 16-year-old mother went to cash her welfare check. A neighbor responded to the cries of the infant and brought the child to Central Hospital, where he was treated and released to his mother's custody. The mother, Angela Burns of the South End, explained softly, "I was only gone five minutes. I left the door open so my neighbor would hear him if he woke up. I never thought this would happen in daylight."

Version 2: Rats Bite Infant: Landlord, Tenants Dispute Blame
An eight-month-old South End boy was treated and released from Central Hospital yesterday after being bitten by rats while he was sleeping in his crib. Tenants said that repeated requests for extermination had been ignored by the landlord, Henry Brown. Brown claimed that the problem lay with tenants' improper disposal of garbage. "I spend half my time cleaning up after them. They throw the garbage out the window into the back alley and their kids steal the garbage can covers for sliding in the snow."

Version 3: Rat Bites Rising in City's "Zone of Death"
Rats bit eight-month-old Michael Burns five times yesterday as he napped in his crib. Burns is the latest victim of a rat epidemic plaguing inner-city neighborhoods labeled the "Zone of Death." Health officials say infant mortality rates in these neighborhoods approach those in many third world countries. A Public Health Department spokesperson explained that federal and state cutbacks forced short-staffing at rat control and housing inspection programs. The result, noted Joaquin Nunez, M.D., a pediatrician at General Hospital, is a five-fold increase in rat bites. He added, "The Irony is that Michael lives within walking distance of some of the world's best medical centers."

Each of these versions directs the reader to think about the subject in a different way. The issue, responsibility, and solution to the problem vary according to how the facts were framed. In the first account, the mother is responsible. In the second, the responsibility revolves around the conflict between the landlord and tenants. The third version presents the broader social context in which these problems occur. All three of these versions are the result of a subjective interpretive concept. Each account offers only a *version* of reality.[26]

Point of View in Film and Television

In film, the POV informs the audience who is telling the story and determines how much information the audience has about the characters and situation. For example, the director may choose to isolate and follow the protagonist, whose image monopolizes the screen. The camera then takes the vantage point of a character or narrator in the film, showing us what the character sees.

Films and television programs can assume a *first-person* perspective, which presents the action as interpreted by one character. For instance, the film *Ponette* (1996) recounts the story from the perspective of a four-year-old. The film follows Ponette (Victoire Thivisol) as she struggles to cope with the death of her mother. Director Jacques Doillon uses close-up shots of Ponette to capture her expressions of a grief she cannot understand. This child's-eye view is powerful, both in its meaning (children feel as adults but think differently) and in its ability to evoke feelings of empathy within members of the audience.

A camera shot commonly employed in first-person POV is known as *the gaze*. This shot, frequently used in soap operas, draws the viewers' attention into the character's mental state. Instead of glancing at an external entity, the character presents a blank stare, suggesting an inward glance. When the character just stares into space, his or her eyes glaze over or speech suddenly falls silent; the camera may move in to a close-up, signaling that the object of the character's gaze is inward. What follows may be a dream sequence, memory image, intersubjective, reasoning or flashback. The gaze, then, informs us of the character's mental state.

Another POV found in films and television programs is the *second-person* perspective, which makes the reader the primary participant in the story. The second-person POV, says Bruce Kawin, "tell[s] 'you' the audience what to do."[27] According to Art Silverblatt, the second-person POV makes the reader (viewer) the primary participant in the story. Obviously, the second-person ("you") perspective is nearly impossible to achieve in television and film unless you actually appear on the screen. However, TV producers and filmmakers simulate the second-person perspective by selecting performers to represent you. For example, advertisements that use phrases such as "people like you" and "your friends" link the people shown in the ads with you, the viewer. This approach sends the message that we, the viewers, are like the people in the ads, and therefore, by extension, we *are* the people in the ads. Silverblatt suggests that advertising's "man in the street approach" casts everyday people as stand-ins for "you" because they theoretically reflect our values and concerns.[28]

In the third-person POV, the media communicator follows the thoughts and activities of one character but retains some critical distance and is therefore not accountable for the behavior of the character. The third-person POV emphasizes the "separateness and individuality of the camera." Sometimes a camera lingers on a scene that a character either has not entered or has already left. The purpose is to emphasize the environment over character and action, context over content. James Monaco says in this third-person POV, "[T]he camera takes on a personality all its own, separate from those of the characters."[29]

Another perspective is the third-person-omniscient POV, in which the narrator observes or comments on the actions and characters or reveals the inner thoughts and motivations of a character. Examples include the off-screen narrations in the films *Big Fish* (2003) and *The Age of Innocence* (1993).

Finally, the ensemble POV allows the spectator to observe points of view from several characters on the screen. This perspective offers the audience a comprehensive exposure to the people and events depicted in the work. In this POV, the audience frequently is aware of the situation on-screen even though the individual characters themselves remain unaware. For example, *Crash* (2004) examines the theme of racial tension and racially motivated clashes (crashes), but the story is viewed from the POV of several characters with varied ethnic and racial backgrounds. As the story moves between characters, the viewing audience is obliged to shift its identification from one character to another, allowing the viewer to assume each character's perspective while the other characters in the film remain limited to a single POV, their own.

Laura Mulvey looks at point of view from a feminist perspective. For Mulvey, the dominant POVs in film narratives are overwhelmingly male: "[The] . . . pleasure in looking has been split between active/male and passive/female. The determining male gaze projects its fantasy onto the female figure, which is styled accordingly. . . . [W]omen are simultaneously looked at and displayed. Women displayed as sexual objects is the leitmotif or erotic spectacle: from pin up to strip-tease from Ziegfeld to Busby Berkeley, she holds the look, plays to and signifies male desire."[30]

The power of the male gaze results from the fact that in most instances men control both the business and the apparatus (director, cinematographer) of representation. As a result, most eroticized female images depicted in the media create a visual bias that affects women in two ways. First, men control how women are portrayed, and this implies ownership. Second, representation from a male-dominated perspective objectifies women and diminishes female agency.[31] As John Berger remarks, "Men act and women appear. Men look at women. Women watch themselves being looked at. This determines not only most relations between men and women but also the relation of women to themselves."[32]

For example, in *A History of Violence* (2005), Director David Cronenberg positioned the camera to linger on Edie's (Maria Bello) body as she stands outside the doorway giving her husband, Tom (Viggo Mortensen), and the audience a steadfast gaze. Similarly, in *Monster's Ball* (2001) director Marc Forster holds the camera on the prostitute Vera's (Amber Rules) breasts while Hank (Billy Bob Thornton) fumbles with his wallet searching for money to pay her. It can be argued that these nude scenes were not needed to understand or support the narrative but appeared gratuitously for the benefit of the male gaze, including the actors, directors, and audience.

In addition, the director of *Monster's Ball* said that he wanted the sex scenes between Leticia (Halle Berry) and Hank to be "very raw, very real, and very graphic."[33] In this scene, Leticia throws herself on Hank and begs him in a panting voice to "make [her] feel good." The film and, specifically, this scene have been criticized for exploiting African American female beauty as mythically sexualized to satisfy the white male fantasy of eroticized interracial sex. In fact, Angela Basset rejected the role of Leticia, saying, "I wasn't going to be a prostitute on screen. I couldn't do that because it's such a stereotype about black women and sexuality."[34]

Angle

Angle refers to the angle at which the camera is pointed at the subject: high, low, or eye level. Camera angles can be manipulated to comment on the status of the individual on camera. If the position of the camera is low, then the subject appears more powerful than if the camera angle is at eye level. With a low camera angle, the spectator, seeing from the camera's perspective, must look up at the subject or event. To the viewer, on an emotional level, the superior position of the subject confirms his or her authority. To dramatize the struggle for power and dominance in the film *Beowulf* (2007), director Robert Zemeckis employed low angle shots in the battle scene between Beowulf and Grendel. As the low camera angle changes from Beowulf to Grendel, the illusion of who commands the position of dominance and strength shifts, creating a sense of heightened intensity in the viewer as to the battle's outcome.

In automobile ads, cars photographed at a low angle appear larger and more dynamic, while filming war missiles from a low angle conveys a sense of their destructiveness and enhances their speed.

When the camera takes a superior position, above eye level, the subject seen below appears smaller, inferior, frightened, or diminished psychologically. The viewer sees the subject as beneath him or her.

Cameras adjusted for straightforward viewing at eye level put the viewer on an equal plane with the subject. In television, newscasters and commercial actors look straight into the camera. It becomes synonymous with a face-to-face interaction, whereby the communicator seems to be addressing the viewer personally. The direct address at eye level creates an intimacy between the viewer and the performers, conveying a sense of trust so the viewer will listen closely to the communicator.

Keith Greenwood analyzed 194 published photographs of presidents from Harry S. Truman to George W. Bush, to determine how U.S. presidents were framed in photographs. All the photographs were deemed examples of photographers' best work and were taken during a campaign or while the president was in office. Of these photographs, 130 were taken at eye level with a medium camera-to-subject distance. Greenwood posits that "the dominance of eye-level photographs suggests photographers generally frame the President as someone on an equal footing with the rest of society . . . as another citizen or 'one of us.'" "The frame of equality," he continues, "supports the cultural beliefs in this country that no one is above the law and any child can grow up to be President." The rare presidential photograph from a high angle was to include the faces in a crowd of people. Occasionally the president has been pictured as a symbol of power with a low angle shot, but here again, the angle was employed to include significant contextual elements (such as inclusion

Bill Clinton

The close personal distance of former president Clinton in this photograph suggests feelings of intimacy. The horizontal angle implies an equal relationship between the subject and the viewer, and Clinton's tilted head and animated gaze create a strong sense of involvement. (*Getty Images; photographer: Jonathan Torgovnik*)

of the American flag) that would be missing with an eye-level angle. The medium camera-to-subject distance overwhelmingly reflects an equal relationship between the president and the audience. Greenwood points out that the award-winning photographs reflect the views of the editors who chose them for publication and may not reflect the views of the photographers who took the photos.[35]

Camera Shots

The three basic camera shots are the *wide shot,* the *medium shot,* and the *close-up.* In addition, cinematographers can use numerous variations on these three shots to convey nuanced information within the narrative. The wide shot, which is sometimes referred to as the *establishing shot* or *long shot,* captures the whole person or object and, usually, the surrounding environment. The purpose of the wide shot is to orient the viewer as to the location, situation, or surrounding context in which the performance takes place. To direct the viewer's attention closer to the subject, as in an interview, the camera moves in closer to the subject, usually from the waist up. The medium shot narrows our focus of the person being interviewed.

When the filmmaker wishes to direct our attention to a small aspect of the scene, he or she will use a close up shot, which is the visual equivalent of saying "Pay close attention." For example, Mel Gibson wanted to heighten the effect of Jesus' scourging in his film *The Passion of the Christ* (2004). Just prior to the instant when the whip strikes Jesus and rips out his flesh, Gibson includes a shot of Jesus from a low camera angle with a close-up of Jesus' side, which serves to heighten our anxiety about the brutal scourging that is to follow. A quick cut to the crowd's reaction accompanied by dramatic music adds to the intensity of the scene. Stephen Prince contends that the strategic combination of production elements (angle, shot, computer-generated imagery, editing, and music) to depict the physical violence heightens the perception of realism.[36]

Word Choice

Words are not neutral. They are a mode of communication and a medium for representing the world. Words carry both a dictionary meaning (denotative) and a connotative meaning. For instance, the word "house" simply describes a structure. However, "home" suggests a much richer meaning—a family gathered around the hearth, children playing video games, and the smells of dinner wafting in from the kitchen.

Sociologist Dorothy Nelkin claims that public perceptions about science are shaped by connotative word choice. In the reporting of science and technology, war metaphors such as *battles* and *struggles* create judgmental biases that underlie public policy. Medical research mobilizes more enthusiastic support when the media tout *revolutionary breakthroughs,* a much more inspiring term than *recent findings.* Consider the difference between *bacteria,* a germ, and *bacteria,* the enemy; whether we battle diseases with weapons or treat them with medicine. This choice of words, Nelkin says, not only evokes powerful battle images but influences public policy decisions, promoting the belief that technological progress should not be challenged and should be allowed to proceed without being questioned or regulated.[37]

In addition, choosing words that overstate scientific findings tends to mislead the public and can lead to false hopes, especially for those individuals who are vulnerable. This is specifically relevant when the results of a study are preliminary and need further research to confirm or negate its findings. A reader seeking valid information, however, might ask, Who financed the research? How many subjects participated in the research? What type of study was it—controlled, randomized, blind, or double-blind? In short, where is the data to back up the sensational claims?

Word choice plays a particularly important role in politics. Words such as *hope, change, strength, value,* and *security* are strategically inserted into candidates' speeches. These word choices are determined by focus groups that listen to numerous speeches. Upon hearing words they like, they turn a dial one way; they turn the dial in the opposite direction when they hear words they dislike. During the Iowa caucus, the *Des Moines Register* noted that Senator Barack Obama used the word *change* twenty-three times in one speech, and Senator Hilary Clinton used it seventeen times in a speech one hour later.[38]

Connotation

Connotation refers to the meaning associated with a word or image beyond its literal, dictionary definition. The connotative meaning of a word is universally understood and agreed upon. For example, the word *rose* carries the denotative meaning of a flower. But depending on the context and culture, a rose also suggests love, passion, perfection, or sexuality. Also, the color of a rose, whether it is yellow, red, or white, adds a further dimension to its meaning. Moreover, if the rose has thorns, the implication may connote the duality of pleasure and pain.

Media communicators depend on connotative meanings to influence our thinking and feeling not only about ourselves, but also about others and the world around us. The more an audience brings to a message, the easier it is for the communicator to inform, persuade, entertain, and so forth.

Political campaigns carefully craft connotative images with words and phrases to convey conceptual ideas that support their platforms. Republican political strategist Karl Rove utilized his rhetorical tools to frame contentious issues in a positive way to garner support for the Bush administration's agenda. Linguist George Lakeoff points out that these conceptual frames obscure reality. For example, Lakeoff tells us that when President George W. Bush started speaking about tax relief, it made people think of relief; following this line of thought, people thought there must be an affliction or burden to be relieved from. Connotatively, one starts to associate the tax reliever as a rescuer or savior. In reality, however, framing taxes as "relief," obscures the fact that taxes pay for our parks, highways, police protection, flood control, air-traffic control, and the Food and Drug Administration, a small list of what we expect and take for granted. In fact, the *Wall Street Journal* reported that the cost of repair for the deteriorating U.S. infrastructure is $1.6 trillion, all of which needs to be financed with tax revenue.[39] Other deceptive framing concepts include:

Clear Skies Act	versus	Clean Air Act
Death Tax	versus	Estate Tax
Healthy Forest Initiative	versus	No Tree Left Behind

Incorporating the wrong analogy into a speech can also be connotatively misleading. Analogy is a rhetorical device whereby complex information is compared to a familiar shared source of knowledge. The correspondence established between the two situates the complex information in an understandable mental concept. Analogy is often used to convey difficult concepts in science and technology to the general public. Starting with George Tenet's "slam dunk," journalist and editor Tom Engelhardt analyzed the rhetorical "war of the words" using sports analogies by military and Washington officials to explain the conflict in Iraq over the past four years. Some of these include:

- "It's important to defend this country on the extremist's 10-yard line and not our 10-yard line."[40]
- "I don't think that the goal post has changed at all."[41]
- "I think it's all still in the same ballpark."[42]
- "We're racing against the clock, certainly, again, we're racing against the Washington clock, the London clock, a variety of other timepieces up there, and we've got to figure out how to speed up the Baghdad clock."[43]

The use of sports terminology to describe the Iraq war situates the highly politicized discussion in a natural context. It encodes knowledge that relates to peoples' personal experiences.[44] In the American psyche, the conceptual images of sports, especially basketball, football, and horse racing, are social interactive rituals of shared collective joy. In short, these uses of analogy take the highly politicized domain of war and connotatively situate them in the joyfully shared realm of sports, which connotes public spectatorship and rooting for the home team. The sports analogy, however, is a false one. It obscures the reality that war, a form of deadly play, is not a game of fair play, and winning brings no gain.

In addition to words and analogies, images carry connotative meanings that derive not from the image itself, but from how society has learned to use and value the image. For example, car commercials aren't just about cars. Depending on the viewer, they can connote virility, power, or freedom. If a beautiful woman is in the scene, it adds a sexual dimension to the image.

Images in beer, cigarette, and alcohol advertisements are laden with connotative meanings that promote product use. By combining words and images, advertisers strengthen the commercial messages. The combination of images acts much like joining a subject and a verb to make a sentence, conveying a meaning very different from a single word or single image.

For example, most alcohol and cigarette advertisements position young models with their products. The models appear successful, and are attractive and engaged in a fun activity. Beyond the denotative level (the image itself) there is a suggested meaning that using these products brings enjoyment and secures friendships, attractiveness, and pleasure. The ads present a social image that appears as reality. Connotatively, they offer personal transformation through the use of the product: The purchaser will be desirable and happy if he or she uses the product.

When media images draw the viewer into identifying with the media presentation, the inner vision of the viewer connects with the outer representation in the media. This creates a world within the imagination of the viewer that reaches beyond what appears on-screen. This identification with the media image makes the media presentation appear natural. It unifies the viewer with the image, and the viewer begins to think of the media image as part of the natural world. In other words, the boundaries between the viewer and the media presentation are blurred. When an image elicits a response, we are aware of its effect on us; however, an important question to consider is why this particular image generates a certain emotional response.

Media communicators often rely on connotative images as a dramatic device. Sometimes the use of images foreshadows events. For example, in one scene in *Titanic* (1997), a crewmember standing beside the captain looks out over the motionless, dark sea and remarks that the waters are so calm that they won't be able to detect any icebergs. The camera immediately cuts to a close-up of the cup of black tea in the captain's hands. The tea is dark and motionless, like the ocean. As the captain rotates the cup, the liquid "waves" back and forth and a slice of lemon emerges. This edit not only is a visual metaphor for the difficulty of detecting icebergs at night in a calm sea, but also foreshadows the coming tragedy. Some additional ways to read image combinations are as follows:

- *Condensation.* Condensation refers to the process by which images are condensed and move beyond the connotative meaning to signify qualities of emotion that are linked to cultural beliefs, or what Roland Barthes calls mythic forms of cultural ideology. According to Barthes, this mythic signification "points out, notifies and makes us understand something and imposes it on us."[45] For example, in a Marine recruitment video, a young man scales a monolithic mountain face as an American flag billows in the wind while a steady montage of historical Marine Corps images are projected onto the mountain during the climber's treacherous assent. As the climber nears the top, a Marine on the mountain peak bends and extends a helping hand. At the top, the two men face each other and salute, which triggers a bolt of lightning, causing the figures to merge into one. At this point, the climber is transformed into a Marine dressed in full uniform. The narrator reinforces this sequence, saying "The passage is intense, but if you complete the journey, you will find your destiny among the world's greatest warriors. The Few, The Proud, The Marines."[46]

  The montage of images, music, and voice-over blend to impose a sensory reality of the system of American values: individualism, self-reliance, discipline, and power—symbolic attributes that ensure success and membership in a group of men who have journeyed to the pinnacle of power. Sergeant Cynthia Atwood, recruiting commander for the Marines, reinforces this concept, saying "We're selling intangibles. . . . Yes, we offer [educational and enlistment] incentives like everybody else, but you couldn't be a Marine if that's all you came in for."[47]

The Climb

The climber finally reaches the top of the mountain after his long treacherous journey indicating that he has conquered all the challenges in his quest to become a member of the Marine Corps. *United States Marine Corps and JWT Atlanta.*

- *Displacement.* Displacement is the process by which we transfer meaning from one sign or image to another. Displacement images often have strong sexual associations. Displacement is a device frequently used in commercial advertising whereby nonsexual objects are used in place of sexual ones in order to avoid censorship. For example, in a Disaronno liqueur commercial, a woman orders a Disaronno on the rocks. When she has finished with her drink, she takes an ice cube from the glass and licks it while glancing seductively at the young bartender across the counter. In the midst of the scene, the narrator says, "Disaronno's warm and sensual taste makes you wish it would never end."
- *Metaphor.* Metaphor employs the substitution or comparison of one idea or object with another to facilitate understanding. For example, in the broccoli–ice-cream-cone ad, broccoli, metaphorically, takes on the qualities of ice cream. In other words, the qualities of ice

cream are transferred to broccoli. The photo for the ad visually implies that broccoli is a tasty treat.

- *Metonomy.* Metonomy is a device whereby an image signifies a group of attributes that have become culturally associated with it. For example, in liquor and beer advertisements, the consumption of the product is associated with happiness and attractive physical appearance, and references a chain of events that results in having friends and fun times. Similarly, drug advertisements for antidepressants trigger an associative link between taking the drug and the attributes of wellness, activity, happiness, energy, and vigor.

Graphics

In addition to content, a publication's form (all graphic elements combined) sends messages about the quality, clarity, and authority of the publication. Graphic representation is a sign system—in essence, a language for the eye. Charts, graphs, illustrations, and maps visually display complex data, making it easier for the viewer to understand and store information. Like language, these figurative images tell stories. Producers of graphic material assign meaning to each sign element before it is presented. The perception of these visual displays is a process in which the viewer considers the relationship between the signs and their predetermined meaning.

Jeremy Black asserts that, in this respect, graphics "play a major role in politics, both international and domestic, reflecting the ability of visual images and messages to contribute to the discourse of power."[48] They are symbols of belief—mental images—that guide our thinking about politics, economics, society, and medical care. Charts, graphs, and statistical analyses are the culture's *symbolic flashlights,* influencing decisions such as insurance rates, interest rates, and public policy. Graphic representations also categorize people, places, and things. This includes class, wealth, and social environment. These symbols, printed in newspapers and broadcast on television, help solidify the agenda of those in power by colonizing the belief of readers and viewers.[49]

Artist and newspaper cartoonist Bob Staake contends that, in the print medium, graphic images are becoming the dominant form of expression, overwhelming the written word. According to Staake, "It's already obvious as we look at the newspapers on the Internet. You can't just put a bunch of words up on the screen. There has to be plenty of illustrations, graphics, and pictures. . . . Artists are going to be part of the decision process."[50]

However, graphic representation cannot provide a comprehensive or realistic depiction of reality. Journalist Victor Cohn cautions that charts and graphs displaying survey results or polls are just "snapshots of the scene at the moment." These frozen moments do not represent time over a continuum, nor do they define the quality of the studies, questionnaires, or answers, written or verbal.[51]

In addition, charts showing statistical analyses do not necessarily indicate a direct cause and effect. For example, several statistical charts reveal that the incidence of delinquent behavior is higher in families where the father is absent. There is a correlation, but not causation. What is hidden and obscured are numerous other variables such as the size of the population being studied and the study population's socioeconomic level and quality of education. In other words, viewers should ask, Are there other factors that would have a significant link to the high rate of delinquency in children without fathers?

Pie graphs also can be easily manipulated. Percentages in a pie graph may not add up to 100 percent. When a viewer looks at visual graphs, charts, and diagrams, questions of concern should include the following:

- Who says so?
- Does the source of information have any bias?
- What is missing?
- Who are the groups being represented?
- What is the purpose?
- Whose agenda does it support?
- How does the title relate to the content?
- Do the numbers make sense?

For example, when newspapers print graphs showing how much the unemployment rate is down, the viewer needs to examine these graphics closely. Does the graph indicate full-time employment, or does it include those people in part-time employment receiving the minimum wage and limited, if any, benefits, such as health care?

The visual presentation of graphics also can distort the information being introduced. For example, when the Florida court ordered a feeding tube removed from Terri Schiavo, who had been brain dead and in a coma for more than ten years, a USA TODAY/CNN/Gallup Poll queried

Media Matters

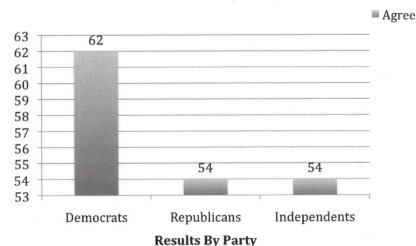

CNN/USA Today/Gallup Poll
Results by Party

■ Agree

Results By Party

Visual presentations of graphics can influence our perception of messages. The graphics shown above present identical information, however, the numerical spacing in the first bar conveys a greater difference of opinion between the Democrats and the other two groups regarding the Florida court's decision on the Terri Schiavo case.

Source: mediamatters.org/items/200503220005.

Democrats, Republicans, and Independents as to whether they agreed with the decision. Even though the results were within the poll's margin of error (+/–7 points), the published graph visualized the gap between the Democratic respondents and the other two parties as overwhelming. CNN corrected the graph only after Media Matters, a Web-based research center that monitors and corrects conservative misinformation published in the U.S. media, highlighted the error.[52]

Sometimes statistics are buried within the narrative, imposing misleading statistical information without our conscious input and setting false expectations. For example, medical researchers from Duke University found that CPR (cardiopulmonary resuscitation) performed on entertainment television programs blurred the line between fact and fiction. On medical shows such as *ER*, 65 percent of patients survived CPR. Rates for long-term survival after cardiac arrest vary from 2 to 30 percent for arrests outside the hospital and from 6.5 to 15 percent for arrests that take place inside the hospital. Even if they survive, patients often suffer some degree of brain or neurological damage due to the extended lack of oxygen to the brain during the attack.[53]

Typography

How do print publications attract and maintain their audience? The magnetic force, according to graphic designers and typographers, begins in the art of typography and layout. Graphic designer Erik Spiekermann and typographer E.M. Ginger observe, "The artistry comes in offering the information in such a way that the reader doesn't get side tracked. . . . Designing . . . has to be invisible. Typefaces used for these hard working tasks are, therefore, by definition 'invisible.'"[54] Kevin Barnhurst elaborates further: "In a sort of visual onomatopoeia, the form of typography can mimic sizes, weights, shapes and postures from the environment. Large, bold headlines are mimetic of dramatic events. In whimsical featured articles, letterforms might take the shape of ghosts, or cooking utensils. . . . Turning a word upside down [in headline] can suggest the state of the world. When the new sense and the content of the text coincide, meaning can be reinforced or expanded."[55]

Spiekermann and Ginger add that even before we read a word, its shape and thickness can trigger an emotion. Depending on the space surrounding the letters, "[D]ark emotions call for a black typeface with sharp edges; pleasant feelings are best evoked by informal, light characters." Emotions such as anger are best illustrated in a heavy black typeface with an irregular shape. Typefaces that are casual and look like handwritten letters suggest surprise. Surprise needs to carry a feeling of spontaneity. Joy, on the other hand, needs a "generous feel . . . open forms with confident strokes and a sense of movement."[56]

Albert J. Kastl and Irvin L. Child's studies reveal that advertisers use typefaces to enhance certain moods. Light, ornate typefaces promote a sprightly, sparkling, dreamy, or calm mood. Simple bold typefaces conveyed a sad, dignified, and dramatic mood. Typefaces are also associated with gender, race, and nationality. Roy Paul Nelson observes, "The meaning assigned to type by readers and typographers seems to spring not from some objective code but from cultural experience common to both groups."[57]

Both newspapers and magazines express their personalities through the accumulation of visual clues. Readers recognize a publication by

Typefaces

walk,   (Century Bold Condensed, 24 pt.)

run,   (Party Plain, 72 pt.)

jump,   (La Bamba, 36 pt.)

or *dance.*   (Party, 48 pt.)

Party says "Surprise"   (Party, 30 pt.)

Franklin Gothic says "Urgent"

(Franklin Gothic, 18 pt.)

Randumhouse says "festive"

(Randumhouse , 24 pt.)

Treehouse says "playful"   (Treehouse - Plain, 30 pt.)

Examples of how fonts can be used to express a range of emotions and feelings.

GREECE
JAMAICA
Ceylon
China
MEXICO
Tahiti
Canada
Ireland
Scotland
Denmark
Japan
PORTUGAL
BRITAIN

Over time, certain letter forms have become associated with particular countries (e.g., Greece capturing the early Greek lettering).
Source: Roy Paul Nelson, Publication Design. Dubuque: Wm. C. Brown Company, 1989, p. 79. *Reprinted with permission of McGraw-Hill Companies, Inc.*

its logotype (nameplate). One glance at a newsstand will reveal the numerous personalities vying for recognition among the cornucopia of offerings. The logotype gives the publication a personalized visual identity, which becomes an important identifying symbol for the reading audience. For example, the nameplate of the *New York Times* uses narrow bold serif letters, imitating the old gothic script (Textura). This type conveys the *Times*' long-standing claim to authority and championing of progressive values rooted in nineteenth-century visionary values.

Mastheads

𝔗𝔥𝔢 𝔑𝔢𝔴 𝔜𝔬𝔯𝔨 𝔗𝔦𝔪𝔢𝔰

THE PLAIN DEALER

In contrast, local and regional papers like the *St. Louis Post-Dispatch* and Cleveland's *Plain Dealer* sport nameplates with broad, open, black letters, conveying a more accessible spirit.

Entertainment Weekly is a good example of how design presents a distinctive voice to attract an audience. *Entertainment Weekly* uses a consistent typography to give readers a sense of familiarity. The magazine is organized into sections—"Film," "TV," "Music," and so forth—each graphically identified by a color-coded tab. Each of these sections is presented in the same typographic hierarchy. The lead story is followed by shorter reviews, sidebars, and graphic inserts that combine charts, illustrations, and text and follow the lead story. To attract attention, the cover employs large pictures and introduces the lead stories with attention-grabbing gothic headlines, which are designed differently from the rest of the magazine.

Graphic titles play an important role in film and television, whether it be the blasting fire and neon graphics of *Casino* (1995) or the vintage *Spider-Man* comic montage with the credits trapped in a web like flies for *Spider-Man 2* (2004). Like the overture to a symphony, the title sequence introduces the film's theme. It is integral to the film's whole.

Graphic designer Saul Bass, who reinvented the art of title sequences with films like *The Man with the Golden Arm* (1955), *Psycho* (1960), *North by Northwest* (1959), *Vertigo* (1958), and *Casino,* said that the film's title sequence must express the film's story and deliver us into the film in a single reductive, metaphorical way. For Bass, *Golden Arm*'s animated title with its distorted arm represented the "disjointed life, schizophrenic life of the addict."[58]

Following in the Bass tradition, Kyle Cooper used surveillance-type photography and kerning fonts to establish Johnny Depp's outsider status in the opening credits of *Donnie Brasco* (1997), which hinted at the character's obsession with the mafia and his infiltration into its dark, underworld of crime and murder. In referencing Cooper's "rousing, majestic" opening montage for the *Ghosts of Mississippi* (1996), film critic Janet Maslin remarked, "None of what follows matches the impact of this title sequence."[59] Among numerous other films, Cooper is also noted for his title sequences for *Se7en* (1995) and four *Spider-Man* films (2002–2007), *Spider-Man 4* to be released 2010.

Codesigners Oliver Kuntzel and Florence Deygas created a playful, animated Bass-like title-credit sequence for *Catch Me If You Can* (2002). The sequence presents silhouetted figures representing Frank Abagnale Jr. (Leonardo DiCaprio) and FBI agent Carl Hanratty (Tom Hanks) in a chase-and-hide motif as Hanratty pursues Abagnale through multiple locations: airport, library, swimming pool, bar, hospital, and highway. Each locale is presented in a different color scheme, while little arrows track the pursuit until the final "gotcha" frame, where they are together.

This opening sequence is a minimovie capturing the escapades of the young con artist, Frank Abagnale, who impersonated an airline pilot, a doctor, a lawyer, and a college professor. Before being caught by the FBI, Abagnale, a master of deception, managed to forge $2.5 million in checks and led law enforcement representatives on a wild goose chase throughout the globe.[60]

Logos

Logos are symbols of identity. Logos are placed on products and serve as a face, communicating the company's essence and personality. Gerry Rosentsweig says logos reflect social changes and changing images of American businesses. Effective logos share the following characteristics:

- Originality
- Wit
- Accessibility
- Mythicness
- Idiosyncrasy
- Emotiveness
- Memorability[61]

Graphic titles, *Donnie Brasco*

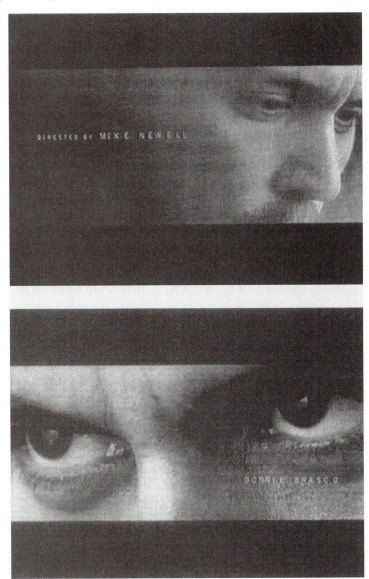

Graphic titles often foreshadow significant themes and events in media presentations. For example, in the opening credits of *Donnie Brasco* (1997) directed by Mike Newell, the combination of graphic titles and visuals introduces the main character's role as an FBI agent who infiltrates the mob. This graphic style is seen throughout the movie, as Brasco types his reports on mob activities and sends them to the FBI.

Globalization necessitates that logo design be instantly recognizable and convey meaning, regardless of cultural and language barriers. For example, the ubiquitous Nike swoosh breaks through all the clutter and is easily recognized all over the world. In fact, the swoosh may be more recognizable than the name Nike itself.

The name Nike stands for the Greek goddess of victory. According to a Nike consumer affairs statement, "The Nike swoosh embodies the spirit of the winged goddess who inspired the most courageous and chivalrous warriors at the dawn of civilization."[62]

The swoosh logo is a visual shorthand that embodies the company's ideology, in that the swoosh may be considered the face of Nike. Its natural curved form creates a sense of perpetual motion. Nike CEO Phil Knight asserts that the swoosh logo symbolizes "never giving up . . . never slowing down . . . not being afraid to try something new. . . . It stands for passion, pride, and authenticity, innovation and courage."[63] Nike spent $1.7 billion, including $476 million for celebrity endorsements, in 2006 marketing its products with the swoosh logo to ensure that its emotional appeal reached a worldwide audience. In addition to Nike's paid advertisements, fifty-nine easily identifiable swooshes were counted in the editorial pages of a ninety-page pro football magazine.[64]

Color

Colors evoke a wide range of emotional responses in the viewer. Warm colors (red, orange, and yellow) can cause an aggressive reaction. Psychological research has found that extroverted personality types often prefer these colors; in contrast, introverts are attracted to cooler, subtler tones such as blue, green, and purple. Warm colors such as yellow and orange also can heighten nostalgic feelings. Researchers have found that muscle reaction is measurably faster under the influence of red, whereas bubblegum pink, when used as a decoration scheme, lowers heart and pulse rates.[65]

Practically every religion, tradition, and superstition has assigned symbolic meaning to specific colors. In some cultures, red has been viewed as the vigorous color of health. For healing purposes, red wool was applied to sprains in Scotland and sore throats in Ireland and was used to reduce fever in Macedonia. The Chinese wore brilliant red rubies to ensure long life. Conversely, red also signals blood and danger, and, for Valentine enthusiasts, red symbolizes love and passion. Since the days of heraldry, yellow has been associated with gold. Religious painters have shrouded the Virgin Mary in blue, signifying her piety. Since Roman times, purple has been symbolic of power, leadership, royalty, and respect.

The University of Basel in Switzerland compiled the following associations and responses to color from subjects in Western Europe and the United States:

- Blue—trust, sensitivity, loyalty, nurturance, piety, and sincerity
- Brown—vitality, receptivity, and sensuality (the color of Mother Earth)
- Green—regeneration and growth, harmony, and abundance (associated with hope)
- Orange—competition, a color of excitability and activity
- Red—impulse and intensity, blood and sexuality, youthfulness and forcefulness
- Yellow—philosophical, intellectual (associated with anticipation)[66]

The *shade* of a color can also affect its meaning. In Western cultures, dark blue is associated with peace, security, and contentment. Violet (a variation of purple) represents magic, imagination, and romance. Depending on the context, green can symbolize either nature or jealousy.[67]

Since the meaning of color varies among cultures, media communicators must be sensitive to the cultural language of color when attempting to convey a message. For instance, when an Irish beer producer aired his beer commercial in Hong Kong, sales dropped dramatically. The commercial featured the tossing of a green hat. The company quickly pulled the commercial off the air when representatives were informed that wearing a green hat was a Chinese symbol for being cuckolded.[68]

While each culture may ascribe its own distinctive meaning to colors, there is often considerable overlap between cultures, reflecting some level of consensus. For example, Xerox recently unveiled its new logo, but the bright red color remained. The uppercase letters are now lowercase, and a red sphere sporting a white stylized X has been appended to represent worldwide connection, energy, and youthfulness. The color red stayed because it is associated with Xerox, said brand strategist Maryann Stump, and the bonus is that in the Asia-Pacific market, red "'resonates as good luck, prosperity, and good will.'"[69]

In film and television dramas, color often sets the mood and tone of a production. Cold blue colors with harsh edges can produce ominous futuristic settings. Subdued colors reflect conservative values, while vibrant red can warn of danger and violence. For example, in *Munich* (2005), a film recounting Israel's revenge after the massacre of Israeli athletes at the 1972 Munich Olympics, production designer Rick Carter placed the color red in numerous scenes throughout the film, especially in scenes before a murder occurred. Red functioned as a leitmotif (a reiteration) throughout the film and, as Carter says, is a subliminal reminder of what the film is really about—"which is the spilling of blood."[70] In addition to the significance of the color red, Janusz Kaminski, *Munich*'s cinematographer, filmed each country in a different color pallet. Kaminski wanted color to define the individual character of the various countries depicted.[71]

Color formed the key element in "carry[ing] the narrative burden" of two parallel stories in *Pan's Labyrinth* (2006), one fantasy world and one reality world. The story revolves around ten-year-old Ofelia, who, along with her mother, joins her vicious fascist stepfather, captain in charge of hunting down rebels hiding in the mountains in rural Spain.

Struggling with the real-world cruelties and feeling powerless, Ofelia retreats to an inner life of fantasy to cope, only to realize the fantasizing must end when she turns and confronts the evil of the real world. Ofelia's fantasy was told in warm colors of "deep crimson and golden ambers, almost like amniotic fluid," to suggest a "womblike" environment, said director Guillermo del Toro. Conversely, the harsh real world of Spain's fascist government was portrayed using sharp angles and cold hues of blue and green. At one point in the film, when Ofelia's imaginary world became as real to her as the fascist world, the colors intermingle. Cinematographer Guillermo Navarro explained that in making color a language unto itself, the filmmakers could "help the audience understand the complexity of the movie."[72]

Black-and-white as a contrast to color can also be used to distinguish the imagined from the real when depicting a dream or imaginary sequence. For example, in Kasi Lemmons's film *Eve's Bayou* (1997) the character Mozelle (Debbi Morgan) has a gift for telling fortunes. Mozelle's psychic visions of the future are presented in black-and-white, while the remainder of the narrative is presented in color. Tim Burton, in contrast, used accentuated color with warm, soft lighting for flashbacks and imaginings in *Sweeney Todd* (2007) to contrast with demon Todd's

(Johnny Depp) revenge-oriented environment, represented in a somber, overcast, monochromatic palette.

A recent Tavist-D (antihistamine) commercial thematically uses black-and-white and color to convey the effects of its product. The black-and-white opening scene shows a tight close-up of a woman frowning, obviously in discomfort. The caption and voice-over ask, "Where do you go for help?" In the next scene the woman emerges from the car on a cold, rainy evening and walks into a drugstore. As she reaches for the Tavist-D, color sweeps over the screen. Next, we see the same woman in a bright red coat, hair coiffed and makeup applied, energetically run down the steps. Sporting a vibrant smile, she greets a man passing her on the steps with a cheerful "Good morning." Within sixty seconds, Tavist-D magically changes your life both from sickness to health and from drab monotony to a "full-color," lively existence.

Lighting

Light has been laden with symbolism since the remote mists of time. Importantly, in visual media those objects or people who are "in the light" attract our attention and are presumed to be the most important characters in the frame. Lighting composition not only directs the viewer's attention to a particular subject, but also elicits certain emotional responses to the scene.

Bright lighting in comedies and musicals evokes feelings of joy, security, and optimism, while film noir's harsh, dark lighting drapes the world in inky black shadows, reinforcing the genre's gloomy, fatalistic worldview and the shadowy motivations of its characters.

Dark or harshly lit pictures can also trigger fear, tension, and a sense of impending doom. *Children of Men*'s (2006) bleak lighting depicts a dystopian London in the year 2027. It is a city of melancholy and despair whose infrastructure has deteriorated to the point of collapse, a situation further aggravated by a global infertility crisis; no child has been born in the last eighteen years. While TV monitors flash images of other nations ravaged by the destructive consequences of war, pollution, natural disasters, disease, and globalization, London, even though a sight of social oppression, presents the last stronghold. A blue-gray, dusty haze blankets scenes of destroyed buildings and piles of debris lying in the streets. Emigrants locked in cages line the city streets awaiting deportation. Director Alfonso Cuarón says that through the prism of the protagonist Theo (Clive Owen), who journeys from apathetic bystander to active engagement, the audience sees the bleak, chaotic surroundings more sharply. For Cuarón, the background visualizes the "ideological despair of late capitalism."[73]

The type of lighting used depends on the story being told. In his political thriller *Syriana* (2005), director Stephen Gaghan chose light as the unifying factor for the five interlocking stories and multiple locations. Cinematographer Robert Elswit said that he and Gaghan, "'wanted to minimize the contrast between the West [the United States and Geneva] and the Middle East, but not to exaggerate the difference. Stephen wanted the storylines and all of the locations to feel connected.'" The goal was to allow the physical environments to register difference, but for the lighting to emphasize their similarity.[74]

To symbolize parallel stories of struggle between death and rebirth and despair and hope, *World Trade Center*'s (2006) cinematographer, Seamus McGarvey, employed light and dark lighting throughout the movie. In the nine scenes where John McLoughlin (Nicolas Cage) and Will Jimeno (Michael Peña), two Port Authority police who were buried beneath slabs of concrete and twisted metal (the "hole") after the collapse of the World Trade Center, the initial scenes were very dark, with each subsequent scene becoming progressively lighter. To warm up and lighten the dark hole, McGarvey made strategic use of fires and the flashlights of the rescuers, until the final scene when John is raised from the hole into the daylight. Director Oliver Stone wanted the lighting in the entrapment and rescue scenes to symbolize the men's psychological journey from a near-death or dying experience to their recovery, a death-and-rebirth motif.

Simultaneously, as the scenes inside the hole grow lighter, outside New York goes from the bright morning light of early day before the attack to the darker, drearier light of night, where John's and Will's anxious wives and families wait, with dwindling hope, for any news of their survival.[75]

Shape

Lines and shapes are major structural elements of media presentations. Vertical lines impart a sense of dignity, class, and power. Advertisers for business and financial services construct images featuring vertical lines, block graphs, and towering skyscrapers to convey a sense of power, wealth, and stability.

Horizontal lines present a relaxed, calm, quiet, serene impression.

Mini Cooper

The large, bulging oval headlights, along with its "cute" name invoke a warm, happy response that makes the Mini Cooper appealing.

Travel and leisure advertisers design their ads with wide, horizontal, tranquil vistas, inviting the viewer to expand his or her horizons in a relaxed environment. In contrast, advertisements for products such as cars and sports equipment usually position the products on a diagonal trajectory to evoke a sense of escape, movement, or speed.

Diagonal lines are dynamic, which suggest action. Curved lines evoke a natural feeling of warmth and humor. Converging lines add depth and perspective to a presentation. Although individual lines have their own core meanings, they may be combined to make shapes such as circles, squares, and triangles, which carry added significance. Media communicators use line and shapes, both literally and symbolically, to construct their media productions, and their subsequent meanings. Advertisers, in particular, have homed in on scientific research that has identified "cute cues." Cuteness, as distinct from beauty, is round and soft and catches an appealing eye from observers.

Consequently, marketers, wishing to beef up sales, use graphics or design products that feature the "cute factor" to make their products appealing and increase sales. For example, "Sales of petite, willfully cute cars like the Toyota Prius and Mini Cooper soared, while those of noncute sport utility vehicles tanked."[76]

Circle

The circle is a geometric form that represents wholeness. It has no beginning or end. Its shape reminds us of the sun and the moon, symbolizing the vital aspect of life that psychologist Carl Jung calls the ultimate wholeness of the self.[77]

In magic lore, the circle is a protected and consecrated space that keeps out evil spirits. Ancient civilizations built walls around their cities for protection against potential enemies. In terms of interpersonal interactions, "social circles" exclude people by setting them apart.

For example, during a breakfast scene in Martin Scorsese's *The Age of Innocence* (1993), the diners discuss who is to be included in or excluded from their elite social circle. Throughout the conversation, the camera circumnavigates the table, symbolically marking the boundaries of inclusion and exclusion.[78]

Symbolic circles sometimes appear in a subtle artistic expression. After several episodes covering Mafia warfare, assassination plots, and numerous killings both inside and outside the mob circle, the last episode of the HBO series *The Sopranos* takes us to a family meal in a local diner. In the last scene, Tony (James Gandolfini) orders onion rings for the family (Tony nods approvingly after eating his). In the background, Journey's "Don't Stop Believin'" plays on the jukebox. Why the onion ring, a circle? One might think of the ring as symbolic of Tony's journey, a return to the beginning of his continuous cycle of Mafia violence. His life has been spared. He can return to his cycle of mob rule and violence. This concept is reinforced as singer Steve Perry bellows out the final line "Oh, the movie never ends / It goes on and on and on." Also, since many images of the Iraq war were seen on a TV within the series, it could be thought of as a larger metaphor referencing our U.S. foreign policy, or "global Mafia." Like the series itself, it is a symbolic recognition of violence's universal presence and eternal return, a symbol that is ingested but never discussed.[79]

Square

The square represents the material world. In contrast to the circle, the square is associated with four spatial orientations of horizontal and vertical directions. Navigation around the square's perimeter symbolizes the need to find one's way in a chaotic world. The right angle symbolizes justice and the true law.[80] Psychologically, its form gives the impression of firmness and stability, which explains its frequent use in symbols of corporate organizations.

In his treatise on democracy, Aristotle suggested that each town establish an *agora*. Agora is the Greek name for a marketplace, a consecrated open space that became the center of commercial, political, and religious activity. As time progressed, these agoras became known as public squares even though the ancient Greek agoras were rectangular. People assembled in locations such as the town hall, coffeehouse, and taverns for open and robust political debates and action.

Significantly, the television screen is either a square, or a rectangle. The engaged viewer symbolically enters the square and vicariously participates in the exchange of ideas. The electronic display of squares in television presentations has become the modern counterpart of the public square. For example, when on-site reporters converse with off-site guests, the off-site guests are framed in squares. Within these squares, dialogues occur, ideas spew out, and, sometimes, heated words are exchanged. These visual icons evoke images (illusions) of democracy where political discussions and community action take place. It should be noted that these off-site guests are chosen by the specific program's producers and may not address the larger issues and consequences in a political issue or debate. Instead of the either/or debate over military strategy dealing with Iraq and terrorism, a true democratic forum might include discussions about what terrorists want, what the root causes of terrorism are, and how to eliminate these causes.

Triangle

The triangle carries a wide variety of interpretations. In pre-Christian times, the philosopher Xenocrates viewed the equilateral triangle as "divine" and the isosceles as "demonic."[81] The Greek letter delta, triangular in form, was a symbol of cosmic birth. Early Christians used the triangle as a symbol of the Trinity, signifying the Father, the Son, and the Holy Ghost.

When triangles began to appear on ceramics, those pointing downward traditionally were interpreted as water symbols, suggesting falling rain:

Those pointing upward were seen as fire symbols, the direction of flames:

These triadic structures with three angles and three sides are recognizable patterns that help organize the visual world around us, producing a sense of psychological closure. Accordingly, Harry Remde says, man is a triadic creature and his unity and sense of wholeness depend on the balance of shapes like the triad.[82] The triangle exemplifies the intricate intertwining of the head that thinks, the body that performs, and the feeling that unites. Claude Bragdon explains, "Three is preeminently the number of architecture, because it is the number of our space, which is three-dimensional, and, of all the arts, architecture is most concerned with the expression of spatial relations. The division of a composition into three related parts is so universal that it would seem to be the result of an instinctive action of the human mind."[83]

The laws of polarity, which is the tension of two opposites, are never static. The dynamic interaction of two parts causes them to react upon each other to produce a third. Translated into metaphysical terms, the human conscience can be viewed as the third principle, the duality and tension between good and evil within each individual.[84] The conflicting images of the triangle's opposing sides (horizontal and vertical) are conjured up in such phrases as the Oedipal triangle, the love triangle, and the Bermuda triangle.

Media communicators effectively utilize the tensions created by *triangular relationships* in their presentations to comment on the dynamics of human relationships. Talk shows like *The Jerry Springer Show* frequently feature couples with problems. Either the host, acting as a third party, will provoke the tension, or a third party who is involved with the couple will serve as the catalyst.

Finally, the media are structured on an active triangular relationship revolving around the media communicator, the production, and the audience. Several interactive tensions regulate the flow of this relationship. First, the relationship between the communicator and his or her production depends on economic, political, and technical factors. Second, the production must attract an audience, which implies that there is a relationship between the work and the audience. The production must in some way respond the needs of the audience or it would not be produced or realize wide distribution. This leads to a third relationship, that between the communicator and the audience. The communicator must balance the tension that connects his own creative expression, economic viability, and meeting the needs of the audience. Finally, the communicator's work must attract an audience to ensure continued production of his or her work.

Movement

Motion is a unique characteristic of television and film. Movement has a dramatic impact on the spectator's viewing position. Art Silverblatt observes, "The principle of movement reduces the distance between illusion and reality and, in the process, also narrows the distinction between media and reality."[85] One category of movement in media presentations is *camera speed.* The variable speed of the camera allows the filmmaker to alter the rate at which events are depicted on-screen in order to send a desired message to the viewer. Slow motion stretches time, revealing details of motion that would not be perceptible in real time. Media communicators sometimes employ slow motion to create a romantic or poetic mood. Time-lapse photography shows the subtle nuances of changes over a period of time: The metamorphosis of a caterpillar or the opening of a flower can be condensed into a few seconds or minutes of screen time. Fast motion speeds up and condenses time. It is also frequently used for comedic effect, making normal actions look absurd. All these techniques allow us to comprehend events that happen too quickly or too slowly under normal time.

Camera movements establish the relationship that connects the camera, the subject, and the viewer:

- In a *pan shot,* the camera rotates on its axis, giving a panoramic view of the scene and situating the viewer within the scene's environment. A pan shot can also be used to follow the movement of characters across the screen.

- *Tilting* moves the camera up and down to follow the movement of the screen subject.
- In *tracking shots,* the camera moves on the ground in a vertical line, a horizontal line, or a vector.
- *Crane shots* are taken by cameras mounted on a cherry-picker, which allows shots to be taken from several directions. In both tracking and crane shots, the subject within the frame can be moving, or the camera can move while the subject remains still.

Combinations of these mechanical movements provide opportunities for the media communicator to reinforce themes and convey messages. Television's medical drama *ER* uses a fast, careening Steadicam that grabs viewers' attention, pulling them into the scene and engaging them in the journey as the camera swoops through crowded corridors and zooms in and out of trauma rooms. The rapid-pulsed camera movement evokes a feeling of vitality and flux that captures the tension and chaos of the emergency room.

Character movement constitutes a second type of motion employed in film and television. Because the audience's frame of reference is the camera, a character's movement toward or away from the camera triggers an emotional response in the viewer. The meaning behind a particular movement often is defined by the context of the situation. If the character is a villain, his or her movement toward the camera can seem aggressive, hostile, or threatening. The same action by an attractive character will feel friendly, inviting, or seductive. In general, forward movements by both types of characters are strong and confident. In contrast, movement away from the camera lens (and the audience) lessens the intensity of feeling, diminishes the threat of a villainous character, or signals abandonment.

Movement from the top to the bottom of the screen often has a negative connotation, suggesting moral transgression, failure of some sort, or unhappiness. A pivotal scene in *Raging Bull* (1980) is a brutal boxing match between Jake La Motta and Sugar Ray Robinson. At the end of the scene, there is a close-up of the rope that surrounds the boxing ring. The rope, resembling a blood vessel, crosses the entire screen. On the right side of the rope (screen), we see La Motta's blood transmitting a visceral resonance as we watch the blood's rhythmic descent from the top of the screen to the bottom (drip, drip, drip).

Similarly, lateral movement can carry significant meaning. In western

Raging Bull

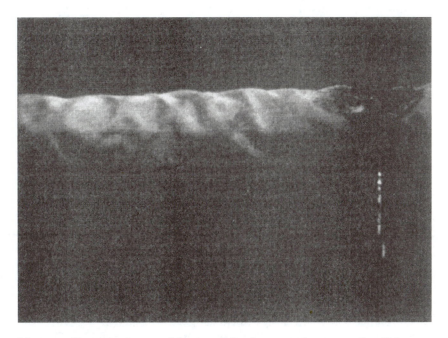

Movement from top to bottom of the screen often has a negative connotation. This scene from Martin Scorsese's *Raging Bull* (1980) features a close-up of blood dripping from the rope surrounding the ring. This movement symbolizes the brutality of the sport and its terrible cost to the two boxers. (*United Artists, 1980*)

cultures, movement from left to right is considered more natural, legitimate, and appropriate (in part because of the direction in which we read). Conversely, movement from right to left moves against the natural flow and connotes awkwardness, abnormality, or contrivance. For example, in *The Walker* (2007), the opening credits move across the screen from right to left, providing both a cue as to the sinister narrative that follows and a metaphor for the corrupt political arena in Washington, D.C.

Automobile commercials frequently rely on movement to dramatize the performance of the advertised vehicles. One study of 250 commercials concluded that 113 contained unsafe driving sequences; aggressive driving accounted for 85 percent, and speeding 55 percent of these sequences.[86] For example, the use of movement in an ad for the Cadillac Catera equates the movement of the automobile with speed, power, excitement, freedom, and risk taking. The ad shows the car suddenly swerving into the oncoming lane, crossing a double yellow line to pass a BMW and a Lexus. This pass takes place while the car is going uphill on a two-lane road. An approaching vehicle coming over the hill would have difficulty slowing down or avoiding a head-on collision with the Catera.[87] The movement of the automobile offers a sense of rebirth—that owning the car is a regenerative experience. The slogan for the ad—"Born to be alive"—reinforces this nonverbal cue.

The commercial also equates the movement of the vehicle with a sense of purpose, direction, and progress. This visual message bolsters the voice-over, which announces that people who drive a Catera are "born to lead." In order to be a leader, however, the ad visually shows that you must break the rules—the car is speeding and crossing the double yellow lines. Drivers in these types of commercials seem to be exempt from the law, since they are never apprehended by the police for speeding. Indeed, the risky driving style (accelerating rapidly, swerving around curves, etc.) appears normal, safe, and commonplace in the ad.

Scale

Scale refers to the relative size of two objects on a page or screen. Scale determines how the audience responds to the people and objects depicted and influences our perception of the events portrayed.

Epic films utilize scale to illustrate the adventures of heroic or legendary heroes and themes. Grand epic films such as *The Ten Commandments* (1956), *Star Wars* (1977), *Gandhi* (1982), *Dances with Wolves* (1990), *King Kong* (2005), and *Beowulf* (2007) contain striking contrasts between mortals and the vast landscape, enabling the viewer to experience the magnitude of grand themes such as humans' relationship with God and nature and the conflict between good and evil.

The relative size of objects on screen can also reveal cultural dynamics. Zhang Yimou's *Raise the Red Lantern* (1991) presents a confined world, as the camera repeatedly looks down on an enclosed courtyard. On either side of the courtyard, houses are adorned with red lanterns where the master's four wives live. The master resides in a large house situated at the end of the long courtyard. Throughout the film, the four wives can be seen through the confining frames of doorways and archways.

Occasionally we get a glimpse of an open vista from the rooftop, which is lit in cold twilight grays. Any sense of freedom quickly vanishes when the camera shifts to the secret tower on the roof. Murmurings

Raise the Red Lantern

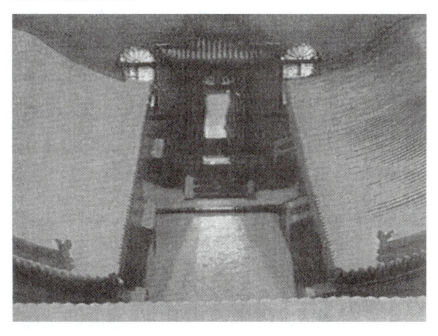

In *Raise the Red Lantern*, director Zhang Yimou uses space to reinforce the feeling of confinement and tension. (*Orion Classics, 1991*)

suggest that the tower holds previous wives who did not adjust well to the master's whims. The scale speaks powerfully to the stifled lives and emotions both of the women and the larger Chinese population who live under the "master" government.

In Robert Zemeckis's *Beowulf* (2007), the monstrously scaled Grendel and the larger-than-life dragon represent external evil and chaos. Beowulf represents order and has assumed the task of killing the marauding enemies who disrupt the social order in the Danish community of Heorot. This epic poem on which the film is based was written around 1100 C.E. and symbolically resonates with contemporary Western cultures, in which Grendel and the monster are metaphors for the anxieties centered on the larger-than-life "monsters," such as 9/11 and terrorists, that threaten boundaries and the status quo of a society.

Scale also refers to shots. According to film theorist Jacques Aumont, Alfred Hitchcock insisted that shot scale is "the single most important element within the director's arsenal for manipulating the audience's identification with a character."[88] In *No Country for Old Men* (2007), the wide-angle shots in the opening montage survey a vast, idyllic Texas landscape that lulls the audience into the mythical timelessness of pastoral tranquility. The close-ups, in contrast, command our attention as if to say, "Take notice." Directors Ethan and Joel Coen's syntax of close-ups represents the nature and existence of unrepentant, unrelenting evil as it intrudes on the boundaries of this bucolic western expanse. "This country is hard on people. You can't stop what's comin'," Ellis (Barry Corbin) informs Sheriff Bell (Tommy Lee Jones). Anton Chigurh (Javier Bardem) is an iconic creature symbolizing evil's random behavior. Bell muses that "he's just pretty much a ghost," while Bardem understands Chigurh as everything "but a human being."[89] Evil in this film is represented in the following ways:

- It sneaks up behind you. Chigurh strangles the sheriff's deputy from behind.
- It makes arbitrary decisions. Chigurh tosses a coin. The arbitrary heads or tails landing dictates the life or death outcome.
- It approaches at random on the highway. Chigurh shoots a man and steals his car.
- It penetrates locked doors and barriers. There is nowhere to hide.
- It travels in any direction. Overhead or boot-level shots of Chigurh's booted feet walking either to the camera or away indicate movement, not direction.
- It is dispassionate, has no feelings or empathy. Chigurh cleans his bleeding wound and removes a bullet from his leg devoid of any expression. He stares blankly at the ceiling after killing the sheriff's deputy.

Collectively, these close-ups visualize evil's arbitrary, ubiquitous presence and chart its course throughout the film, leaving it wandering free-floating at the film's ending.

The degree of attention, shared emotion, and viewer identification with a character depends on the relative size of the actors on the screen and the varying proximity of the camera's eye to each character. Depending on the type of shot, the viewers may focus total attention on one character or see the character as merely one figure within a larger context.

Currently, two shots in one frame, known as the split screen, are employed frequently in the TV series *24,* specifically during Jack Bauer's (Kiefer Sutherland) cell phone conversations. This storytelling technique allows viewers to focus on two characters and situations simultaneously.

Sound

Sound occurs in three different forms in media productions: dialogue, background sound, and music. Dialogue is written material that is intended to sound like conversation. A script may contain a great deal of information and complex layers of meaning. This material is presented very rapidly, like speech, so that the audience must pay attention to the message being delivered.

Background sound consists of the noises that normally occur within a given setting (e.g., crowd noise at a baseball game). Frequently, natural sound is added to the audio tracks of media presentations to add a feeling of realism. *Literal sounds* are directly connected to the visual source on the screen. For example, when you see an actor talking, you hear him at the same time. Because these events occur within the same space, time, and sound environment, literal sounds lend authenticity and furnish essential information to the narrative.

Films depicting a specific time period must use sounds particular to that era to bring authenticity to the story. For example, cars, rotary phones, and weapons such as Uzis and AK-47s produced different sounds in the 1970s than they do in the present day. Each city or location is also identified by its characteristic visuals or noises. You wouldn't see the Eiffel Tower or hear London's Big Ben in the background for a film taking place in Italy, nor would you hear crickets and frogs in bustling New York.

*Nonliteral sound*s are not source connected but instead support the image by adding meaning and emotional energy to the on-screen event. For example, loud, frightening noises may act as a cue, anticipating an action on-screen. Romantic music adds atmosphere to a love scene. A cartoon character's actions are punctuated by *bangs, pows,* and *whams.* Car chases, space battles, and martial arts fights frequently are energized by sound effects.

When media communicators construct images, they carefully select the right sounds to fit predetermined visual patterns. Herbert Zettl declares, "The sound rhythm acts like a clothesline on which you can hang shots of various length without sacrificing rhythmic continuity."[90] For example, quick edits may be hung on a line of staccato beats. Hanging a slow edit sequence on a fast rhythm or a fast edit sequence on a slow rhythm not only will add interest and texture to the montage but also will influence our emotional responses.

Sound may also reflect internal states of consciousness. *Dissonant* sounds can inform the audience of tensions stirring within a character, while melodic music can indicate tranquility. Music can also dramatize the visuals by punctuating the action, delineating characters, and providing a counterpoint to individual scenes.

By unlocking emotions, music can set a romantic mood, cue tension, and heighten suspense. In that sense, musical cues tell viewers how to feel about what they are watching. Music is also a way for media communicators to establish cultural, ethnic, or historical context in association with the images projected on-screen. For instance, Terence Blanchard, who composed the film score for *Eve's Bayou* (1997), combined jazz and regional folk into a traditional classical orchestration to capture the romantic epic life of the story's southern black family living in the Gothic bayou country of Louisiana.

Film director Martin Scorsese has a clearly defined purpose for each musical selection performed in his productions. For *The Departed* (2006), Scorsese wanted a "very dangerous and lethal" tango conveying "the idea of different themes of fate" played on guitars. He felt that "all the characters are sort of intertwined in a web, almost as if they tried to get away from each other. They're tied together almost like in a dance of death in a way, or like a tango, a very dangerous and lethal tango which ultimately does everyone in, in the story."[91]

When image and sound do not harmonize, however, the viewer must make an effort to reconcile this tension or ambiguity. Famed Russian film director Sergei Eisenstein designed many of his montages around what he called a "collision of opposites." He reversed the usual pattern of matching image with music by placing jarring music under placid images or vice versa.

Material Objects

Material objects (clothes, tools, weapons, art, furniture) in films not only indicate the time period in which the film takes place, but also inform the audience as to the social status of the characters and provide a deeper understanding of social interactions taking places within the film. Artifacts such as trains, weapons, and technology serve as metaphors for abstract ideas such as conflict, man versus machine, technology versus nature, and civilization versus wilderness, along with numerous other political, economic, and social changes taking place outside the world of the film.

For example, in *Talk to Me* (2007), a film about Washington, D.C., African American radio personality "Petey" Greene, African American station manager Dewey Hughes (Chiwetel Ejiofor) wears impeccably tailored suits with coordinating shirts and ties. His role model growing up was Johnny Carson, host of the *Tonight Show*. In the midst of a heated exchange over reasons for not hiring Petey as a talk show host, Petey acerbically spits out that Dewey is attempting to deny his blackness; Dewey, he remarks, acts and dresses like white man with tan skin. Later, as the bond between the two solidifies, Dewey emotionally reconnects with his heritage. His sartorial choices become more casual, reflecting those of his radio audience, signifying his comfort with his cultural roots as well as himself.

Special Effects

Special effects encompass a wide variety of techniques that can create almost whatever can be conjured by the imagination. Essentially, the art of special effects originates from three principal premises.

- Although film runs continuously, each frame of film can be photographed separately.
- Paintings, artwork, and miniature models can be filmed in a way that makes them appear as reality.
- Images and elements can be composited.[92]

At the turn of the century, Stuart Blackton realized that since film was a sequence of individual frames, he could stop the camera, alter the props and drawings, and then resume filming. The result was a continuous movement of letters, words, and faces. Blackton's imaginative experiment, entitled *Humorous Phases of Funny Faces* (1906), has been cited as the first animated cartoon, and, for the viewing audience, challenged the credo that "seeing is believing."[93]

Hollywood filmmakers then discovered that they could build miniature models and make them appear real if they "overcranked" the camera at faster than normal speeds. George Melies, credited as the father of special-effects filmmaking, combined stop-action with miniature models to create his famed image of a rocket ship in *A Trip to the Moon* (1902). Films such as Fritz Lang's *Metropolis* (1927) presented its gothic futuristic city with filmed models. The Emerald City and seventy other models were constructed and painted to perfect *the Wizard of Oz* (1939). Even in the original *King Kong* (1933), the mammoth gorilla, who stood towering over the Empire State Building in the film, was a mere eighteen-inch model.

Another notable special effect was rear-screen projection, in which a film is projected onto a screen behind the actors. Many a Hollywood car ride with scenic routes or city streets were scenes projected onto a matte screen, while actors sat "wheeling" a stationary car in the studio. Eventually, matte, blue, and split-screen shots allowed separate images to be composited into a single shot. For example, *Jurassic Park* (1993) managed to keep the massive dinosaur in the same frame with the characters rather than cutting from a shot of a dinosaur to a separate shot showing the actors' reactions.

Motion-controlled photography was a significant development in special-effects technology. Rather than keeping the camera stable and manipulating the model (set, figures, etc.), the camera moves through a stationary model. The use of this technique enabled the audience of *Star Wars* (1977) to travel with the characters through the star fields, planets, and laser bursts.

Today, computers composite many digitalized elements in the same frame, giving animators the ability to create (or destroy) entire worlds. Various elements (e.g., insects, spaceships, planets, people) can be inserted into a film without loss to the picture's quality. For example, the actors' physical presence was the only "real" thing in the film *300* (2006). Director Zack Snyder enlisted ten special-effects companies to create landscapes, creatures, and entire armies. He then blended the special-effects footage with the actors' performances, which were filmed before a blue screen on a digital back lot. To fully re-create Frank Miller's comic-book representation of the Spartans' battle on the cliffs of Thermopylae, "[e]very frame was manipulated and color shifted to create an intense color storm palette . . . computer generated elephants rear up and plummet off computer-generated cliffs . . . times speeds up for dramatic effect, then slows down to capture a balletic spear thrust," Snyder explained. [94]

Other special effects such as digitally recorded movements (motion-capture) situate human movements on computer-animated animals or computer-generated people. For example, in the film *Happy Feet* (2006*)*, penguin Mumble's toe-stomping performance was the digitally recorded "happy feet" of tap virtuoso Savion Glover. Taking the motion-capture a step further to a process known as "performance capture," the creators of *The Polar Express* (2004) used computerized cameras to record three-dimensional facial expressions and body movements from multiple actors. They used these images as a blueprint to build digital characters (the boy, the father, the conductor, the hobo, and Santa Claus). A single actor, Tom Hanks, voiced these five roles in the film.[95]

In *The Matrix Reloaded* (2003), the climatic fight scene begins when the real characters Neo (Keanu Reeves) and Agent Smith (Hugo Weaving) face off before launching into intricately choreographed martial arts warfare. As the combat progresses, Neo and Agent Smith, along with Smith's 100-plus reproductions, are undetectably transitioned into computer-generated virtual selves. Neo pivots in midair, hurls the black-tied Smith bodies skyward, flips, and shifts positions as he single-handedly battles the attacking Smith clones.[96]

Because special effects allow people to experience things they never experienced before, sometimes the viewer erroneously perceives this art of illusion as true. For example, in Mel Gibson's *The Passion of the Christ* (2004), Christian viewers familiar with the biblical narrative felt that Gibson's portrayal of the scourging and crucifixion "showed it the way it really was." Many American Catholics and their spiritual leaders claimed their faith was deepened and renewed after seeing the vivid presentation of the scourging and crucifixion on the screen.[97]

Yet these images perceived as authentic and truthful were, in fact, the result of digital wizardry. To achieve this "gospel truth," the film depicted 135 digital effects shots along with the traditional armory of cinematic tricks. An actor pantomimed the flaying of Jesus (Jim Caviezel). The whip that ripped through Jesus' body, dislodged his flesh, and created open wounds was a composited addition. Stephen Prince illustrates: "When the flagrum's teeth wrap around Jesus' side and rip out a large chunk of flesh, Caviezel was filmed clean, without corresponding wound prosthetics on his body, and he pantomimed Jesus' reaction. A body double was outfitted with the wound prosthetic (with the flagrum's teeth embedded in it), and was then filmed as the teeth were ripped out. This element was then digitally tracked onto

Caviezel's body with some digital painting used to hide the seams of the composite."[98]

Ultimately, special effects are the contemporary elements that deliver the same themes common to the earliest forms of literary endeavors. These effects are woven into stories that recount how people navigate obstacles, overcome fears (real or imagined), conquer demons (personal or political), and triumph over adversity.

Syriana: Media Literacy Analysis—Production Elements

Syriana (2005), inspired by Robert Baer's book *See No Evil*, recounts Baer's experience as a CIA operative. The film weaves a complicated tapestry of five interconnected stories:

- CIA operative Bob Barnes (George Clooney) bungles an assignment and begins to question his life's work.
- Corporate lawyer Bennett Holiday (Jeffrey Wright) finds a scapegoat (the illusion of due diligence) to satisfy the Department of Justice's probe into an oil company suspected of malfeasance.
- Middle Eastern prince Nasir Al-Subaai (Alexander Siddig) aspires to initiate economic and social reforms in his country. In a desperate attempt to curtail the hemorrhaging oil profits pouring out of his country, he awards a drilling contract to China, eliminating U.S. oil company Connex.
- Economic analyst Bryan Woodman (Matt Damon) becomes Nasir's confidant after the accidental death of his son at a party given by the aging emir.
- Pakistani emigrant worker Wasim Khan (Mazhar Munir) joins a charismatic fundamentalist group after being fired from his job.

The narrative moves in and out of several countries, following an ensemble cast in short, tense scenes that often end abruptly. The merger of the two Texas oil companies Connex and Killen is the running thread that binds these seemingly unrelated global events and disparate characters together.

Emerging from the circumstances of present-day complexities and global expansion, the film demonstrates how America's historical metaphors have extended into the Middle East. In *Syriana,* the Middle East is presented as the outgrowth of the American historical imperative, as expressed through beliefs and concepts of manifest destiny, as symbols of America's "mission" embedded in U.S. foreign policy.

Within this context, the triumvirate of oil, law, and the CIA form a tightly knit power structure with a unified mission to continue America's thirst for expansion, thus extending the cultural myth that it is "the right of our manifest destiny to overspread and to possess the whole of the continent which Providence [God] has given us."[99] It is this belief, formulated in 1845, that has become the symbol of expansion and progress throughout the world that fuels American life and America's dream.

The film shines its light on white supremacy participating in what America represents. As in the past, privileged white males dictate these cultural expressions of America. Bennett Holiday, the only black male in this elite enclave of men, is included because he has assumed the behavior, dress, and attitudes of the power players. In a scene at Jimmy Pope's (Chris Cooper) ranch, Holiday informs Pope that finding another sacrificial scapegoat will satisfy the U.S. Treasury's investigation and ensure the Connex/Killen merger, thus making Connex/Killen the fifth-largest oil and gas industry company in the world. Pope hands Holiday a plate of Texas barbecue, smiles, and responds, "Call me, Jimmy," signifying Holiday's inclusion in the "club."

Like manifest destiny's expansion of the American frontier, *Syriana* represents America's vision to remake the Middle East in the image of the United States. The future Middle East, "with its boarders redrawn on 'rational lines' and its governments all democratically elected, peace-loving, respectful of human rights—and their economies always open to the inroads of global (i.e., American) capitalism,"[100] will extend America's manifest mission under the rubric of spreading democracy.

In a scene reminiscent of the American frontier, we see a herd of wild animals running across the vast uncultivated expanse of Killen's president Jimmy Pope's ranch in Texas. While shooting one of the animals, Pope tells Holiday, "My granddaddy was a wildcatter; so was my daddy. That's how I got my start. Luck and hard work; nobody handed me shit." Jimmy then proceeds, "China's economy ain't growing as fast as it needs, and I'm damn proud of it." In a subsequent scene, while eating around the fire, Pope discusses the "proud members of the committee to liberate Iran." These scenes are rooted in the cultural expression of American individualism and competitiveness, and the myth of the American dream that through hard work you can achieve wealth and success. The wilderness expanse of Pope's ranch corresponds with America's vision for territorial expansion.

Syriana connects this idea of manifest destiny to present-day global expansion. For example, in a hunting scene early in the film, Pope aims his rifle and shoots his moving target (symbolizing the taming of the West). This foreshadows a later scene, in which the CIA, from a distant monitor, pinpoint their targets (Prince Nasir and his entourage) as they move across the vast expansive desert, and blow up Nasir's car.

Nasir, who thwarted America's expansion and control of oil profits, informs Woodman, "I accepted the Chinese bid, the highest bid, and suddenly, I'm a terrorist, a godless communist." This rejection of America's vision gives the CIA reason to identify Nasir as hostile to American interests and a threat to national security. The CIA places Nasir on their high-priority hit list. Symbolically, both sequences represent the reenactment of the taming of the frontier and extend the notion of American expansion to the global frontier in order to secure the national dream of progress.

Ironically, Nasir's brother Prince Meshal (Akbar Kurtha) is shown catering to U.S. business interests. The differing U.S. attitude toward the two brothers speaks to our concept of liberalness. If foreigners sign on to the American ideological mission, they are considered good and, therefore, included, but anyone resisting America's ambition is deemed evil and targeted for assassination.

Significantly, all of this global manipulation takes place in natural light rather than hidden in dark shadows. Director Stephen Gaghan employs natural lighting to provide continuity throughout the film's multiple locations, to make them "feel connected," and "to emphasize their similarities."[101]

Gaghan also contends that "[t]here are no good guys and bad guys." The film, he says, avoids creating a black-and-white world.[102] Baer notes that *Syriana* "became the vehicle for the things I [Baer] couldn't say in writing." The book, he said, needed CIA approval, but information shared with Gaghan did not. According to Baer, the film reveals "a lot more truth" about the "illusion of intelligence," and the "form of corruption . . . we live by."[103]

Consequently, the film's quasi-documentary style and natural lighting illuminates clearly what America is up to and what America is about. Emerging out of the circumstances of present-day complexities and global expansion, the film demonstrates how America's historical metaphors are reconfigured and acted out with the expanding frontier into the Middle East. Throughout the film, the characters associated with Connex and Killen oil, Whiting law firm, and the CIA stay on message. They form a tightly knit power structure with a unified mission that runs straight through the multiple story lines involving corruption, obsession, greed, deception, torture, and murder that are delivered in bits and pieces with choppy editing, and whisks the audience in and out of locations almost in midsentence, conveying a sense of instability and fragmentation.

The subjective camera POV and blocking "create a personal perspective that [Gaghan] wanted with each story." They reinforce ideological differences between the characters, said cinematographer Robert Elswit, and allow the audience to establish an intimate connection with each character's point of view.[104]

As the scenes move to various locations around the globe, *costumes* inform the audience about the position, status, and ethnicity of each character and country. The emir wears the traditional Arab clothing, while his two sons, who were educated in Europe and America, wear both tailored Western suits and traditional Arab garb. Barnes's rumpled clothes befit his aging veteran CIA status. In contrast, lawyer Bennett Holiday wears stylish, expensive suits, representing his meticulous nature and due diligence.

In a scene in his garden, Whiting (the great white father) is trimming away dead roses. He wears a white brimmed hat and gloves. Symbolically, he deselects what does not enhance his and America's privileged environment. The protective attire symbolically shields him from any "damaging rays" or "thorns" that might diminish his and America's power. As Connex oil's chief counsel, he is to remove any "thorns" that will interfere with the merger. One of these thorns is the Justice Department, which is probing Killen for suspected shady dealings when the firm acquired its drilling rights in Kazakhstan and, consequently, threatening the merger. Whiting instructs Bennett, "If there is something to find, I expect you to get it before they [the U.S. attorney's office] do." He then looks up and remarks, "At my firm I have a lot of sheep who think they're lions." He pauses, makes eye contact with Bennett, and continues, "Maybe you're a lion who everyone thinks is a sheep."

In addition, costumes reveal Nasir's desire to initiate social and economic reforms within his own country. His sincerity is indicated by his wife's attire. She wears a head covering, but her clothing is modern and Western. She also speaks freely when present in male gatherings.

Thus, in *Syriana,* production elements are used to reinforce the message that progress, free enterprise, and expansion are a cluster of concepts that America has internalized as reality and actualized as if they were ordained by divine providence to advance America's cry of liberty, justice, and equality. In reality, however, they are the enduring symbolic strategies manifested in the actions of those who wish to maintain dominance and power.

Conclusion

I. Editing
  A. One way to understand the editing process is to examine a variety of newspapers or television programs appearing on the same day.
    1. How much information can be covered in these brief segments?
    2. What important stories have been ignored or downplayed?

3. What important details are left out and why?
4. Who orders the segments and to whom are they important?
5. What is the primary purpose of most lead segments?
B. Which *topics* have been included or omitted from a program?
   1. Are the segments informative or are they sensationalized?
C. When looking at film or television, examine how shots are pieced together (edited) to convey the story being told.
   1. Emphasis: Are there any individual shots inserted to convey messages that are independent of the story being presented?
   2. Contrast: How does a sequence of shots relate to the sequence connected to it?
   3. Editing for rhythm: What is the duration of each shot in the edited sequence?
      a. What effect does the duration of the shot have on the viewer?
   4. Spatial rhythm: How does the content of each shot differ from the others?
   5. Temporal and spatial continuity: What do the juxtaposed images say about chronological time, physical space, and relationship with people, places, and events, past or present?
D. Arrangement
   1. In what order are the news segments arranged?
   2. Are lead stories of national, international, or local importance?
   3. Are the segments informative or are they sensationalized?
II. Composition: This refers to how the elements are placed within the frame.
A. Where are the images placed within the screen or page?
B. What is the audience's emotional response to the images?
C. Where does the article appear on the page?
D. How does the composition direct the audience's viewing?
E. Is the composition set up to help the audience envision what is outside the frame?
III. Colors: Colors convey symbolic meanings that evoke a wide range of emotional responses.
A. How does the color set the mood and tone of a production?
B. What feeling do the colors evoke?

C. Do the colors convey meanings that correlate with or contrast with the content of the production?
IV. Lines: Lines are basic structures employed in media productions to convey meaning.
  A. What lines are used?
  B. How do they support the message given by the media communicator?
  C. What is the purpose of the vertical lines in the production?
    1. Horizontal lines
    2. Diagonal—movement
    3. Curved—natural
    4. Converging—depth perspective
V. Shapes. Shapes carry symbolic meanings that support the overall meaning of the production.
  A. What are the major shapes employed in the production?
  B. Do the shapes emotionally support the message of the media communicator?
VI. Lighting. The style of lighting sets the tone and helps focus our attention. It supports moods and themes in the production and impacts the viewer's emotions.
  A. What types of lighting are used: dim, bright, hard, or soft?
  B. How does the lighting support the mood and theme of the production?
  C. Does the lighting cast shadows?
  D. What do the shadows represent?
VII. Scale. Scale refers to the relative size of two sets of dimensions.
  A. How does the size of the production relate to the theme being communicated?
  B. How do the shot scales relate to the overall theme?
VIII. Angle. Angle refers to the position the camera takes in viewing the object or subject on the screen.
  A. Are you looking up or down at the subject or object, or viewing the image at eye level?
  B. How does the use of angles reinforce themes in the presentation?
IX. Movement. Movement is a unique characteristic of television and film.
  A. Camera speed refers to the ability of the camera to alter the rate at which events are depicted on-screen.
    1. Is the production in fast, slow, or time-lapse motion?

     B. Camera movements establish the relationship among the camera, the subject, and the viewer.
        1. How does the camera follow the subject or object on the screen?
        2. What is the movement of the camera—up or down, side to side?
     C. Character movement refers to how the character moves in relation to the camera's lens.
        1. Which direction does the character move in relation to the lens?
        2. How does the character's or object's movement affect the audience's emotions?

X. Point of view. Point of view refers to the source who conveys the information.
     A. Who is telling the story?
     B. What information is being conveyed?
     C. How does it orient the viewer to the story?
     D. How does it affect the audience's sympathies?
     E. Whose view is missing, and is it important?

XI. Sound and music. Sound and music refer to the sounds that are either directly related to or support the visuals on the screen.
     A. What information do the sounds convey?
     B. Are the sounds directly related to the screen images?
     C. Do the sounds signal an off-screen event?
     D. How do the sound and music cue the audience's emotions?
     E. Does the music correspond with the image on the screen, or is it directly oppositional to what is being presented?

XII. Graphics. Graphics refers to the figurative images used to illustrate the text.
     A. Graphic representations
        1. What is the source of this information?
        2. Does the source information have any bias?
        3. Who are the groups being represented?
        4. Does the graph or chart set up a "we" and "us"?
        5. What is the function of the graphic representation?
        6. How does the title relate to the content?
        7. Do the visuals accurately present the information?
        8. Does the graphic representation leave out significant details? Explain.

    B. Typography
        1. Is the type plain or decorative, heavy or light?
        2. What meaning does the typeface convey?
        3. Does the typeface convey any emotion?
        4. What is the spacing between the type?
        5. Are the headlines in lowercase or uppercase letters?
        6. What does the typeface in the headline say about the event?
        7. How are the headlines arranged?

XIII. Connotation
    A. Connotative words refer to the meaning associated with a word beyond its literal, denotative definition.
        1. What associated meanings are attached to the word?
        2. What cultural associations are attached to the word?
        3. What personal association is attached to the word?
    B. Connotative image refers to the meanings given to the image through its use in a society.
        1. What are the cultural associations of the image?
        2. Is there a universal meaning attached to the image?
        3. Does the image evoke an emotional response?
        4. Can you identify why the image evokes the specific response?
        5. Does the combination of images change the meaning?

XIV. Special effects. Special effects are the technical activities that are manipulated and combined to deliver images.
    A. Why does the media communicator use special effects in the program?
    B. What emotions do the special effects evoke?
    C. What is the role of the special effects in the film?
    D. What is the relationship between the created world of special effects and the real world?

Notes

CHAPTER 1

1. Raymond Williams, *Keywords: A Vocabulary of Culture and Society* (London: Oxford University Press, 1995), p. 118.

2. Linda Holtzman, interview by Art Silverblatt, St. Louis, MO, January 23, 1998.

3. Nikolai Zlobin, interview by Art Silverblatt, St. Louis, MO, December 2, 1997.

4. Len Masterman, "Shifting the Power, Addressing the Ideology," *Mediacy* 13, no. 2 (Spring 1991): 1–6.

5. "World Development Report 2002," Brookings Institution, http://www.brookings.edu/global.aspx, accessed September 29, 2007.

6. Neil MacFarquhar, "In Tiny Arab State, Web Takes on Ruling Elite," *New York Times,* January 16, 2006.

7. Ibid.

8. Aleksander Grigoryev, interview by Art Silverblatt, Washington, DC, November 2001.

9. Frederic M. Sherer and David Ross, *Industrial Market Structure and Economic Performance,* 3rd ed. (Boston: Houghton Mifflin, 1990).

10. Ben Bagdikian, *The Media Monopoly,* 5th ed. (Boston: Beacon Press, 1997), pp. 47–48.

11. Katrina vanden Heuvel, "Postal Rates Increase," DemocracyNow! June 6, 2007, http://www.Democracynow.com.

12. David Wallis, "Malice in the Middle," *Slate,* December 27, 2006.

13. James Barron and Campbell Robertson, "Page Six, Staple of Gossip, Reports on Its Own Tale," *New York Times,* May 19, 2007.

14. "The State of the News Media, 2006," Project for Excellence in Journalism, http://www.stateofthenewsmedia.org/2006.

15. "FCC OKs Laxer Media Ownership Rules," DemocracyNow! December 19, 2007, http://www.Democracynow.com.

16. Jeremy Iggers, "Get Me Rewrite!" *Utne Reader,* September 1, 1997, p. 46.

17. Ibid.

18. Frank Rich, "The Price Is Right," *New York Times,* January 10, 1988, p. A25.

19. Scott Collins, "Looking for Buzz, ABC Will Show Madison Avenue Its Scripts."

20. Ibid.

21. Michito Kakutani, "Portrait of the Artist as a Focus Group," *New York Times Magazine,* March 1, 1998, p. 26.

22. Jacques Steinberg, "After the Peaks of Journalism, Budget Realities," *New York Times,* June 14, 2004, p. C1.

23. Howard Kurtz, "The Big News: Shrinking Reportage," *Washington Post,* March 13, 2006.

24. "Cuts in Personnel," Democracy Now! http://www.democracynow.org/2007/2/19/headlines (July 19, 2007)

25. "Chicago Deal to Pay $20 Million in Police Torture Case Hits Roadblock," Democracy Now! December 13, 2007, http://www.democracynow.org.

26. Ibid.

27. Tripp Frochlichstein, interview by Art Silverblatt, St. Louis, MO, March 10, 1998.

28. Ibid.

29. Robert Pear, "Ruling Says White House's Medicare Videos Were Illegal," *New York Times,* May 20, 2004, p. A24.

30. "Minorities Gain on Local Television News Staffs," Radio and Television News Directors Association, July 6, 2006, www.aaja.org/news/releases/2006_07.

31. Ibid.

32. Fewer Women in Newsroom," DemocracyNow! June 6, 2007, http://www.Democracynow.com.

33. Kim Gordon, interview by Art Silverblatt, St. Louis, MO, December 8, 1997.

34. "During Wartime," Editorial, *New York Times,* June 13, 2006, p. A22.

35. Scott Shane, "For Liberal Bloggers, Libby Trial Is Fun and Fodder," *New York Times,* February 15, 2007.

36. Ibid.

37. Joe Baltake, "On Internet, Everyone Is a Critic," *St. Louis Post-Dispatch,* July 4, 1997, p. E1.

38. Gordon interview, December 8, 1997.

39. Doreen Carvajal, "1,000 Journalists Killed in 10 Years While Reporting," *New York Times,* March 7, 2007.

40. Gordon interview, December 8, 1997.

41. Seth Faison, "In China, Better Unread Than Read," *New York Times,* September 7, 1997, section 4, p. 5.

42. Randy Dotinga, "Are You a Public Figure?" *Wired,* November 9, 2005. www.wired.com/politics/raw/news/2005/11/69411, accessed May 23, 2009.

43. "TV Networks Devote Attention to Ramsey Trial," Democracy Now! August 21, 2006, http://www.democracynow.com.

44. Harold D. Laswell, *Power and Personality* (New York: W.W. Norton, 1948), chap. 6.

45. John C. Merrill, John Lee, and Jonathan J. Friedlander, *Modern Mass Media* (New York: Harper and Row, 1990), p. 428.

46. David S. Cloud and Jeff Gerth, "Muslim Scholars Were Paid to Aid U.S. Propaganda," *New York Times,* January 2, 2006.

47. John Tierney, "The Pentagon's Vanity Press," *New York Times,* December 3, 2005, p. A.19.

48. Cloud and Gerth, "Muslim Scholars Were Paid."

49. Abby Goodnough, "U.S. Paid 10 Journalists for Anti-Castro Reports," *New York Times,* September 9, 2006.

50. Josef Joffe, "America the Inescapable," *New York Times Magazine,* June 8, 1997, pp. 38–43.

51. Panrawee Pantumchinda, "Cosmopolitan Magazine in Thailand" (unpublished paper, Webster University, March 5, 1998), p. 8.

52. Marc Lacey, "Why They Booed Her in Mexico," *New York Times,* June 3, 2007, section 4, p. 7.

53. Tyler Cowen, "For Some Developing Countries, America's Popular Culture Is Resistible," *New York Times,* February 22, 2007, p. C3.

54. Pankaj Mishra, "Hurray for Bollywood," *New York Times,* February 28, 2004, p. A15.

55. Cowen, "For Some Developing Countries."

56. Art Silverblatt, *Media Literacy: Keys to Interpreting Media Messages,* 3rd ed. (Westport, CT: Praeger Publications, 2008).

57. Sut Jhally and Justin Lewis, "Enlightened Racism: The Cosby Show," *Audiences, and the Myth of the American Dream* (Boulder, CO: Westview Press, 1992).

58. Scott Simon, "Affluenza," KETC/PBS, September 19, 1997.

59. Ibid.

60. Ibid.

61. Eduardo Porter, "Happiness for Sale," *New York Times,* December 26, 2007, p. A26.

62. Ibid.

63. Simon, "Affluenza."

64. Stuart Ewan, "The Public Mind: All Consuming Images," Public Broadcasting Service, November 8, 1989.

65. Simon, "Affluenza."

66. Ibid.

67. Robin Anderson, *Consumer Culture and TV Programming* (Boulder, CO: Westview Press, 1995), p. 15.

68. James Melvin Washington, ed., *A Testament of Hope: The Essential Writings of Martin Luther King, Jr.* (San Francisco: Harper and Row, 1986), p. 286.

69. Michael Schaller, "Godzilla, Present and Past," *New York Times,* May 16, 1998, p. A27.

70. Ibid.

71. Sharon Waxman, "A Hollywood 'Candidate' for the Political Season," *New York Times,* July 28, 2004, p. E1.

72. Ibid.

73. Michael Parenti, *Make Believe Media* (New York: St. Martin's Press, 1992), p. 60.

74. Simon Romero, "Chávez Takes Over Foreign-Controlled Oil Projects in Venezuela," *New York Times,* May 2, 2007.

75. Richard Paul and Linda Elder, *The Thinkers Guide to Fallacies: The Art of Mental Trickery and Manipulation* (Dillon Beach, CA: Foundation for Critical Thinking, 2004), p. 2.

76. Christopher Goodwin, "Ku Klux Klan Cleans Up Image," *London Sunday Times,* August 18, 1996.

77. Fredrick McKissack Jr., "Nike Memo Details Abuses in Asian Factory," *St. Louis Post-Dispatch,* November 21, 1997, p. C19.

78. Ibid.

79. "Nike: Key Statistics for Nike," Yahoo Finance! http://finance.yahoo.com/q/ks?s=nke, accessed August 22, 2006.

80. Ibid.

81. "Cheney Criticizes 'Sensitive War' Idea," *St. Petersburg Times* (Florida), August 13, 2004, p. 15A.

82. Paul Krugman, "Three-Card Maestro," *New York Times,* February 18, 2005, p. A23.

83. Ibid.

84. Paul and Elder, *The Thinkers Guide to Fallacies,* p. 18.

85. Clark Hoyt, "Fact and Fiction on the Campaign Trail," Public Editor, *New York Times,* December 2, 2007.

86. Daniel Okrent, "Numbed by the Numbers, When They Just Don't Add Up," *New York Times,* section 4, p. 2.

87. Michael Cooper, "Giuliani Boasts of Surplus; Reality Is More Complex," *New York Times,* August 25, 2007.

88. "Bush Says U.S. Will Keep Current Troop Level of 138,000 in Iraq," Xinhua, May 25, 2004, http://www.xinhua.org.

89. Paul and Elder, *The Thinkers Guide to Fallacies,* p. 22.

90. George Orwell, *Nineteen Eighty-Four* (New York: Harcourt Brace, 1949), p. 200.

91. William Lutz, *The New Doublespeak: Why No One Knows What Anyone Is Saying Anymore* (New York: HarperCollins, 1996), pp. 6, 7, 176, 241, 258, 190.

92. Jim Drinkard, "Lobbying Groups Play Distracting Name Game," Associated Press, *St. Louis Post-Dispatch,* December 23, 1997, p. B1.

93. Molly Ivins, "Who Is Funding Those Who Are Debating Global Warming?" *St. Louis Post-Dispatch,* December 16, 1997, p. B7.

94. Drinkard, "Lobbying Groups," p. B1.

95. Nikolai Zlobin, interview by Art Silverblatt, St. Louis, MO, February 3, 1998.

96. Joe Williams, "A Behind-the-Last-Scenes Look at Hollywood Endings," *St. Louis Post-Dispatch,* May 5, 2002.

97. Ibid.

98. Internet Movie Database, http://www.imdb.com./Pretty Woman, "Tagline."

100. Henry A. Murray, "The Possible Nature of a 'Mythology' to Come," *Myth and Mythmaking,* ed. Henry A. Murray (New York: George Braziller, 1960), p. 338.

100. Daniel Chandler, "Semiotics for Beginners," www.aber.ac.uk/media/Documents/S4B/semiotic.html, accessed April 1, 2006.

101. John Cawelti, "Myth, Symbol, and Formula," *Journal of Popular Culture* 8 (Summer 1974): 1–10.

102. George Gerbner, "The 1998 Screen Actors Guild Report: Casing the American Scene," November 16, 1999, http://www.media-awareness.ca/english/resources/research_documents/reports/diversity/american_scene.cfn, accessed May 23, 2009.

103. Douglas Kellner, "TV, Ideology, and Emancipatory Popular Culture," *Socialist Review* 9, no. 3 (1979): 13–53.

104. James M. Collins, "The Musical," in *Handbook of American Film Genres,* ed. Wes D. Gering (New York: Greenwood Press, 1988), p. 272.

105. Ibid.

106. Theo Emery, "In Nashville, Sounds of Political Uprising from the Left," *New York Times,* August 19, 2006.

107. Ibid.

108. Gloria Goodale, "Reality TV's Fall Mix: Dogs, Dating, and Circus Stunts," *Christian Science Monitor,* August 9, 2002, p. 18.

109. Darlene Wagner, "Production Analysis: Titanic" (unpublished paper, Webster University, 1997).

110. Jane Caputi, "Charting the Flow; the Construction of Meaning Through Juxtaposition in Media Texts," *Journal of Communication Inquiry* 15, no. 2 (Summer 1991): 32–47.

111. Gary Schwitzer, "Doctoring the News: Miracle Cures, Video Press Releases, and TV Medical Reporting," *Quill,* November–December 1992, pp. 19–21.

112. "Top Reporters Are Ignoring the Top Issue," Video: "What Are They Waiting For?" http://www.whataretheywaitingfor.com.

113. Angela Rollins, "Tommy Hilfiger and the American Ideal" (unpublished paper, Webster University, March 2, 1998).

114. Bill Nichols, *Ideology and the Image* (Bloomington: Indiana University Press, 1981), pp. 3–5.

115. Frank J. Prial, "We'll Have the Chateau Cuervo," *New York Times,* March 15, 1998, section 4, p. 2.

116. Nichols, *Ideology and the Image,* p. 290.

117. Religious Tolerance, Ontario Consultants on Religious Tolerance, http://www.religioustolerance.org/jud_blib.htm.

118. Britney, "Review of Cinderella II," Internet Movie Database, http://www.imdb.com.

CHAPTER 2

1. *Mediacy* (Winter 1990): 10.

2. Byron Reeves, "Children's Understanding of Television People," in *Children Communicating,* ed. E. Wartella (Newbury Park, CA: Sage Publications, 1979), p. 132.

3. Diane Toroian, "The Impact of Pop Lyrics Depend on Who's Listening," *St. Louis Post-Dispatch,* January 22, 1998, p. D1.

4. Charles W. Turner, Bradford W. Hesse, and Sonja Peterson-Lewis, "Naturalistic Studies of the Long-Term Effects of Television Violence," *Journal of Social Issues* 42 (1986): 51–73.

5. Richard Frost and John Stoffer, "The Effects of Social Class, Gender, and Personality on Psychological Responses to Filmed Violence," *Journal of Communication* 37 (Spring 1987): 29–46.

6. David Buckingham, *Moving Images: Understanding Children's Emotional Responses to Television* (Manchester: Manchester University Press, 1996), p. 3.

7. Barrie Gunter, *Dimensions of Television Violence* (New York: St. Martin's Press, 1985).

8. Reeves, "Children's Understanding of Television People," p. 143.

9. David Buckingham, *Moving Images,* p. 145.

10. Frost and Stoffer, "Effects of Social Class," p. 30.

11. David Buckingham, *Moving Images,* p. 145.

12. Ibid., p. 150

13. Ibid.

14. Buckingham, *Moving Images,* pp. 110–12.

15. Len Masterman, *Teaching the Media* (New York: Routledge, 1988), p. 239.

16. Ibid.

17. Masterman, *Teaching the Media,* p. 239.

18. Douglas Kellner, *Media Culture—Cultural Studies, Identity and Politics Between the Modern and the Postmodern* (London: Routledge, 1995), p. 32.

19. Masterman, *Teaching the Media,* p. 239.

20. Kenneth Burke, *The Philosophy of Literary Form: Studies in Symbolic Action,* 2d ed. (Baton Rouge: Louisiana State University Press, 1967), p. 304.

21. John W. Hesley and Jan G. Hesley, *Rent Two Films and Let's Talk in the Morning: Using Popular Movies in Psychotherapy,* 2d ed. (New York: John Wiley and Sons, 2001).

22. Jane Anne Phillips, "Premature Burial," in *The Movie That Changed My Life,* ed. David Rosenberg (New York: Penguin Group, 1991), pp. 37–49; here p. 42.

23. Gloria Johnson Powell, "The Impact of Television on the Self-Concept Development of Minority Group Children," in *Television and the Socialization of the Minority Child,* ed. Gordon L. Berry and Claudia Mitchell-Kernan (New York: Academic Press, 1982), p. 107.

24. Esther B. Fein, "The End of 'Seinfeld' Has Hit Show's Fans Grieving," *New York Times,* December 27, 1997, p. A28.

25. Ibid.

26. Buckingham, *Moving Images,* p. 161.

27. Aimee Dorr, "Television and Its Socializing Influences in Minority Children," in *Television and the Socialization of the Minority Child,* ed. Gordon L. Berry and Claudia Mitchell-Kernan (New York: Academic Press, 1982), p. 27.

28. Ibid.

29. W. Andrew Collins, "Children's Comprehension of Television Content," in *Children Communicating,* ed. Ellen Wartella (Beverly Hills, CA: Sage Publications, 1979), pp. 72–73.

30. Ibid., pp. 71–72.

31. Ibid., pp. 76–77.

32. Judy McMillan, interview with the author, St. Louis, MO, February 26, 1998.

33. Jane Sumner, "Isabella Rossellini—Without Makeup," *St. Louis Post-Dispatch,* July 16, 1997, p. 3E.

34. Camille Sweeney, "In a Chat Room You Can Be N E 1," *New York Times Magazine,* October 17, 1999, pp. 66–70.

35. Tony Pierro, "Local Blogs Offer Variety of Outlooks on Life," *Charleston Gazette* (West Virginia), February 4, 2007, Forecast, p. P3J.

36. Vanessa De Groot, "Life Is an Open Book," *Courier Mail* (Australia), February 12, 2007, Today section, p. 33.

37. 97. John Tropea, "Blogs: the man ways 'many' come together," Newstex Web Blogs. Newstex LLC: Copyright 2007 Library Clips. June 7, 2007.

38. Ellen Schneider, "'E.C.U.': Home for Video Diarists," *Current,* March 6, 1995, p. 2.

39. Aspen Institute, National Leadership Conference on Media Literacy, Queenstown, MD, December 7–9, 1992.

40. Elizabeth Thoman, "Blueprint for Responsive-Ability," *Media and Values* 35 (Spring 1986): 12–14.

41. Jeffrey A Chester and Anthony Wright, "A Twelve Step Program for Media Democracy," *Nation* (June 3, 1996): 9–15.

42. Masterman, *Teaching the Media,* pp. 31–32.

43. Barry Duncan, "Media Literacy at the Crossroads: Some Issues, Probes and Questions," *History and Social Science Teacher* 24, no. 4 (Summer 1989), pp. 205–209.

CHAPTER 3

1. Dale G. Leathers, *Successful Nonverbal Communication: Principles and Applications* (Boston: Allyn and Bacon, 1997), p. 6.

2. Alex Williams, "Live From Miami, a Style Showdown," *New York Times,* September 26, 2004.

3. R. Rosenthal, J. Hall, M.R. DiMatteo, R. Rogers, and D. Archer, *Sensitivity to Nonverbal Communication: The PONS Test* (Baltimore: Johns Hopkins University Press, 1979).

4. K.L. Burns and E.G. Beier, "Significance of Vocal and Visual Channels in the Decoding of Emotional Meaning," *Journal of Communication* 23 (1973): 118–30.

5. R. Ekman, W.V. Friesen, and R. Ellsworth, *Emotion in the Human Face* (New York: Pergamon, 1972).

6. Ibid.

7. Joshua Meyrowitz, *No Sense of Place.*

8. Remarks by Barbara Cubin, YouTube, http://www.youtube.com.

9. Erving Goffman, "Gender Advertisements," *Studies in the Anthropology of Visual Communication* 3, no. 2 (1976): 100.

10. Ibid., p.102.

11. Ibid., p. 105.

12. Ibid., p. 121.

13. Ibid., p.123.

14. Jane Bruns, interview by Art Silverblatt, St. Louis, MO, March 17, 1998.

15. Associated Press, "Study of Immigrants Links Lighter Skin and Higher Income," *New York Times,* January 28, 2007, p. A19.

16. "Global Lip Customs," Blistex Web site, http://www.blistex.com.

17. Elizabeth Olson, "Better Not Miss the Buss," *New York Times,* April 6, 2006, section G, p. 1.

18. Joan Vennoch, "Bush, Merkel, and the Quickie Neck Rub," Op-Ed, *Boston Globe,* July 23, 2006, p. E9.

19. Ibid.

20. Lorri Antosz Benson, "Jerry Is King of the Talk Show World, but His Show May Be Springing a Leak," *New York Times,* March 22, 2004, p. E1.

21. Judy Foreman, "A Conversation with Paul Ekman; the 43 Facial Muscles That Reveal Even the Most Fleeting Emotions," *New York Times,* August 5, 2003, p. F5.

22. Erving Goffman, "Gender Advertisements," *Studies in the Anthropology of Visual Communication* 3, no. 2 (1976): 121.

23. Tripp Frohlichstein, *Media Training Handbook* (St. Louis: MediaMasters, 1991), p. 31.

24. Jan Hargrave, *Let Me See Your Body Talk* (Dubuque: Iowa: Kendall Hunt, 1995), p. 209.

25. Erving Goffman, "Gender Advertisements," *Studies in the Anthropology of Visual Communication* 3, no. 2 (1976): 116.

26. Desmond Morris, *Bodytalk* (New York: Crown Trade Paperbacks, 1994), p. 189.

27. Olson, "Better Not Miss the Buss," p. 1.

28. Dale G. Leathers, *Successful Nonverbal Communication: Principles and Applications,* 3d ed. (Boston: Allyn and Bacon, 1997), p. 403.

29. Richard E. Porter and Larry A. Samovar, *Communication Between Cultures,* 2d ed. (Belmont, CA: Wadsworth, 1995), p. 203.

30. Mattias Thuresson, http://www.imdb.com/title/tt0031359/plotsummary.

31. Pamela Cooper, *Speech Communication for the Classroom Teacher,* 3d ed. (Scottsdale, AZ: Gorsuch Scarisbrick, 1988).

32. Leathers, *Successful Nonverbal Communication,* p. 122.

33. Stephanie Rosenbloom, "Holding Hands: A Simple Touch of Intimacy Never Fades Away," *New York Times,* January 15, 2007.

34. Leathers, *Successful Nonverbal Communication,* p. 145.

35. Kathryn Perkins, "Study: Sex, Age, Work Against Women," *Sacramento Bee,* November 30, 1996.

36. Tom Zeller, "Word for Word/Preppies and Hipsters; Taxonomies of Style: It Takes More Than Scoots and Berries to Be Deck," *New York Times,* January 12, 2003, section 4, p. 7.

37. Eugene Rosow, *Born to Lose: The Gangster Film in America* (Oxford: Oxford University Press, 1978), p. 185.

38. Farid Chenoune, *A History of Men's Fashion,* trans. Richard Martin (Paris, France: Flammarion, 1993), p.196.

39. Harriet Worobey, interview by Art Silverblatt, St. Louis, MO, October 10, 1997.

40. Stephanie Rosenbloom, "The Obscure and Uncertain Semiotics of Fashion," *New York Times,* March 5, 2006.

41. Ibid.

42. Ibid.

43. Ibid.

44. Guy Trebay, "Campaign Chic: Not Too Cool, Never Ever Hot," *New York Times,* July 22, 2007.

45. Ibid.

46. Ibid.

47. Ibid.

48. Robin Givhan, "Condoleezza Rice's Commanding Clothes," *Washington Post,* February 25, 2005, p. C01.

49. Alex Williams, "Live from Miami, a Style Showdown," *New York Times,* September 26, 2004.

50. Cherie Bank, interview by Art Silverblatt, WCAU-TV, Philadelphia, PA, November 3, 1997.

51. Ruth La Ferla, "A Return to That Drop-Dead Year 1960," *New York Times,* August 23, 2007.

52. "Read or Listen, But Don't Look; Eyes Will Lie, Says TV Researcher," *St. Louis Post-Dispatch,* February 2, 1995, 2A.

53. Leathers, *Successful Nonverbal Communication*, p. 161.

54. Tripp Frohlichstein, *Media Training Handbook* (St. Louis: MediaMasters, 1991), p. 33.

55. "Read or Listen, But Don't Look," p. 2A.

56. Clyde Taylor, "New U.S. Black Cinema," in *Movies and Mass Culture*, ed. John Belton, (New Jersey: Rutgers University Press).

57. Phil Wilson (international performer and lecturer of jazz currently at Berkeley School of Music, Boston, MA), interview by Jane Ferry, May 1997.

58. Terry Corpal, interview by Art Silverblatt, October 1, 1997.

59. Foreman, "A Conversation with Paul Ekman."

60. Ibid.

61. Deputy Tom O'Connor, interview by Art Silverblatt, St. Louis, MO, December 8, 1997.

62. Ibid.

63. Ibid.

64. Allan Pease, *Signals* (Toronto: Bantam Books, 1981), p. 69.

65. Morris, *Bodytalk*, p. 182.

66. O'Connor interview, December 8, 1997.

67. Pease, *Signals*, p. 130.

68. Hargrave, *Let Me See Your Body Talk*, p. 72.

69. Morris, *Bodytalk*, p. 152.

70. Hargrave, *Let Me See Your Body Talk*, p. 73.

71. Morris, *Bodytalk*, p. 154.

72. Samantha L. Harms, "Magazine Advertisements: What Do They Tell Us About Gender?" (Unpublished paper, Webster University, October 15, 1997).

73. Andre Picard, "Hollywood Women Model Smokers: Study," *Globe and Mail* (Toronto).

74. Clair Weaver, "Smoking Rife in Films," *Sunday Telegraph*, March 5, 2006, p. 27.

75. Kim Rahn, "Smoking Scenes Frequent in Movies," *Korea Times*, March 6, 2006.

76. Pease, *Signals*, p. 159.

77. Ibid., p. 75.

78. Richard Klein, "After the Preaching, the Lure of the Taboo," *New York Times*, August 24, 1997, section 2, p. 1.

CHAPTER 4

1. Max Muller, "The Philosophy of Mythology, *Science of Religion* (London, 1873) pp. 353–355.

2. Mircea Eliade, *The Sacred and the Profane*, trans. Willard R. Task (New York: Harper Brothers, 1957), p. 205.

3. Rollo May, *The Cry For Myth*. (New York: WW. Norton, 1991), p. 27.

4. Campbell, Joseph, with Bill Moyers, *The Power of Myth* (New York: Doubleday, 1988), p. 5.

5. Gilbert Highet, *The Classical Tradition: Greek and Roman Influences on Western Literature* (New York: Oxford University Press/Galaxy Books, 1957), p. 540.

6. Henry A. Murray, "The Possible Nature of a 'Mythology' to Come," in *Myth and Mythmaking,* ed. Henry A. Murray (New York: George Braziller, 1960), p. 337.

7. Rayshawn Campbell, "The Story of Jim," unpublished, 1998.

8. D'Auaires' *Book of Greek Myths* (New York: Doubleday, 1962), pp. 14–15.

9. May, *The Cry For Myth,* p. 294

10. Roland Barthes, *Mythologies* (New York: Hill and Wang, 1957), p. 129.

11. Campbell, Joseph. *Historical Atlas of World Mythology,* pp. 8–9.

12. Rollo May, *The Cry for he Myth,* p. 282.

13. Bruner, Jerome S. "Myth and Identity," in *Myth and Mythmaking,* ed. Henry A. Murray (New York: George Braziller, 1960), p. 280.

14. Harry Levins, "Original Sin Sells," *St. Louis Post-Dispatch,* February 1, 1998, p. A2.

15. Jeff Zeleny, "Testing the Water, Obama Tests His Own Limits," *New York Times,* December 24, 2006.

16. Ibid.

17. May, *The Cry For Myth,* 50–51.

18. Henry A. Murray, "The Possible Nature of a 'Mythology' to Come," in *Myth and Mythmaking,* ed. by Henry A. Murray. (New York: George Braziller, 1960), p. 337.

19. Joseph Schuster interview. Webster University, December 20, 1997.

20. Henry A. Murray, "The Possible Nature of a 'Mythology' to Come," p. 338.

21. Foster R. McCurley, "American Myths and the Bible," *Word and World,* 8, no. 3 (1988): 226–227.

22. Charles Herold, "It's Nice to Have Minions, Whether for Good or Evil," *New York Times*, July 12, 2007.

23. Ibid.

24. Rob Owen, 'Revelations Taps into a Biblical Theme," *Pittsburgh Post-Gazette* (Pennsylvania) April 10, 2005, p. TV-5.

25. Bruce Weber, "Hollywood Help Wanted: Classicists with Style," *New York Times*, May 23, 2004, Section 4; Week in Review Desk; Ideas and Trends; p. 12.

26. Phillip McCarthy, "Pitt abs-olutely has the Achilles Feel," Fairfax Digital. http://www.theage.com.au/articles/2004/05/12/1084289745473.html.

27. Henry A. Murray, "The Possible Nature of 'Mythology' to Come," p. 324.

28. Ronald B. Tobias, *20 Master Plots* (Cincinatti, OH: Writer's Digest Books, 1993), p. 57.

29. Joseph Campbell, *The Hero with a Thousand Faces,* 2d ed. (Princeton: Princeton University Press, 1949), p.22.

30. Linda Seger, *Creating Unforgettable Characters* (New York: Henry Holt, 1990), p. 185.

31. Holland Cotter, "On My Road," *New York Times,* September 2, 2007.

32. Campbell, *The Hero with a Thousand Faces,* 146.

33. Ronald B. Tobias, *20 Master Plots* (Cincinnati, OH: Writer's Digest Books, 1993), p. 138–139.

34. "36 Plots" is based on a classroom handout, the source of which is unknown. All efforts to track the original or author have proven unsuccessful.

35. Tobias, 99.

36. Ibid.

37. Murray, "The Possible Nature of a 'Mythology' to Come," pp. 316–317.

CHAPTER 5

1. Mark Shields, "And Now for the Outrage of the Week," http://atrios.blog-spot.com/2002_12_01_archive.html#390026589, March 5, 2008

2. Joshua Marshall, "Hard-Hitting Coverage. We Report, You Decide," http://www.talkingpointsmemo.com/archives/week_2002_12_01.php, March 5, 2008

3. Paul Krugman, "The Other Face," *New York Times,* December 13, 2002, p. A39.

4. Rahul Kumar, "Bloggers Versus the Mainstream Media: A Study on Iraq," *OneWorld South Asia,* https://www.comminit.com/en/node/243160/2754, October, 2005.

5. Ibid.

6. Ann Curry, "Next Steps for Former Conjoined Twins: Carl and Clarence Aguirre Learn to Sit Up, Talk, Walk," *NBC News,* 26 September, 2005, http://www.msnbc.msn.com/id/9483659/, March 25, 2008.

7. National Coalition on Health Care, "Facts on Health Insurance Coverage," http://www.nchc.org/facts/coverage.shtml, March 25, 2008.

8. Amy, Goodman, "All Anna Nicole Smith, All the Time," *Democracy Now* http://www.democracynow.org/2007/2/19/headlines, February 19, 2007.

9. Steve Rendall, "Wrong on Iraq? Not Everyone: Four in the Mainstream Media Got It Right," http://www.fair.org, February 12, 2008; Todd Gitlin, "All The President's Friends," *American Prospect* 1, no. 1 (January 2006): 47–49; Rich Frank, "All The President's Flacks," Op-Ed, *New York Times,* December 4, 2005.

10. Judith Miller and Michael R. Gordon, "U.S. Says Hussein Intensifies Quest for A-Bomb Parts," *New York Times,* September 8, 2002, p. 1.

11. Rendall, "Wrong on Iraq?"; Gitlin, "All The President's Friends"; Frank, "All the President's Flacks."

12. Susan D. Moeller, "Media Coverage of Weapons of Mass Destruction," *CISSM Monograph,* http://www.cissm.umd.edu/papers/files/wmdstudy_full.pdf.

13. "Cablers Interrupt Paris Coverage for Pace," *TVNEWSER,* 6 June,2008, http://www.mediabistro.com/tvnewser/top_stories/cablers_interrupt_paris_cover-age_for_pace_60654.asp (January 26, 2009); Oliver Willis, http://www.oliverwillis.com/2007/06/from_paris_hilt.htm video of news cast (June 8, 2007) (no longer available), "MSNBC Cuts Away from Pentagon to Paris," (8 June, 2007) *Huffington Post,* 8 June, 2007, http://www.huffingtonpost.com/2007/06/08/msnbs-cuts-away-from-pent_n_51315.html.

14. Mark Jurkowitz, "Paris Has the Media Burning," PEJ News Coverage Index, June 3–8, 2007, http://www.journalism.org/node/6001.

15. Gary Schwitzer, "Ten Troublesome Trends in TV Health News." December 4, 2004, http://www.bmj.com/cgi/content/extract/329/7478/, April 2, 2008.

16. Martin Scorsese, "Made Men," *Film Comment,* interview by Kathleen Murphy, September–October 1990, 30.

17. Christopher Rouse, interview by Author Unknown, "The Bourne Unti-matium: Assembling the Missing Pieces to Create Character," *Avid,* 2007 http://www.avid.com/showcase/bourne-ultimatum-editing-workflow.asp (December 13, 2007).

18. Mark Harris, "Which Editing Is a Cut Above?" *New York Times,* January 6, 2008, Arts & Leisure pp. 15, 17.

19. Jacques Aumont, Alain Bergala, Michel Marie, and Marc Vernet, *Aesthetics in Film,* trans. Richard Neupert (Austin: University of Texas Press, 1992), p. 13.

20. Walter J. Ong, *Orality and Literacy: The Technologizing of the Word* (New York: Routledge, 1996), pp. 127–132.

21. *Albany Times Union,* December 24, 2007, p. A1.

22. Clinique, term used in advertising copy, http://www.clinique.com/templates/products/sp_nonshaded.tmpl?CATEGORY_ID=CATEGORY4914&PRODUCT_ID=PROD767.

23. Marcelo Duran, "SF Examiner Changes Look with New Tabloid Format," *Newspapers and Technology,* July 2002, http://www.newsandteck.com/issues/2002/07–02/nt/07–02 examiner.htm, October 15, 2007.

24. Mario Garcia, "The Mario Scenario," http://www.reveries.com/reverb/media/garcia/index.html, April 12, 2008.

25. L. Gordon Crovitz, "Embracing Change to Build on a Tradition of Excellence," *Wall Street Journal,* http://www.wsj.com/public/article-print/SB//6767372393163913-cvq. January 2, 2007.

26. Charlotte Ryan, *Prime Time Activism* (Boston: South End Press, 1991), pp. 53–56.

27. Bruce Kawin, *Mindscreen: Bergman, Godard, and First-Person Film* (Princeton, NJ: Princeton University Press, 1978), quoted in Edward Brannigan, *Point of View in the Cinema* (Berlin: Mouton, 1984), p. 221.

28. Art Silverblatt, *Media Literacy: Keys to Interpreting Media Messages* (Westport, CT: Praeger, 1995), p. 111.

29. James Monaco, *How to Read Film* (New York: Oxford University Press, 1981), p. 173.

30. Laura Mulvey, *Visual and Other Pleasures* (Bloomington: Indiana University Press, 1989), p. 19.

31. E. Ann Kaplan, "Is the Gaze Male?" in *Women and Values: Readings in Recent Feminist Philosophy,* ed Marilyn Pearsall (Belmont, CA: Wadsworth Publishing, 1986).

32. John Berger, *Ways of Seeing* (London: Penguin, 1972), p. 47.

33. *Monster's Ball,* DVD, Directed by Marc Forster, (USA, Lions Gate Production, 2001), commentary by Marc Forster.

34. Melissa Anjiwa, "Monster'Ball" *Scope,* no. 12, October 2008, http:www.scope.notingham.ac.uk/filmreview.php?issue=6&id=176&section=film_rev&q=midn ster%5c%27s+ball, April 20, 2007.

35. Keith Greenwood, "Picturing Presidents: A Content Analysis of Photographs of Presidents from the Pictures of the Year," manuscript presented to the Political Communications Division of the International Communication Association, 2005, p. 12.

36. Stephen Prince, "Beholding Blood Sacrifice in *The Passion of the Christ:* How Real Is Movie Violence?" *Film Quarterly* 59, no. 4 (2006).

37. Dorothy Nelkin, *Selling Science* (New York: W.H. Freeman, 1987).

38. Matt Taibbit, "To the Best of Our Knowledge," National Public Radio, January 13, 2008, http://www.wpr.org/book/.

39. George Lakeoff, *Don't Think of an Elephant: Know Your Values and Frame the Debate,* (White River Junction, VT: Chelsea Green Publishing Company,2004); Thaddeus Herrick, "U.S. Infrastructure Found to Be in Disrepair," *Wall Street Journal,* May 2, 2007, p. 4; Bill McKibben, "The Environment," *Harpers,* June 2007, p. 49.

40. General Gates, quoted in Paul Richter, "Bush Sees Long-Term Role for Troops," http://articles.latimes.com/2007/May31/world/fg-bushiraq31, May 31, 2007.

41. Secretary of Defense Robert Gates and Commander, Pacific Command, Admiral Timothy Keating, U.S. Department of Defense, Press Conference with Secretary Gates and Adm. Keating from Camp Smith-Honolulu, Hawaii, June 1, 2007, http://www.defenselink.mil/transcripts/transcript.aspx?transcriptid=397442.

42. Ibid.

43. General David Petraeus, quoted in Sig Christenson, "Will Iraq Surge Work? Inshallah," *San Antonio Express News,* June 3, 2007, http://www.mysanantonio.com/news/MYSA060307-01A_Inshallah_35f70d9)html; Tom Engelhardt and Nicholas Turse, "Take the 11-Quote Quiz on the Bush Administration's War of the Words," 12 June, 2007, http://www.tomdispatch.com/post/174809/engelhardt_and_turse_the_bush_administration_s_fighting_words.

44. Isabelle Blanchette and Kevin Dunbar, "Analogy Use in Naturalistic Settings: The Influence of Audience, Emotion, and Goals," *Memory and Cognition* 29, no. 5 (2001): 730–35.

45. Roland Barthes, *Mythologies,* trans. Annette Lavers (New York: Hill and Wang, 1972), p. 117.

46. U.S. Marine Corps recruitment video, *The Climb,* 21 November, 2005, produced by JWThompson, http://www.google.com/search?hl=en&q=http%3A%2F%2Fwww.youtube.com%2Fwatch%3Fv%3DS2MeLM2Sz34&btnG=Google+Search&aq=f&oq= (October 25, 2007).

47. Staff Sergeant Alicia Borlik, "Recruitment Ads: New Strategies, New Messages," *USA American Forces Press Service,* March 31, 1999, http://www.defenselink.mil/news/newsarticle.aspx?id=41606.

48. Jeremy Black, *Maps and Politics* (London: Reaktion Books, 1997).

49. Victor Cohn, *News and Numbers* (Ames: Iowa State University Press, 1989).

50. Don Corrigan, "Future of Newspapers Belongs to Visual Artists," *St. Louis Journalism Review* 28, no. 206 (May 1998): 1.

51. Cohn, *News and Numbers,* p. 45.

52. "CNN.com Posted Misleading Graph Showing Poll Results on Schiavo case," *Media Matters,* March 22, 2005, http://mediamatters.org/items/200503220005.

53. Susan J. Diem, John D. Lantos, J.A. Tulsky, "Cardiopulmonary Resuscitation on Television: Miracles and Misinformation," *New England Journal of Medicine* 334, no. 24 (June 13, 1996): 1578–1582.

54. Erik Speikermann and E.M. Ginger, *Stop Stealing Sheep and Find Out How Type Works* (Mountain View, CA: Adobe Press, 1993), p. 15.

55. Kevin Barnhurst, *Seeing the Newspaper* (New York: St. Martin's Press, 1994), p. 156.

56. Speikermann and Ginger, *Stop Stealing Sheep,* pp. 47–48.

57. Roy Paul Nelson, *Publication Design,* 3d ed. (Dubuque, IA: Wm. C. Brown, 1989), p. 79.

58. Pamela Haskin, "'Saul, Can You Make Me a Title?': Interview with Saul Bass," *Film Quarterly* 50, no. 1 (Autumn 1996): 10–17; here, p. 14.

59. Janet Maslin, "True Story, Dipping into the Classics," *New York Times,* December 20, 1996.

60. "Catch me if you can," *YouTube*, May 8, 2008, http://www.google.com/ search?hl=en&q=http%3A%2F%2Fwww.youtube.com%2Fwatch%3Fv%3DiVE gK3nCkao.&btnG=Google+Search&aq=f&oq=.

61. Gerry Rosentswieg, *The New American Logo* (New York: Madison Square Press, 1994), introduction.

62. Anna Notaro, "Swoosh Time: Nike's Art of Speed Advertising Campaign and the Blogsphere," *Nebula* 5.4 December 2008, www.nobleworld.biz/images/ Notar02.pdf.

63. M. DeMartini, "The Great God Nike: Good or Evil," *Sporting Goods Dealer,* March 1997, p. 36.

64. Betty B, "Nike, Sweatshops and Slave Labor," *Heartland Diary of Betty B.,* 10 July, 2007. http://heartlanddiaryofbettyb.blogspot.com/2007/07/nike-sweat-shops-and-slave- labor.html

(December 10, 2007.

65. Rosemary Sadex Friedman, "Psychological Aspects of Color Choices in House," *St. Louis Post-Dispatch,* May 2, 1998, p. L-15.

66. Ibid.

67. Ibid.

68. David A., Ricks, *Blunders In International Business* (Malden, MA: Black-well, 2006) p. 71, http://amygdalagf.blogspot.com/search?q=green+cap+cuckold.

69. Maryann J. Stump, quoted in Claudia H, Deutsch, "Xerox Hopes Its New Logo Doesn't Say 'Copier,'" *New York Times,* January 7, 2008.

70. Rick Carter, *Munich,* directed by Steven Spielberg DreamWorks SKG, U.S. 2005, DVD.

71. Ibid.

72. John Calhoun, "Fear and Fantasy," *American Cinematographer,* January 30, 2007, pp. 34–45; here, p. 36.

73. *Children of Men,* directed by Alfonso Cuarón Universal Pictures, USA, 2006, DVD.

74. Roger Elswit interview by Elina Shakin "Blood, Oil and a Global Economy," *International Cinematographers Guild,* January, 2006, http://www.cameraguild. com/index.html?magazine/0601/stoo.htm~top.main_hp.

75. *World Trade Center,* directed by Oliver Stone, Paramount Pictures, USA, 2006, DVD.

76. Natalie Angier, "The Cute Factor," *New York Times,* January 3, 2006.

77. Carl G. Jung, *Man and His Symbols* (New York: Doubleday, 1964), pp. 240–52.

78. Jane Ferry, *Food in Film: A Culinary Performance of Communication* (New York: Routledge, 2003), p. 23.

79. *Sopranos,* HBO, directed by David Chase, June 10, 2007.

80. Hans Biederman, *Dictionary of Symbolism: Cultural Icons and the Mean-ings Behind Them* (New York: Meriden, 1994).

81. Ibid.

82. Harry Remde, "Inner Surface," *Parabola* 14, no. 4 (1989): 15.

83. Claude Bragdon, "An Architecture of Changeless Change," *Parabola* 14, no. 4 (1989): 38–39.

84. Harry Remde, "Inner Surface," pp. 14–15.

85. Art Silverblatt, *Media Literacy: Keys to Interpreting Media Messages* (Westport, CT: Praeger, 1995), p. 108.

86. Phillip C. Shin D Hallet, ML Chipman, C Tator, J Cranton, "Unsafe Driving in North American Automobile Commercials," *Journal of Public Health* 27, no. 4 (2005): 318–325.

87. Center for Science in the Public Interest, "Bad Ads 'Win' Lemon Awards," Thirteenth Annual Harlan Hubbard Lemon Awards, December 4, 1997 (Washington, DC: Center for Science in the Public Interest, 1997), http://www.cspinet.org/new/hubb97.htm.

88. Aumont et al., *Aesthetics in Film,* p. 229.

89. Lynn Hirschberg, "Coen Brothers Country," *New York Times Magazine,* November 11, 2007, p. 72

90. Herbert Zettl, *Sight Sound and Motion: Applied Media Aesthetics,* 2d ed. (Belmont, CA: Wadsworth, 1990), p. 335.

91. Martin Scorsese interview by Rebecca Murray. "Director Martin Scorsese Discusses *The Deaparted,* http://movies.about.com/od/thedeparted/a/depart-edms93006_2.html, April 25, 2000.

92. Monaco, *How to Read Film* (New York: Oxford University Press, 1981), p. 106.

93. Leonard Maltin, *Of Mice and Magic: A History of American Animated Cartoons* (New York: Plume Printing, 1987), pp. 1–4.

94. Lev Grossman, "The Art of War," *Time,* March 12, 2007, p. 58.

95. Devin Gordon, "Making 'The Polar Express,'" *Newsweek* Next Frontiers http://www.msnbc.msn.com/id/6261181/site/newsweek/, accessed September 5, 2007.

96. Steve Silberman, "Matrix[2]" *Wired, 11.05, May 2003,* http://www.wired.com/wired/archive/11.05/matrix2_pr.html.

97. Phillip French, "A Vision of Hell on Earth," *Observer,* 28 March, 2004, http://film.guardian.co.uk/News_Story/Critic_Review/Observer_Film_of_the_week/0,,1179452,00.html.

98. Stephen Prince, "Beholding Blood Sacrifice" in *The Passion of the Christ: How Real is Movie Violence?" Film Quarterly,* vol. 59, no. 4, 2006: pp.11–22.

99. John O'Sullivan, quoted in Alan Brinkley, *American History, A Survey,* vol. 1, 9th ed. (New York: McGraw-Hill, 1995).

100. Ray Cassin, "The World Where You Live," *The Age* (Melbourne, Australia), February 18, 2006, p. 20.

101. Robert Elswit, interview by Elina Shatkin, "Blood, Oil and a Global Economy," *International Cinematographers Guild,* January 2006, http://www.cameraguild.com/index.html.

102. *Syriana,* DVD, directed by Stephen Gaghan., U.S. Warner Brothers, 2005.

103. Robert Baer interviewed by Susan A De Guzman, "From 'See No Evil' to 'Syriana,'" 18 February, 2006, *George Clooney-Clooney Studio,* http:www.clooneystudio.com/see_no_evil_syriana.html (January 29, 2008); source: *Manila Bulletin online,* http:www.mb.com.ph/source (February 2, 1009).

104. Elina Shatkin, "Blood, Oil and a Global Economy."

Index

About the Authors

Jane Ferry, PhD, is an academic adviser and adjunct professor in the School of Communications at Webster University in St. Louis, Missouri. She is the author of *Food in Film: A Culinary Performance of Communication* (2003).

Barbara Finan has an MA in management and leadership, served as academic coordinator for Webster University's School of Communications from 1990 to 2001, and is currently an academic adviser in the Webster University School of Communications Graduate Program.

Art Silverblatt is a professor of communications and journalism at Webster University, St. Louis, Missouri. He earned his PhD in 1980 from Michigan State University. He is the author of numerous books and articles, including *Media Literacy: Keys to Interpreting Media Messages* (2007), *The Dictionary of Media Literacy* (1997), *Approaches to the Study of Media Literacy* (2009), *International Communications: A Media Literacy Approach* (2004), and *Approaches to Genre Study* (2008). Silverblatt's work has been translated into Japanese, Korean, Chinese, and German.